THE
LOG CABIN

THE LOG CABIN

An Adventure in Self-Reliance, Individualism, and Cabin Building

By Len McDougall

The Lyons Press
Guilford, Connecticut
An imprint of The Globe Pequot Press

The Lyons Press is an imprint of The Globe Pequot Press.

10 9 8 7 6 5 4 3 2 1

Printed in the United States of America

ISBN 1–58574–459-X

Library of Congress Cataloging-in-Publication data is available on file.

This book is dedicated with my sincerest gratitude and thanks to Cheanne Chellis, the Wolf Lady. She believed in me when others did not, and she gave me hope when I had none left. If not for her friendship and support this book would never have become a reality.

Note from the Publisher

The publisher unequivocally endorses adherence to all national and state firearms, hunting, and environmental regulations. Neither the author nor the publisher advocates in any way disregard for the law of the land. Both the publisher and the author are also enthusiastic supporters of conservation of wildlife and natural resources.

Some of the actions described in this narrative are not permitted on state-regulated land. However, the author built his cabin and undertook these actions subject to tribal regulation, on tribal land, under the supervision of tribal officials, and at all times with utmost reverence for the wild.

CONTENTS

INTRODUCTION

I don't believe there has ever been an American boy (and a few girls, too) who didn't at some period of adolescence proclaim that he was going to one day build a cabin far back in the woods, and then live there like a frontiersman. It's an almost universal boyhood fantasy, this desire to homestead a wilderness, because living from the land, dependent only on one's own wits and skills, represents the self-sufficiency, strength, and independence of manhood that all boys crave.

In nearly every instance this primal desire to forge a home from untamed wilderness fades, then dies away almost entirely when a boy reaches manhood. The fantasy is never really gone, but the world of civilization—known as reality to those who are resigned to living in it—leaves no time to pursue profitless childhood dreams. The fiery allure of becoming a self-sufficient frontiersman is doused more with each passing year of car payments, mortgages, and responsibilities, until only dim embers remain.

That it does remain is evidenced by the timeless popularity of movies and books about mountain men, trappers, and cowboys. We're entertained by tales of high adventure in a wilderness, I think, because we ourselves envy the thrills and trials those early pioneers must have experienced. Many of us crave the excitement enough to become weekend outdoorsmen, but only rarely can a man or woman break the chains of civilization and actually live the frontiering dream full-time. Instead, the fantasy passes to the next generation of boys and girls, who are also unlikely to realize it before a sea of responsibilities washes it to that mournful place of surrendered dreams.

Like every youngster who ever got starry-eyed over the idea of living the life of Davy Crockett, the boy who grew to be me also boasted his intent to live in a remote log cabin built by axe and arm. And like other kids who shared that dream, I too spent my most active years of adulthood having never fulfilled it. The dream was never abandoned, but for long decades the demands of family, social responsibilities, and a technical career in manufacturing caused me to be preoccupied with other matters. During that chapter of my life, my passion for wilderness—referred to as an obsession by wives and friends—was kept alive, but barely fed, by weekend backpacking trips.

It wasn't until age forty-four that my own spark of passion for homesteading was rekindled into a blaze that did indeed look something like an obsession. I'd been struggling along as a full-time outdoor writer for ten years, lived in the same apartment for six years, and had been divorced from my second wife for two years. The kids I'd raised were doing well on their own, and a couple of them had made me a grandfather. My small success as an author had come at the expense of time spent getting the experiences I wrote about, and now seemed an ideal time to break the chokehold of social conformity that civilized life had been trying to get on me. My life had become less than I thought a life should be, and I needed an adventure to remind me that there were still good reasons to wake up each morning.

When I told my family and friends that I was going into the deep forest to build a cabin and then live in it for a year, none of them had much to say. I knew some were using terms like "midlife crisis" in private, but relatives generally chalked it up to just another eccentric endeavor in the life of a family member who was always a bit off anyway. Friends, for the most part, simply gave me a blank look, and probably most didn't believe I was serious.

But I was as serious as the heart attack my nephew said I would have if I actually tried to do this homesteading thing. I'd grown up cutting firewood to heat our house, I'd run a for-profit trapline as a kid, canned vegetables from my own garden, gillnetted fish with local Indians, and I'd rendered about every edible animal into meat for the pot. I figured there would be a lot of new things to learn from a homesteading project, but I hoped that I already possessed the most fundamental skills that this endeavor would demand.

I also knew that, despite my best intentions, there was no possibility of fully duplicating what the homesteading experience must have been when area highways were just rutted wagon trails and nighttime was actually dark. There was no denying that my traps and truck, from the boots and clothing I wore to the dried foods I bought at the supermarket, were products of modern technology. The entire planet had been mapped by satellite, all roads to town were paved, and many more objects glittered in the night sky than had been there when Lewis and Clark forged their way across the Great Divide.

Besides that, there was a real disparity in knowledge between twenty-first-century humans and pioneers of even a century ago. Unlike early frontiersmen, I knew there were microscopic parasites in the water, and I knew how to avoid infestation from them. I knew that microbial organisms caused a wound to become infected, that Jupiter would be bright enough at night that year to serve as a navigation beacon, and that air traffic in the area would respond to international emergency ground-to-air signals should I get into trouble. I knew which herbs had proven medicinal value, and I knew which plants were edible, as well as their scientifically validated nutritional worth. There was no forgetting the accumulated knowledge that gives modern humans so many survival advantages over mountain men of old, and that alone made it impossible to live an authentic nineteenth-century lifestyle.

I figured I could accurately duplicate the spirit of homesteading, however, and learn the hows and whys of the pioneers' daily routines by falling into those same routines as a matter of course. Circumstances would dictate that I learn to live without plumbing, refrigeration, and on-demand lighting and heat, while necessity would compel me to adapt the best I could. Despite having an education that our forefathers could not have possessed, I'd be forced to learn many lessons about matters they'd simply accepted as part of life.

I guess I'll never know for sure what my motivation was. Maybe it was indeed a midlife crisis, or possibly just the desire to fulfill a lifelong fantasy before my aging body took away that option forever. A number of people have told me that I must be a masochist, and a few have even accused me of having some sort of death wish. Whatever my reason for taking on the hardships and joys that I now know are a part of homesteading, it was an experience, and sometimes an adventure, that I know I'll never forget. I hope you'll enjoy my story.

THE
LOG CABIN

1

GEARING UP TO LEAVE

Having made the decision to become a twenty-first-century homesteader, I then needed the tools with which to accomplish the many tasks that would lay in store for me in the woods. I didn't truly know what might have awaited an 1800s frontiersman who set out to create a home in wilderness where human footprints rarely, if ever, fell. But then, I reckoned that neither could most of them have known what to expect.

Probably like most of those first pioneers, I entered into this wilderness odyssey with no real instructions other than old books and pictures about homesteading to guide me. The *Foxfire* book series was helpful, but even those books didn't get as primitive as I'd have to live. I hoped to draw heavily from my childhood in northern Michigan, where I'd learned to put up food for winter, swing an axe, smoke fish, and hunt for meat. Thanks to the old timbermen, farmers, and especially Indians I grew up knowing, I reckoned on having at least the fundamentals of whatever skills my homesteading adventure would demand. Thirty-three years of backpacking and camping in all seasons would doubtless prove beneficial, too.

My most basic and immediate needs, like shelter, bedroll, and water purification, would be supplied by the same backpacks that were geared to keep me living comfortably for up to a week at a time, and to keep me at least living for an indefinite period beyond that. A large Moss Olympic 4-season tent would be my house until the cabin was finished, while its smaller cousin, a 2-person Starlet, would serve as a closet of sorts to keep spare clothing out of the elements. My bed was a Peak 1 Crestone 15-degree sleeping bag lying on a Cascade Designs closed-cell foam pad. A well-used MSR Blacklite mess kit cooked the first meals I ate, backed up by the old classic GI canteen and cup outfit. Clean drinking water would be provided by PUR Voyager and SweetWater Guardian+ Plus purifier pumps until I could get a well dug. I figured to spend a week or so hauling in a half ton of tools and equipment that would complement these basics and make life easier, but my backpacks already contained the gear I'd need to immediately establish a permanent foothold in the wilderness.

It was spring now, but much of my comfort, if not survival, during the next year would depend on the clothing I took. My trousers consisted of six pairs of military BDU (Battle Dress Uniform) trousers with large button-down thigh pockets, chosen for their loose-fitting comfort and rugged

Layered Cold-Weather Outfit

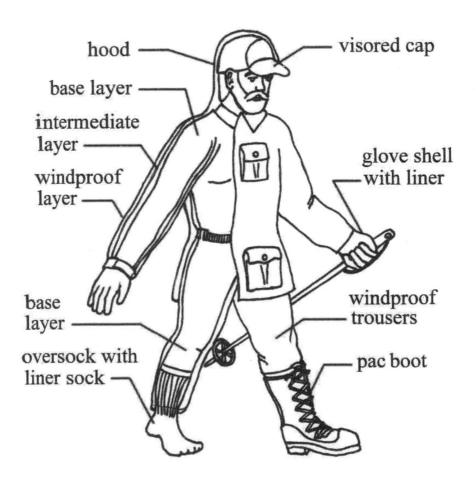

construction of ripstop fabric. Summer undershirts were mostly T-shirts and tank tops, with heavyweight BDU overshirts in case the bugs or the terrain got too rough. Summer boots included my comfortable old Merrell M2s for hiking, and La Sportiva's brutally heavy Pacific Crest mountaineering boot for lumberjacking chores. For camp slippers I took a pair of Teva's sneaker-like water shoes.

In winter I'd continue wearing the BDUs, except that I'd add more layers of insulation. Good synthetic long johns were a critical item, so I took three pairs of Medalist bottoms with matching zip-neck tops, backed up by a pair of heavyweight L. L. Bean fleece pants. For ice fishing and other long periods of inactivity in subzero weather, I included a pair of heavy wool German border patrol trousers with six pockets, double-layer construction, and waterproof lining at the knees and seat.

I knew from painful experience that proper winter footwear was also critical. For hiking in above-zero weather I took a pair of Rocky's Ozark pac boots with internal liners, which had proved very comfortable for long walks with or without snowshoes. For very cold weather and sedentary winter activities like deer hunting, I took a pair of Sorel's rugged Alaska boots with removable liners that were rated to minus 100 degrees. I also included two spare sets of boot liners to serve as winter camp slippers and to help keep my feet warm while I slept on subzero nights.

In all seasons my socks would consist of Wigwam and SmartWool oversocks with thin acrylic liner socks beneath to help wick away perspiration and provide a slippery shield against friction. I'd been wearing this sock system for years, and it worked as well for hot summer backpacking as it did for snowshoeing.

Primary in importance among the tools I still needed was an axe, and I knew I was going to need a good one to take down the trees needed to build a log cabin. I wanted a large double-edge "timber cruiser" axe with a 5-pound head, like the one I'd used as a boy. A heavy axe is easier to use because it develops more centrifugal force and inertia when swung, which means it hits harder and removes larger chips, and that of course means fewer swings are needed to make one log into two. It was once common practice to keep one edge dull for splitting firewood lengths, while its opposite was kept shaving sharp for chopping trees and delimbing trunks.

To my frustration, I searched practically every hardware store and co-op in four counties, and never did find the axe I wanted. In fact, I almost felt as if I were in a *Twilight Zone* episode because, with the exception of one grizzled old-timer, none of the employees at those stores could recall

Single-Bit Axe   Double-Bit Axe

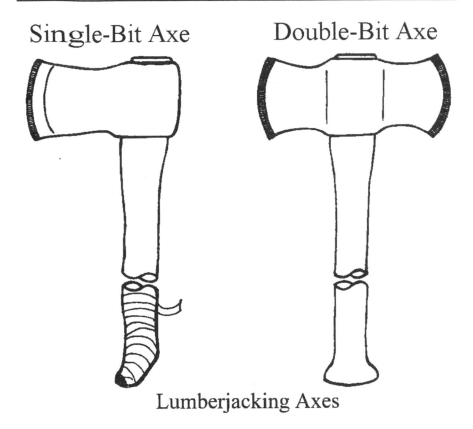

Lumberjacking Axes

ever having seen such an axe. I found an old farmer who, like many old farmers, had turned his land into development property, and he had one. But it had been his father's, and there was no way he was going to sell it to some crazy guy who wanted to actually use it for chopping wood. In the end, I settled for a single-bit Collins axe with a 3-pound head and yellow fiberglass handle from the Home Depot store in Petoskey, but it just wasn't the same.

For light chopping and prying chores, I chose the square-nosed Ontario Knife SP-8 survival machete that already been a part of my backcountry outfit for several years because it was so versatile. For hammering nails and chopping jobs too heavy for the machete, but too light for an axe, I took a large roofer's hatchet with a 2-pound head.

I had some difficulty finding a brace-and-bit hand auger, and when I did find one at the Boyne City Co-Op, they had no drill bits for it. I ordered those from a lumber company in Petoskey, but when I went to pick them up a week later, a beaming salesman handed me two bits that were designed for use with a power drill, not a muscle-powered brace-and-bit. Although I tried my best to explain what I needed the tools for and how I intended to use them, not even the most senior of the hardware professionals I dealt with could envision building a log cabin with hand tools.

Since we all seemed to be equally ignorant on the subject of felling and manipulating large trees without the aid of chainsaws and other power tools, I stopped asking for advice and elected to wing it alone. I had to, because even if the hardware professionals I dealt with had no idea of what I needed to do, most were still willing to sell me a tool with which to do it.

A good handsaw was necessary, but even in the timber country of northern Michigan I knew there was little chance of finding a bucksaw in working condition—most of the real ones had blades painted with wildlife murals and were hanging in someone's living room as decorations. I was looking for a Corona Razor Tooth with an 18-inch blade, like the one I carried in my 4 x 4 for years before making the mistake of leaving it unattended for a few minutes. But no one seemed to have heard of that, either, and there was no time to order one from the manufacturer in California. I settled for a Stanley SharpTooth carpenter's saw from Home Depot, hoping that its next-generation style of sawteeth would help to compensate for a design that was never intended to cut logs, let alone green wood.

Probably because I'd seen too many movies about slaves building pyramids in ancient Egypt, I envisioned moving the logs I cut over the forest floor by placing them on wood rollers, then pulling them to where they were needed by means of a timber-hitched steel cable and a long stout pry bar. For that task I bought 25 feet of plastic-coated aircraft cable with snap hooks at either end and a tensile strength of 4,000 pounds. The pry bar I figured to cut from a stout green maple or ash sapling.

A good, strong rope was going to be important for the innumerable tying, hauling, and hoisting jobs that awaited, even though I wasn't sure just what all of those would be yet. My best lady friend and fellow wolf-team member, Cheanne, said she'd pick that up for me, so I gave her a twenty and told her about a 50-foot length of braided climbing rope that I'd seen on sale at Home Depot. She brought back 50 feet of more expensive ¾-inch nylon marine rope, saying that she refused to buy the rope I'd asked for because it was garbage (her words). I took her word for it, because she's often smarter than I am, and later had cause to thank her for not bringing me a rope that almost certainly would have snapped, perhaps dangerously, under the forces I needed to apply.

Although I'd originally intended to auger through whatever joints needed assembly, and then peg them together with wood dowels cut from green saplings, I hedged my bets with 2 pounds of 8D 3-inch galvanized deck nails. Their spiral design had far more holding power than the squared wrought iron horseshoe nails carried by early settlers, but I figured that was a good thing. I also included a small assortment of heavy ⁵⁄₁₆-inch hex-head lag screws to experiment with, along with a matching socket and a 10-inch breaker bar for driving them.

Shovels were going to play an important part in forging a homestead out of the wilderness, beginning with the excavation of a freshwater well. I took two pointed shovels, one for the cabin and one for the van, the latter in case I needed to dig the big vehicle out of mud or snow. For shoveling snow from around the cabin in the coming winter I threw in a square-nose grain shovel that was stout enough to permit chopping away ice and packed snow from the doorway.

Because I was sure to need a source of light other than my flashlight and campfire, I stocked up on candles. At a local discount store I bought ten 10-count boxes of emergency candles for $1 per box. I also found good deals on dinner tapers and votive candles, all of which would work fine as lamps in the woods.

Used by itself in the open, a candle makes a poor lamp, because the slightest breeze will cause it to flicker or be blown out, and even a small open flame can be downright dangerous in a forest that's literally filled with tinder. For that reason, I included a dozen or so canning jars that would lend themselves well to making candle lanterns, a simple homespun lamp that I'd been using and writing about for more than a decade. A flat-bottom votive candle sitting in the bottom of an ordinary jar will stay lit even in strong wind; it throws enough light to perform emergency medical procedures, and the lamp can be set on the ground without danger of fire. A loop of fencing wire—I've always carried several yards of the stuff in my backpack—twisted around the jar's threaded mouth provides a means of hanging the lamp from an elevated point.

I've always had a few kerosene lamps around my house for use during power outages, and I took four of these as well. The indoor lamps with their delicate glass chimneys wouldn't be of much use until the cabin was built, but the enclosed hurricane lantern my old friend Big John had given me was made for use outdoors. It meant that I'd have to lug fuel out there, but it turned out that six gallons of kerosene in a plastic jerrican was more than sufficient for the next year.

A good knife has been vital to human survival since Cro-Magnon man flaked the first cutting tool from obsidian. We civilized people tend to forget that a large, strong blade was part of a rural man's daily attire right into the twentieth century, but I'd learned that a sharpened length of steel on my hip could mean the difference between comfort and frustration, if not life and death. For a general duty knife I elected to take a next-generation Ka-Bar made from D2 tool steel, backed up by a folding Gerber Gator made from ATS-34 steel for delicate jobs like skinning and filleting fish. The Ontario SP-8 machete strapped to my pack was better than a hatchet for light chopping and prying, while a small Spyderco Native clip knife in my pocket worked for light jobs that I didn't want to dull my Gator by performing.

My guns were far better than any the old-timers had carried, which also gave me a real edge should it become necessary to hunt for food. For larger game I took my beloved Thompson/Center Encore single shot in .308 Winchester caliber. With an effective hunting range of more than 500 yards and proven half-minute-of-angle accuracy, even in my hands, it had the ability to down any deer I might see. The Simmons 2.5–8 power Whitetail Classic scope it was mounted with insured that I could draw down on any critter that poked its head out of the woods. The rifle was carried by a Ranger Sling, comprising 50 feet of nylon parachute cord that could be unwound from its quick-detach swivels to drag out or hang a whitetail without detracting from the sling's utility as a carrying device.

As important as the gun was its ammunition, and here again I had a real advantage over the charcoal-burning muskets and flannel-patched cast-lead balls carried by my predecessors. To cover all the bases, I took 200 rounds of Winchester and Remington cartridges loaded with expanding bullets that ranged from 150-grain Ballistic Tip to 165-grain Match Grade to traditional 180-grain softnose. A few of my more testosterone-laden friends said I was cheating, but I've never considered the killing of a fellow creature to be sport, and if I was going to do it, I was going to do it efficiently.

In fact, I'd considered taking my Thompson/Center Black Mountain Magnum percussion primed .50 caliber, just to keep things as authentic as possible. It was shaped a lot like the old Hawkin rifles carried by 1800s mountain men, but there the similarity ended. It loaded from the muzzle like the smokepoles of old, but it held a whopping 150 grains of black powder, shot saboted .44 bullets accurately out to 200 yards, had a weatherproof synthetic stock, and aimed through fiberoptic sights unless there was a scope mounted. Hell, I thought, I might as well just take a cartridge gun that could be relied on to fire in the rain.

Complementing the Encore was my sixteen-year-old survival rifle, a .22 caliber semiautomatic Armscor 20P with floated barrel, bedded action, Ranger Sling, and 4 x 32 TimberKing scope fitted with Butler Creek Flip-Up scope caps. Considering the amount of small game this gun had put on the spit, I wouldn't think of being without it. For ammunition, I opted to take 200 rounds each of Remington's Yellow Jacket and Viper Hyper Velocity cartridges, both of which had more than proved their worth at ranges out to 100 yards.

Although I've taken deer and smaller game from grouse to squirrels with a handgun, I don't generally consider any pistol to be the best choice for putting meat on the spit. None of them delivers the power, range, and accuracy of a rifle, and all of them require a great deal of skill to be useful for hunting. In spite of those limitations, I included a compact .22-caliber Astra automatic in my kit because a pistol has one advantage over a longarm: it's always available if you need it. I recall a story from my youth in which a whitetail hunter left his blind to answer an urgent call of nature, only to have an 8-point buck walk within 30 feet of where he squatted. Caught literally with his pants down and his rifle well beyond reach, the hunter drew a .38 Special revolver from the holster on his belt and shot the deer dead. I decided it was better to have a handgun and not need it than to need it and not have it.

Having selected the tools I needed to hunt birds and mammals on land, I then needed weapons for hunting animals that lived in water. Fish might play an important part in my diet, just as they had for the earliest settlers in the Great Lakes State. Lake Michigan, French Farm Lake, Carp River, and several beaver ponds lay within 5 miles of my intended homestead site, and I'd fished all of them enough to know where to get a meal.

I already had two poles, a backpack-size outfit made from a stubby Shakespeare ice-fishing pole fitted with a Johnson closed-face reel, and a conventional full-length Zebco rod mounted to a Zebco open-face spinning reel. Both had taken fish weighing better than 6 pounds, and I owned them because they were dependable and sturdy enough to withstand the rigors of backcountry travel. After adding a few dozen hooks of varying sizes, a few dozen split-shot sinkers, a fresh spool of 20-pound test line (I prefer winching a fish to shore over "playing" it), and a half dozen spinnerbaits, I felt I had my fishing needs pretty well covered.

I also threw in a dozen leghold traps of varying sizes, ranging from smaller models for muskrats to a couple large enough to hold the biggest beaver or raccoon. I hadn't run a trapline since the '70s, when the fur market had been scuttled at the hands of utopian animal rights groups, but I knew how to track and read sign, and I figured I could still place my traps to good effect. I honestly had no intention of using them, but the traps provided some peace of mind, just in case things got rough out there.

Although I had absolutely no desire to use it, thirty years of backpacking had taught me the hard way that a good first-aid kit was essential. I was going to be alone most of the time, and I very much needed the ability to repair myself before small wounds could become serious injuries. Because I'd already learned that the most common wounds are lacerations to the hands and fingers, I started with several rolls of Safety Tape, a surgical-grade gauze impregnated with natural latex that sticks tenaciously to itself, but nothing else, even when wet. A tube of triple-antibiotic ointment helped to insure that whatever germs did get under the wraps would do no harm. For larger cuts in places that couldn't be taped shut, I included a box of butterfly sutures—which ultimately proved useless just when I needed them most.

My own endorphins had proved sufficient to endure the pain of bone fractures, but I backed them up with a bottle each of acetaminophen, ibuprofen, and aspirin, all of which have anti-inflammatory properties that help diminish swelling and the throbbing that can rob an injury victim of restful sleep. There are natural painkillers like squaw weed and elecampane available in the woods, and the leaves of plantain are an anti-inflammatory, but the pills were more likely to be immediately at hand when needed.

Then there were the surgical tools that I really didn't want to use. These included forceps for clamping off severed arteries while I sewed them shut with a sterile suture kit, pincer-shaped extractors for pulling blood vessels into the open so they could be worked on, and debridement scissors for cutting away dead tissue. Two feet of surgical latex tubing would serve as a tourniquet to restrict blood flow while I performed these unpleasant tasks. I prayed that I never needed to use any of them, but experience had taught me to expect that I might.

To bolster my limited knowledge of medical procedures, I included a copy of the *US Army Special Forces Medical Handbook* in a Ziploc bag. Cheanne, who makes her living as a paramedic, also gave me a copy of the weatherproof *EMS Field Guide* that is standard equipment for ambulances. Between those two books, I had more medical information than I knew how to use, and certainly more than had been available to any homesteader who'd gone before me.

Despite some ribbing from friends who said that a real woodsman would hunt and gather his own food, I went shopping. No sensible frontiersman of old would have willingly gone into a wilderness to live without provisions, and neither did any of the Indian tribes make an attempt at resettlement without first loading up on nonperishable foodstuffs. Like them, I had the means and the knowledge to obtain food from the environment, but also like them I understood that doing so was always a gamble. Even wild crops can fail, and venturing into unknown territory by definition means that you don't know what you'll find when you arrive. Besides that, there was the question of palatability; anyone who's ever lived on a purely natural diet for even a few days can tell you that dining on wild foods alone takes a lot of the joy out of eating.

Canned goods were out of the question. I needed my foods to not only be nonperishable, but lightweight—I had to carry this stuff on my back. I started with a case of macaroni and cheese, a case of Ramen noodles, a case of baking mix, a 5-pound bag of flour, a 5-pound bag of sugar, and 6 pounds of salt. The only canned goods I took were two large cans of lard and two cans of baking powder.

Although a few people recommended them, I rejected both the military MREs (Meals, Ready to Eat) and civilian freeze-dried preprepared dishes. Based on the times I've tried them, I consider both to be overpackaged, lacking in nutrition and volume, and overpriced compared to meals I could concoct from less expensive grocery store dried goods. Instead, I bought two cases of Betty Crocker freeze-dried scalloped and au gratin potatoes, which are loaded with calories (I was going to be working very hard, that much I knew), yet cost less than half of what an equivalent size "camping" food sold for. Ten pounds of homemade venison summer sausage added taste and protein, and I could supplement potato dishes with whatever wild greens were available.

Besides store-bought dried foods, I dehydrated 20 pounds of raw potatoes, 20 pounds of bananas, 10 pounds of apples, 5 pounds of onions, and even a half-dozen cans of cranberry sauce. In fact, I pretty much emptied my refrigerator, freezer, and cupboards of any fruit, vegetable, or meat that could be dried and taken to the woods with me.

Despite a tendency to overcomplicate the process, dehydrated foods are exactly what the name implies: foods from which nearly all moisture has been removed through evaporation. The only real trick is to accomplish that without applying enough heat to cook the food, which means that whatever food is being dehydrated should be sliced thinly, then dried slowly and as evenly throughout as possible. The potatoes and apples I dried on cookie sheets in my oven for twelve hours at 150 degrees. Venison and lean beef from the freezer I cut into thin strips, salted, and dried in the microwave. The banana chips and cranberries were actually done in an electric dehydrator. Any of these could have been dried using any of the methods described, but I had them all going at once to increase yield and to save time.

Because I'd been drying my own backpack foods for several years, I'd learned that proper storage is essential to their longevity. The most common mistake is putting them into airtight containers (including plastic Ziploc bags), where mold spores and bacteria can thrive. Instead, I placed the foods I'd dehydrated into cloth or mesh bags that breathed well enough to keep microbes from breeding, but provided protection from dirt, bugs, and larger contaminants. So long as the bags were kept dry and exposed to open air, the foods inside remained edible for months, sometimes years, depending on the food.

Beans would be an important source of protein in my diet, just as they had been for the trappers of old. I took 50 pounds of them, pinto, navy, kidney, and split peas. I'd intended to buy them in bulk, but decided that individual 1-pound bags would lend themselves better to long-term storage.

Rice has been a staple in my backpack for thirty years, because not only is it lightweight and nutritious enough to live on indefinitely, it works very well as a base food for numerous main dishes. When I was a kid, it was almost a tradition in camp to eat a stick-to-your-ribs breakfast of canned peaches and rice cooked together in the same pot. The versatile grain also makes a great meal when mixed with fish, meat, berries, fruits, and wild vegetables ranging from bracken ferns and cattail shoots to watercress and wild carrots. I loaded 20 pounds of it into my shopping cart.

From there I prioritized downward. Twenty-four pounds of ground coffee, two cans of baking powder, two boxes of baking soda, a case of peanut butter, Kool-Aid mix, a case of granola bars, 5 pounds of brown sugar, 5 pounds of oatmeal, and so on. I honestly didn't know how much I'd need of most of the stuff I was buying, but I figured I'd have a pretty good handle on my consumption rates and needs by the start of winter.

My cooking utensils were for the most part taken from the stuff I had in my apartment. Cast-iron skillets that were too heavy for backpacking worked great for cooking over fire at a permanent camp. Big aluminum pots were ideal for heating gallons of water for bathing, laundry, or dishes, although Bakelite handles would crack and fall off if overheated. For coffee I bought a Coleman camp percolator for $11. Fire would blacken the outsides of these vessels, but that wouldn't affect their utility, and in fact helped them to absorb heat better than bare metal did.

I also bought a good supply of toilet paper because, like bears, woodsmen do indeed shit in the woods. I'd wiped my arse with enough grass, ferns, and leaves over the years to know for a fact that tissue paper is a much better medium for that purpose, so I bought twenty-four rolls to insure that I wouldn't need to use natural materials. This was one area where I knew my consumption rate pretty well, and I figured that even using some of it for cleaning eyeglass and other lenses, I had enough to last four months. For years I'd made a habit of packing a roll inside a Ziploc plastic bag and carrying it in a cargo pocket of my BDU trousers whenever I was in the woods, so it seemed likely that I'd be making a roll of this handy stuff part of my daily attire from now on.

I suppose I could have made my own soap from wood ashes and animal fat, the way an authentic pioneer would have, but I elected to pack in a large zipper-lock bag of bar soap for personal hygiene, and a 10-pound box of powdered detergent for laundry. I had several recipes for soap making, but I suspected the time and effort required to render animal fat and ashes into soap might be better spent on other construction projects.

Bar soap also makes a superior tooth cleaner, but it doesn't taste very good, so I bought two large tubes of toothpaste and four toothbrushes. In the days before proper dental hygiene, teeth were cleaned (if at all) using a "twig brush," made by chewing the end of a branch cut from astringent shrubs like witch hazel until it was fibrous and brushlike, then using the chewed end to scrub teeth and gums. I'd used both bar soap and twig brushes to clean my teeth in the past, which explains why I chose to include toothpaste and nylon toothbrushes in my homesteading kit.

I didn't have a mule to pack tools and materials in to the cabin site the way a nineteenth-century trapper would have, but I did have my "Indian van," an '89 Chevy three-quarter-ton conversion van, that would serve as an accessible resupply cache. The term was a colloquialism that had actually been coined by local Odawa and Ojibwa Indians, many of whom elected to drive large conversion vans because their roominess and extra seating capacity was sufficient to haul a tribe. In fact, I'd bartered my van from an Indian friend after losing my 4 × 4 pickup to my ex-wife.

I didn't really like the 3-ton Chevy, with its bargelike handling and the fuel economy of a school bus, but it was a three-quarter-ton truck, and it's huge interior made it nearly ideal for use as a resupply station. I wired in an extra battery as insurance that it would start, and made sure I had bottles of engine fluids to replenish its crankcase and reservoirs as needed. The van also carried two Craftsman toolboxes loaded with wrenches, sockets, pliers, and a broad assortment of tools. The spare tire mounted to its rear was serviceable, and those on its axles were in good shape, but I felt safer including a 120-psi hand pump to which I attached a small pouch containing a pencil-type air gauge and a plug kit. So long as the punctures were through the tread, and the sidewalls remained undamaged, I could repair flat tires right in the woods.

I packed all of these and more into the van, until there was barely room to move about inside. I tried hard to compartmentalize everything into categories, the way I've always done in my backpacks, so that whatever I needed would be readily accessible. Milk crates, 5-gallon buckets with covers, and even picnic coolers became individual kits. I still ended up with a mess, but at least it was an organized mess. Finally, I just said to hell with it; at least it was all in there and ready for transport. I slammed the back doors shut, still feeling that were was a whole lot of stuff that I'd overlooked.

During the gearing-up process, I was simultaneously attempting to liquidate my household. I no longer had any use for a microwave oven, VCR, color TV, and most of the other appliances that had been important to civilized life, so I put everything up for sale to help bolster my rather lean grubstake. Most of my office went into storage, because unless something went terribly wrong out there, I hoped to return the following year and resume my writing career. Furniture, dress clothing, bedding, and dozens of other things that were unnecessary to life in the wild had to be left behind. I regretted leaving behind the queen-size Serta bed I'd treated myself to just a year before, but there was certainly no way that could go with me.

Hardest to leave behind were my dog and cat. Buddy, my Samoyed-mix companion of the past six years, was more dear to me than were most humans. I'd gotten him as a month-old puppy when I heard that he was going to be shot the next morning because no one would take him in. I was in the market for a good dog at the time, and I didn't want a mutt, but I couldn't let this little black furrball die just because his parents hadn't had the right genes. So I adopted him, trained him to be the best dog in the woods I'd ever had, and spent literally thousands of dollars I couldn't afford to keep him healthy.

The real problem was that Buddy's constitution had already proved too fragile for the homesteading life I'd be living. He had mange when I adopted him, and had come close to death from pancreatitis when he was two years old. Deerflies considered him a delicacy, and he'd already suffered several allergic reactions to their bites, nearly dying from them once. He was trained to find lost hikers and lead them back to safety, and I often relied on his superior night vision to guide me along vague footpaths in the dark during our frequent backpacking trips, but he was prone to ear infections, skin rashes, and other ailments that made taking him with me a bad idea. When he did accompany me on camping trips, the Benadryl and antibiotic medicines I carried in my pack were for him, not me.

Fortunately, my downstairs neighbor, Big John, and Buddydog had been best friends since they'd first met. A lot of people volunteered to take my dog, but I knew John honestly loved him, and he'd treat Buddy better than he did himself. Besides, I'd get to see both of them when I came to town for supplies.

My cat, Lucky, had been with me for just over a year, succeeding Buster who'd died at ten years of age, but he'd also earned a place in my heart during that time. When Lucky was a mere handful of a kitten I'd detected a feistiness in him that was more pronounced than I'd ever seen in a house cat. People actually came to my house just to see what we dubbed "the cat and dog show," an evening ritual during which the 2-pound kitten would attack my 85-pound dog with all the energy he could muster.

Lucky usually started the fight, stalking purposefully over to Buddy, who was typically in a prone position, and batting his nose with a series of lightning fast blows that would put a champion boxer to shame. As soon as Buddy responded by gently mouthing him, the little tiger would pin his ears back and leap onto the dog's neck with real fury, wrapping his forelegs around as far as they'd reach and biting hard into Buddy's thick mane. Lucky eventually outgrew this game, but most folks credited his fearlessness and genuine love for fighting anything that would fight back—including raccoons and opossums—to martial arts training he'd received from a dog that was ten times his size.

Excepting a few local cat owners, everybody loved Lucky, but my upstairs neighbor, Howard, would probably have paid me to adopt him. We both knew that the cat's extraordinarily scrappy nature would get him killed in no time out there in the woods, probably the first time he encountered a coyote. Lucky seemed to genuinely like Howard—as much as his prickishly independent nature permitted—and I knew Howard would care for him as though here were a child, so Lucky moved upstairs. Mercenary that he was, I don't think the cat even missed me.

I ended up with only a few hundred dollars from the many thousands of dollars worth of goods that I put up for sale. Many people got the items they wanted at bargain basement prices, while I simply gave much of it to needy people who couldn't afford to buy those items at all. My friends tell me I'm a poor businessman, while family members think I'm a fool who lets people take advantage of him with a sob story. Maybe they're right, but I seldom have trouble getting a good night's sleep.

The lowest category, the scavengers, waited until I pulled out, then descended in a flock to grab up and scurry away with whatever was left. Cheanne, who actually had a key to the place, stopped by the apartment to pick up my computer printer just a few hours after I'd left—she'd already taken my computer to storage, thank God—only to find that it had already been carried off, apparently by no one. She said the vultures were everywhere, unscrewing fixtures, taking pictures off the wall, and generally hauling away even things that had been nailed down. The only items that were of no interest to them were books.

In all, my grubstake totaled just over $3,500. It wasn't much to live on for the next year, and while I was in the woods there wasn't much likelihood that I could continue writing the magazine articles I'd counted on so heavily to pay my bills. It would have to do, however, because that was all I had. I knew there'd be tools and other expenses that I hadn't foreseen, I just hoped none of them were too serious or too costly.

LEAVING FOR THE WOODS: APRIL 14, 2001

April 14 dawned bright and sunny, with a promise of spring in the air. There were still a few snowbanks remaining in parking lots where it had been piled high by snowplows over the winter, but warmer weather was definitely on the way.

My departure went without fanfare. There was no one to see me off, even though the people I thought should know had been told when I'd be pulling out. I couldn't blame them, because nobody knew what to make of this apparent bout of insanity, and only those who knew me best actually believed that I meant to go through it. It was an uncomfortable situation for the few people who cared about me, so they just stayed away, hoping I'd return to my senses. Besides, what do you say to a man who has apparently gone off the deep end?

I spent the morning rearranging my gear for the trip north. The old Indian van was loaded to its three-quarter-ton axles with more weight than it had been designed to bear, but I hoped it would hold up for the 35 miles I needed to go. My only real concern was handling the last 3 miles of bumpy, sandy two-track that led to the dam at French Farm Creek, literally the end of the road. From there it would be manual labor, hauling in supplies and tools on my back 1.5 miles to the building site, deep inside the forested glacial dunes around Lake Michigan's northeastern shoreline.

I already had a site on Odawa tribal land in mind for my homestead. I hadn't been to the place in two years, but I recalled that it had seemed to be as ideal a place for homesteading as I could find without crossing the Mackinac Bridge and tribal authorities had granted permission to build there. There was already a cache there in the form of a plastic open-top 55-gallon drum, dragged in and stocked with a few essentials two years earlier, just in case the dreaded Y2K computer bug turned out to be the global catastrophe that some had predicted it would be. Y2K had come and gone without much trouble, but at least I had a food cache already in place, and that saved me the considerable effort of getting one out there.

There were good reasons why I'd chosen that particular spot as a retreat. For one, it was secluded enough to exhibit no sign of ever having been found by hunters, or even Michigan Department of Natural Resources biologists, for more than a decade. Century-old white pines and cedars, lusted after by timber companies, flourished there, hidden by the smaller trees of a forest so thick that hurricane-force winds were reduced to a mere breeze at ground level and anything more than 50 yards distant was out of sight. The ridge I'd be building on was open and sunny enough to grow a garden, yet still had enough canopy to conceal a log cabin from the many helicopters and small planes that flew over the area on a daily basis. The place would never be flooded, would never see a tornado, and winter blizzards would be gentle there, regardless of how much snow fell.

The site wasn't perfect, though. Being springtime, lowlands and swamps around the glacial ridge I'd selected to build on would be flooded with melted snow that I could filter or boil for cooking and drinking, but I knew from experience that as summer progressed the swamp would go dry. The nearest permanent source of water was a very old beaver pond a quarter mile north of the site, and even that was mostly mud in midsummer. I'd need to dig a well to provide a permanent year-round source of water.

I finally left Petoskey at about 11:30 A.M. There was a twinge of regret at leaving behind my home of the last six years—and most of my personal belongings—but there was no looking back now. For the next year I'd be living the life of a homesteader, and the many tasks at hand would require all of my attention and energy. I gassed up at the Speedway station north of Petoskey, and headed the van northward on U.S. 31 toward Mackinaw City, 35 miles away.

When I pulled off the pavement onto the rutted, sandy two-track that led past French Farm Lake's northern shore, I prayed that my overloaded Chevy van would make the 3 miles to the dam without problems. It was slow going at a breakneck speed of 5 miles per hour, but after a half hour of bouncing along and gassing the big 350 V8 hard through sandy spots and a few remaining patches of hardpack snow, I arrived at the dam that separated French Farm Creek from the beaver flooding at the lake's western end.

At the dam, I took a few moments to marvel at the beauty of the country that was to be my home for the next year, even though I'd been visiting there for more than a decade and knew the area as well as any person living. A chill breeze came off the water, cooled by still melting pack ice and remnants of winter snow, but skies over the water were a brilliant blue, and the scene was as breathtaking as any natural environment in the world.

But there was hard work to be done, and plenty of it. I shouldered my backpack, grabbed my axe, saw, and rifle, and headed into the woods. The first mile was through a section of the North Country Trail, an interstate hiking path that extended from the Atlantic to the Pacific across the northern United States, including Michigan's Lower and Upper Peninsulas. The trail was flooded by melted snow where it crossed through low, swampy spots between glacial dunes. It was blocked in places by trees toppled during the sometimes vicious nor'westers for which the straits were infamous, but the going was generally easy.

A mile in, the North Country Trail turned abruptly west toward Carp River, 2.5 miles away, but I continued north on an old logging trail that had been abandoned for more than twenty-five years. It was broken by washouts, flowing springs, and wind-felled trees, and so overgrown in summer that it resembled a subtropical jungle. In the twelve years that I'd been frequenting this section of forest, fewer than a dozen people had traveled this far back, and none had ventured more than a hundred yards from the trail. Despite an abundance of whitetails in the area, even the most enthusiastic hunter balked at dragging a deer more than a few hundred yards, and not many hikers were willing to face the clouds of bloodsucking bugs that filled the air there from spring till fall.

A number of friends, acquaintances, and just plain nosey people had questioned me about the location I'd chosen to homestead, but I honestly couldn't tell them. I described the place, and even gave map coordinates to those who could understand them, but I knew that the most accomplished outdoorsman had virtually no chance of finding the cabin site unless I first led him there. Despite satellite technology and aerial mapping, the remote ridge I'd selected might well have been on another planet, and if you hadn't already been there, you weren't going to find it.

Fortunately, I'd been there, albeit not for a couple of years, and after a minor blunder or two, I walked out onto a relatively open section of dune right where I wanted to be. The blue barrel wasn't where I'd left it, but I figured it had to be close by. When I'd first brought it out, I'd had some troubles with a local black bear that seemed to find the big noisy barrel irresistible, and I suspected that he had bounced it off into the woods nearby.

Sure enough, I found the lidless drum within 50 yards of where I'd left it, lying in a flowing spring, its top and locking ring a few feet away. It had apparently been there for about a year, abandoned once its edible contents had been consumed. I dragged the drum back to the ridge and cleaned it up with a rag and water in preparation for loading it with food, noting as I did so that its heavy polyurethane walls were deeply gouged by the black bear's powerful teeth and claws. I was happy to see that the drum's construction had been proof against the most powerful animal in these woods, and I reckoned it had been just luck that the retaining ring had come loose.

The ridge was as near to perfect for homesteading as I'd remembered. Marsh and freshwater springs bordered it on either side, a plethora of edible and medicinal plants grew close by in summer, and the area teemed with wildlife of all kinds. As Robert Redford said in the movie *Jeremiah Johnson*, "This'll be a good place to live." I dropped my pack and prepared to move in.

I pitched my tent just behind where the cabin would sit, taking more care than normal to insure that it was in a place where I could live with it for the next several months, until I could get a real roof over my head. I made three more trips to the van that day, hauling back shovels, pots and pans, clothing, and the stuff I thought would be most important to getting started with a homesteading project. My second tent, a 2-person Moss Starlet, I erected a few feet from the 4-person Olympic that served as home. The smaller tent would be a warehouse for clothing and equipment that I didn't want exposed to the elements and animals. An ultralight tarp stretched between four spruces kept rain off my tools and other less fragile gear.

It was during my last return trip to the cabin that I heard an unmistakable rustling in the brush to my left. I stopped, backpack on my shoulders and a shovel in one hand, as the rustling came directly toward me. The noise revealed itself as a large opossum—weighing about 15 pounds—that entered onto the trail barely 5 feet from where I stood. The 'possum looked at me unafraid, then veered away to head in the direction from which I'd come.

When it was no more than 10 feet from me, the critter suddenly turned, bared its fifty pointed teeth, and hissed loudly at me, as if contesting my right to use the trail. I was surprised for a moment, then just a little outraged at having been challenged by this brazen scavenger whose species didn't even exist here just a decade ago. I stalked toward the 'possum, intent on giving it a good boot through the air to show it the error of confronting a human, but the animal realized its bluff had been called before I'd taken two steps, and ran off into the brush at trailside.

After humping heavy loads more than 10 miles through rough terrain, it was late afternoon and I'd had enough for that day. After carefully selecting a spot where I could live with it long term, I dug out a fire pit with the shovel and built a warm blaze to fend off the chill of an early spring evening. When it had burned down to a hot bed of coals suitable for cooking, I made a simple supper of macaroni and cheese flavored with slices of summer sausage. I figured on eating a lot of macaroni and cheese over the next year; good thing I liked it so much.

Nightfall found me seated on a closed-cell sleeping pad leaned against a maple, listening with amusement to my shortwave receiver while a seriously stressed-out talk show host named Bill Cooper tried to incite me to violent revolution against the American government. The sky was clear and glittering with stars as temperatures fell toward a nighttime low of 30 degrees Fahrenheit, and a chorus of mating peeper frogs seemed to mock the rantings that came from my radio's speaker.

Recently arrived sandhill cranes and loons called to one another from the beaver pond north of me, and Canada geese honked noisily from their nests in the cattails as local bobcats prowled the shoreline looking for an opportunity to make them dinner. For more than a year newscasters had been reporting that goose numbers were out of control, fouling parks and lakefront properties with their scat, and causing an epidemic of swimmer's itch at beaches around the country. That was true near civilization, where large predators aren't permitted to live, but out here the geese didn't get a chance to overpopulate.

A small peep, like the chirp of a bird, sounded from right next to where I was sitting. I looked down and was surprised to see a tiny tan-colored tree frog—identifiable by suction cups at the ends of its toes—sitting atop my radio, peering upward at me. The little guy had probably been attracted from its arboreal home by the warmth of my campfire, but its appearance certainly dispelled the myth about so-called cold-blooded animals going dormant in freezing weather. I gently placed the little frog on the ground before taking the radio and other items I didn't want to leave outside into the tent with me. I fell asleep to the "thum–thum-thum" engine sound from distant freighters passing through the Straits of Mackinac.

I slept soundly until 9:00 the next morning, when a bright sun rose high enough above the trees to shine into my tent's open door and awaken me. I crawled out of the tent into crisp morning air that was still below the freezing mark. Frost made the reindeer moss and grasses look as if they'd been sprinkled with confectioner's sugar, and my exhaled breath condensed into white clouds before me. The radio, tuned to WJML out of Petoskey, told me that temperatures would reach the mid-50s that day, but right then there was a skin of ice over any water that wasn't flowing. Besides, I knew that temperatures in town were always at least 10 degrees warmer than they were in the woods.

After drawing water from a gurgling spring and perking a pot of coffee in the fire pit, I sat back with a steaming canteen cup and planned my activities for the day. There were still four backpacks in the van, already loaded with pots, tools, and other items that needed to be hauled to the cabin site. Once they were here, I'd empty them and head back out with the largest to refill it with more gear that needed to come out here. I figured it would be a week before I got all the stuff I needed to the site.

But first I thought I'd limber up a bit from the previous day's labors and see how good I was with an axe after so many years. I picked up the Collins axe and walked through the woods surrounding my camp, selecting which trees to cut first for the cabin walls. I'd already decided to build the walls from poplar, a softwood that nearly everyone had told me was a poor choice because it would rot too quickly. They were partly right—poplar does tend to deteriorate quickly from exposure to the elements—but logs used in cabin walls aren't subject to the same conditions as a dead log lying on the ground, and it would rot no more quickly than the pine many old cabins had been made from.

Some also expressed doubts about using green wood because it was bound to warp and twist to some degree as it dried. True again, but a trapper in the nineteenth century would have had no choice if he was to have a roof over his head before winter. Those objections aside, I'd chosen to construct my cabin with poplar because it was both fast growing and abundant in the forest I'd be using for building materials.

Poplar is also one of the straighter trees in a forest, but you wouldn't have known that by the trees I had available. Whether it was because they were so close to the water table, or maybe because there was so much competition from spruces and hemlocks in this thick forest, these trees were as gnarled and bent as a poplar gets. Oh well, there was nothing I could do except make the best of what I had to work with.

First came the foundation logs. Ideally, these were the largest-diameter logs in the walls because they supported the structure's entire massive weight, and because they would be half buried in earth. I picked out a fairly straight 60-footer that was a full 18 inches across, selected a relatively clear path for it to fall without hanging up in other trees, and trimmed away any surrounding limbs that might interfere with my axe strokes. Finally, I planted my feet, and started swinging. The axe, whose edge I had honed to shaving sharpness, bit satisfyingly deep into the green wood, and I started making the first of many thousands of chips that would litter the surrounding area before I was finished.

Cutting wood with an axe has a method. Nothing about it is easy, but there is definitely an easier way and a harder way. The first stroke makes a cut that's perpendicular to the trunk, about 2 feet above the earth; this sets the bottom of the cutting notch. The second stroke is applied downward at a 45- to 50-degree angle, at a distance above the first cut that equals roughly two-thirds the diameter of the trunk being cut. This width insures that there will be sufficient room to remove chips as the notch becomes narrower toward the trunk's center. A hard outward twist of the embedded axe's handle helps to loosen both its head and large chunks of wood.

How the axe is swung is also important, because the more centrifugal force you can develop at the head, the harder it hits. There's a tendency among beginners to choke up on the handle, which serves to limit the amount of force delivered. The most efficient method is to allow the forward hand, the one closest to the head, to slide downward as the axe arcs toward impact, until both hands grasp the handle only at its end. A wider toe at the end of the handle keeps it from sliding free of the wielder's grip.

When the initial notch, which faces the direction of the intended fall, has been opened to a depth that equals about two-thirds of the trunk's diameter, the axe wielder moves to the opposite side, away from the direction of the fall, and cuts the felling notch. This second notch is centered about 6 inches above the apex of the first, creating a ledge of sorts that prevents the tree from falling backward.

Things I'd forgotten about lumberjacking began coming back to me before I'd cut halfway through the big poplar's trunk. One of them was just how much work this was. My chest was heaving and I could actually see my heart pounding in my chest as I leaned against the axe handle, gasping for breath. Among those who backpacked and snowshoed with me, I was considered to be in fine physical condition, but this first tree was kicking my ass. The axe felt like it had gained another pound each time I resumed swinging. By the time I heard the loud crack that told me the tree had lost

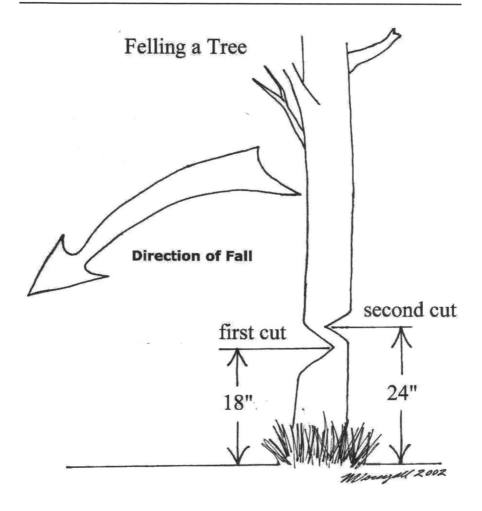

Felling a Tree

Direction of Fall

first cut

second cut

18"

24"

M'Connell 2002

this contest of endurance, I was drenched in honest sweat and so exhausted that I staggered like a drunk. Two tons of green wood came crashing down through the branches of surrounding trees to hit the ground with a force that shook the earth, and I was beginning to wonder if I hadn't bitten off a good deal more than I could chew. One down, twenty-five more to go.

It also occurred to me that every tree had to be cut twice: once to fell it, and once again to make it into a log. I refused to even think about the labor that would be involved in getting it to the construction site. I took a few minutes to catch my breath, already feeling the muscles in my shoulders and arms stiffen, and convinced myself to get moving again.

I'd calculated that each wall log needed to be cut to a length of 15 feet, discounting tapers at the ends, to end up with an interior wall length of 12 feet, and a finished floor space of 144 square feet. I placed the end of the 25-foot tape measure I kept clipped to my belt against the butt end, extended it as far as my arms could reach, then held the tape tight against the log with one hand while I moved down its length. I then extended the tape farther, again pinning it firmly against the bark, until 15 feet of it lay stretched down the tree's length. This method allowed me to get precise measurements without the need to anchor the tape's zero end, and it worked especially well when those measurements were being taken from a tree that had landed in heavy brush where even walking was difficult. At 15 feet, I scratched a mark into the poplar's smooth upper bark with my axe to indicate where the log must remain at full thickness, and began angling the halving cut from there. The length of the taper at either end was inconsequential, but each log had to be at full thickness for 15 feet.

Chopping a downed tree in two is a bit different than felling it, because there is no getting around to cut from the opposite side. The initial cuts need to be at least as wide as the log is thick to keep the V-shaped notch from coming to a point before the length has been severed. Unlike a felling cut, in which the bottom of the notch is kept generally perpendicular to the trunk, both cuts are angled inward from the opposite sides to remove as much wood as possible per swing.

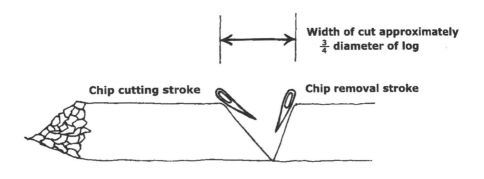

Halving a Log

After the tree had been turned into a cabin log, I had to get it to the building site. I'd purposely chosen a tree that was close, but there was still more than a hundred feet of rugged, uneven terrain over which to drag a huge piece of wood that weighed roughly 800 pounds. Worse yet, it was all slightly uphill.

My plan was to tie a timber hitch around the length with my cable, then place it on rollers made from 2-foot sections of 10-inch-diameter saplings that had shallow notches cut around their centers to keep the log from sliding sideways on them as I pulled it forward using a 10-foot pry bar cut from a white ash sapling. It was harder to do than I'd figured. It took everything I had to lift one end of the log high enough to swing it onto the roller. Then, with the free end of the cable looped around the lower half of the pry bar, I placed the pry bar's end behind a convenient tree and levered it forward about 2 feet at a time, placing another roller under the forward end of the log as I went to keep its nose from pressing directly against the earth. It was backbreaking labor and progress was very slow, but at the end of a long day I had both foundation logs entrenched 12 feet apart at the front and back of the cabin form. The last step was to cut inward-angled notches 1 foot wide and 12 feet apart into the ends of both logs to accommodate the logs that would lie perpendicular to them.

Next came the logs that would cross both foundation logs to tie them together and form the base of what would become the cabin's side walls. I rolled these logs into the notches I'd cut in the foundation logs, levered

Timber-Hitch (Choker) Log-Skidding Knot

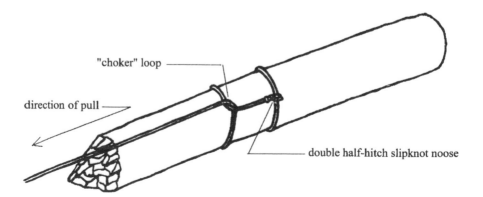

"choker" loop

direction of pull

double half-hitch slipknot noose

them into place so that the overhang was even on both ends, and used the foundation log notches as guides for placing the notches on their ends. It was vital that the end notches of the log being placed match as precisely as possible with the notches in the log below it to keep the walls from becoming skewed as they were built upward. The notches—four per log—needed to be one-third the depth of the log into which they'd been cut, to keep them interlocked tightly against one another at the ends, but not so shallow as to leave a larger gap than was necessary between them and the log directly below on the same wall. Any protuberances that would keep successive logs from sitting as flush as possible atop one another were removed with a few lateral axe strokes.

With a few days of hard labor under my belt—and on my body—I began to feel the need for a bath. Not for the superficial reasons that cause people in civilization to feel embarrassed if they don't have shiny, bouncy hair and a chemical scent on their bodies, but because the sweaty nooks and

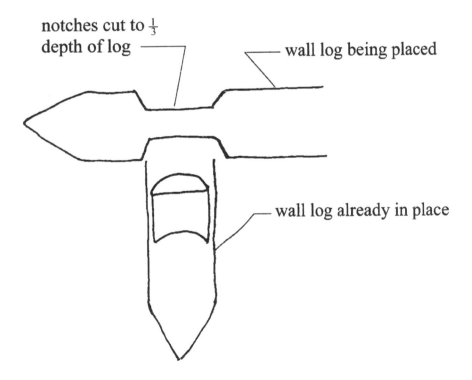

notches cut to $\frac{1}{3}$ depth of log — wall log being placed

wall log already in place

Notching the Wall Logs

crannies of my body needed to be cleaned of potentially infectious bacteria that had accumulated there. It wasn't an attractive proposition, being naked and wet in open air that was cold enough to induce hypothermia, but neither was the possibility of a fungal or bacterial infection.

I heated a pot of water on the fire. When it had warmed sufficiently, I poured it into a 2-gallon plastic tub marked "feet," so designated to keep it from being mixed up with an identical tub that I used for washing dishes. Glad that no one was there to witness what must have been a ridiculous sight, I stood barefoot in the tub, pants legs rolled up to my knees, and stripped to the waist. I washed my hair with bar soap, rinsed it with a canteen cup, then scrubbed the dirt and sweat from my upper torso.

Feeling chilled, I dried myself quickly with the bath towel I'd hung from a nearby branch, noticing as I did that a half-dozen black grass spiders were clinging to its nappy sun-warmed surface. I shook them off, pleased that none of the relatively venomous little buggers had bitten me.

Next, I dropped my trousers and repeated the process on my lower half. I scrubbed my abused feet, clipped my toenails, and put on clean socks. I was shivering slightly as I dumped the bath water and hung my towel to dry over the boughs of a small spruce, but I felt much better. Still, I was in no hurry to take another bath until the weather had warmed up some.

There was also laundry to be done. For this I had a bucket washer, similar to the one I'd learned to use as a kid. This one was made from a 6-gallon plastic bucket with a plastic snap-on lid, and a toilet plunger (unused of course) whose handle extended upward through the lid's pouring hole. I filled the bucket halfway with laundry, added a handful of powder soap, and filled it the rest of the way with water. Then, with the lid snapped in place, plunger inside, I moved the protruding handle forcefully up and down—as if plunging a drain—for 300 strokes. After that, I loosened one corner of the lid and lay the bucket on its side to drain. When it was empty, I refilled it with clear water and plunged for another 100 strokes. The result was laundry as clean as if it had been had it been washed in a machine. Twenty-five feet of parachute cord strung between two trees served as my clothesline.

After two weeks I had eight logs in place, counting the foundation logs, and the cabin had become a box. I was losing track of days, and if it weren't for news broadcasts from my radio receiver, I wouldn't have known what day, or even what month, it was. Dates didn't matter; there were no holidays here, no Sabbath days, and no reasons to celebrate or mourn any events except those that happened in these woods. The presence of God was undeniable, it whispered through the treetops and gurgled in the springs, and there was nothing a church could give me that I didn't already have right here.

I kept track of one date, however, because my friends Cheanne and Pete had told me before I'd left that they would be coming out to visit me in two weeks. I rose that morning, joints and muscles aching from the heavy exertion they'd been subjected to, but feeling much better and stronger with each passing day. My appetite had been tremendous, averaging about 4,000 calories per day, and I could see that I was still losing body fat rapidly. My muscles, though stiff in the morning, had become hard and heavily veined, and there were ridges in my abdomen. I no longer wore my heavy leather work gloves for most chores because thick callouses on my palms and fingers armored my hands against splinters and abrasions. No amount of money could have induced me to perform such brutal labor, but the challenge of creating a home for myself within this untracked wilderness was sufficient to make me work almost obsessively from morning until darkness forced me to stop.

I made coffee and ate a couple of granola bars to get my blood sugar up to working level. I'd built a low bench next to the fire pit out of two 14-inch diameter sections of logs laid parallel with 3 feet between them. A half-dozen 6-inch diameter lengths were laid crosswise on top of them and nailed in place to form a seat that was about 4 feet long. I'd been building this same type of bench at permanent campsites since I was a teenager. It was a functional and expedient means of keeping one's butt off the cold ground, especially in winter.

Cheanne and Pete were due to arrive at 11 A.M., and because no one but me knew how to find the cabin site, I'd told them I'd meet them on the trail in—they both knew how to get that far. It was 9:00 now, and I had time to kill before leaving to meet them, so I decided to use that time to drop a 40-foot poplar that was just behind the cabin. It wasn't a perfect wall log, being somewhat crooked and bumpy, but it was usable, and it was nearby.

For lumberjacking I normally wore my heavy La Sportiva mountaineering boots, but I'd been in these woods long enough to get perhaps just a little too comfortable. Axe in hand, I walked the 20 yards between cabin and tree wearing the sneakerlike Teva water shoes that served as camp slippers.

The poplar had a couple of twists in its trunk, almost like a spiral, caused by the weight of winter snows on its branches as it was growing up. My gut told me that this tree might be tricky to aim, but my ego said that I'd been dropping trees precisely where I wanted them to land for half a month, and this one would be no different. To hedge my bets, I decided to notch the direction of its fall directly away from the cabin—and the very expensive Moss tent that sat just behind its rear wall.

I'd barely broken a sweat when the tree gave out that loud crack that told me it was coming down. I stepped back to avoid getting hit by the butt end if it bounced when it struck the ground, and was horrified to see a sudden powerful gust of wind catch the topmost branches and drive it in exactly the opposite direction, right toward my tent. Shouting a string of expletives that used most of the cuss words I knew, I foolishly jumped to place my body directly under the falling tree. There was no stopping it—I knew that—but I caught the trunk in both hands and heaved it sideways, away from the tent, with all the strength I could muster. It worked, but just barely; the outermost branches struck my tent hard enough to skew its shape in the opposite direction. As reward for this act of idiocy that kept the tent from being flattened, the poplar's trunk bounced upward when it struck earth and landed squarely across my left foot. The pain was exhilarating; I yowled like a lynx in heat and this time I used every one of the cuss words I knew at least once. Fortunately, the trunk had just pushed my foot downward into the soft humus, and I sustained nothing worse than a bruised instep.

The clock on my radio told me it was time to leave anyway. I tied on proper footwear and headed out to the main trail, just in time to find Cheanne and Pete headed off down the wrong ridge in search of my cabin. Although they'd come in separate vehicles, both had showed up early with the intention of surprising me by finding the cabin without my guidance. Good thing I found them when I did, because they were headed into some really rough country.

Back at the cabin, they were understandably unimpressed by my progress, although Cheanne did remark that those were some big logs. After they'd dropped their packs and Pete had pitched his tent—Cheanne shared mine—we sat down to catch up with a bit of conversation by the campfire. The sky was still clear, with a temperature in the mid-60s, but a late-season nor'wester off the straits had begun to kick up, and by sunset the treetops around camp were swaying hard.

We banked the fire and crawled into our sleeping bags at about 10 P.M. As usual, I left the front door of my tent open so that I could see what was happening outside. I might better have zipped it closed so we couldn't see, because the wind picked up to gale force, with gusts in excess of 50 miles per hour. The radio broadcast a travelers' advisory on the Mackinac bridge, while treetops silhouetted against the overcast sky were bending to frightening extremes. Away in the forest we could hear some of them snapping off and crashing to earth. We lay there for several hours, too anxious to sleep until exhaustion overcame us.

Morning dawned calm and sunny, but I perceived that neither Cheanne nor Pete was overly anxious to spend another night. After helping me to haul in the last of my necessities from the van, they left me with a sincere wish that I have good luck. Cheanne told me that in two weeks she and Pete would return with some of our friends—Archie Kiogima, wildlife biologist for the Odawa tribe; tribal conservation officer Al Colby; and Kathy Germain, a biologist friend. Aside from being curious about my well-being, they'd all expressed a desire to help me with the construction of my cabin. Based on what I'd learned about cabin building up to now, I doubted they'd be able to help much, especially in a single day. Still, I'd be happy to see them, and I noted the date in my heretofore unmarked pocket calendar.

Although it was only the first week in May, water was already getting harder to find in the swamp as what was left of the snow melt drained into Lake Michigan through a hundred springs, feeder creeks, and rivers. In a couple more weeks I'd have to walk a quarter mile to make a pot of coffee, and that was unacceptable.

I recalled an old adage from my childhood, usually used in reference to winter weather, about being "colder than a well-digger's ass." I figured that colloquialism had to have stemmed from a time when shovel-wielding workmen made a living digging freshwater wells for homesteaders, and even entire villages. I knew that what most modern people knew only as a "wishing well" had once been a vital source of drinking water in the days before plumbing. A stone or log wall around the well's perimeter had prevented animal feces from washing into it during hard rains, while a roof overhead kept out bird droppings.

But I'd never dug a well, and I'd never met anyone who had. I knew that it was essentially just a hole dug downward through the earth until it reached the water table, but I really didn't know what to expect. Judging from the wet marsh on either side of my homestead, the water table couldn't be too far down, so I picked up my shovel and went looking for a spot to dig.

First, I tried to find a suitable spot using the old divining rod trick. I'd seen it done before, once using an ordinary wire coat hanger, but the Y-shaped stick I cut refused to twitch downward, no matter where I held it. I remembered that it hadn't worked for me before, either, and the old farmer who'd used this method to determine where to drill a well for his house had told me that some people just didn't have whatever it was that made a divining rod work.

Screw it. I might not have the power to divine, but I had logic. There was a giant white birch off the northwest corner of the cabin, and although it was rooted on high ground, I knew that a birch required plenty of water to grow so big. I stepped a few yards off to avoid harming the roots of this magnificent tree, planted my shovel, and started digging.

I started by cutting a circle 5 feet in diameter out of the blueberry bushes that covered my ridge. The roots were thick and tough, and the sandy soil just below was filled with granite stones, most of them too small to be of any use for construction. Below that was hardpan, an orange-brown layer of compacted sand that defies shoveling and must be chopped through. The urine-yellow fiberglass handle of my "professional-grade"

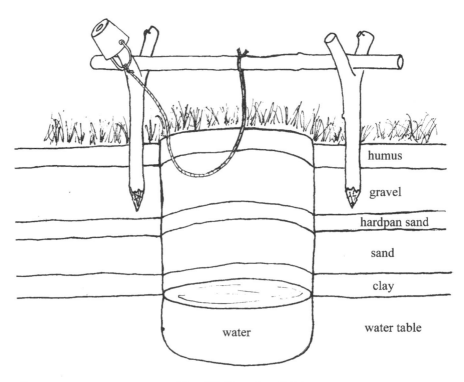

humus

gravel

hardpan sand

sand

clay

water table

water

The Well at the Cabin

shovel gave out a crack, then snapped off at the shovel head before I'd reached a depth of 3 feet.

After throwing a tantrum that I'm glad no one was there to witness, I hacksawed off the shovel head's retaining rivet, drove it out with a hammer and nail, and removed what was left of the broken handle. I replaced the flimsy hollow handle with a much stronger one whittled from a white ash sapling, held in place by drywall screws, and went back to work. Fitted with a proper handle, the shovel did what it was supposed to do.

At 5 feet I hit wet, compacted red clay that had to be pried free in big chunks. That made me happy, because clay is the homesteader's concrete. It can be mixed with water to make a thick slurry that pours like cement, and when it dries completely—over a period of a week or so—it makes a pretty good facsimile of concrete. There wasn't nearly as much of the stuff I needed to make a fireplace box, a hearth, and for all the other uses I had for clay, but I tossed the lumps out the well pit into a small pile by themselves anyway. Enough or not, I'd use them for something.

The few larger stones I encountered were also segregated into their own pile. I thought I might mortar them together with wet clay for the chimney at some point, but the biggest I used right away as cornerstones under the foundation logs.

I hit water at a depth of 6 feet, but continued digging to 7 feet to allow sufficient depth for a bucket to fill. When I'd accomplished that, my feet were cold from standing in spring water, and I'd had enough well digging for one day. I climbed up out of the vertical hole by placing my back against one wall and my feet against the other, then crab-walking upward.

The well's bottom filled with water slowly. By nightfall it resembled a foot-deep mud puddle, too murky to drink. I crawled into my sleeping bag, exhausted from my labors. By morning, the well had settled, and I drew my first pot of coffee from the clean, cold spring water that covered its bottom. It made me grin to think of how many people in the real world would pay good money to drink this water if I put it into a pretty bottle.

The next day marked the beginning of the blackfly hatch. Temperatures rose to the '70s, creating ideal conditions for the minuscule bloodsuckers to rise up in great black clouds from shorelines of lakes and ponds. I was ready for the ferocious little monsters with a head net I'd sewn from no-see-um netting—blackflies are unaffected by any insect repellent I know of—but I sure didn't expect to see the hordes of them that set upon me. From the time the morning sun warmed them enough to be active until sunset drove them into hiding once more, they were literally all over me, biting any exposed skin not too weathered to resist their proboscises. Any soft spots, like the insides of my forearms and elbows, behind my ears, my eyes, and the corners of my mouth had to be physically shielded with fabric.

Years of exposure to swarms of biting insects has given me an immunity to their venom and, thankfully, I don't swell or itch when bitten, but 2001 marked the biggest blackfly hatch I'd seen in more than three decades of roaming the northwoods. A humming aura of them followed me wherever I went, and when I closed my eyes to sleep at night, I could still see dozens of them crawling over the mesh that covered my face during daylight hours.

I recalled the stories of an old lumberjack's disease that was known as "swamp madness," in which usually inexperienced timbermen of the 1800s would suddenly go berserk and run screaming through the forest while flailing wildly at the air, sometimes with their axes. The disease, actually a nervous breakdown caused by long days of hard labor and unceasing torment from flies and mosquitoes around the clock, usually passed when victims were removed to the relatively bug-free environment of a town. My own situation wasn't quite so severe, what with the protection I enjoyed from my head net and having a purposely smoky campfire close by, but I certainly understood how these tiny animals might drive even the strongest man to insanity.

My tent provided a welcome measure of protection, because even with its screen doors open the blackflies wouldn't enter, and those that did fly inside wanted only to get back outside. Something in the makeup of these creatures causes them to shun enclosed places. It was a good thing to know, but not of much real use, because I still had to be outside to perform the labors of cabin building. I disliked having my vision hampered by mosquito netting while I chopped down trees heavier than most automobiles, but working without it would have been utterly impossible, and even more dangerous if a fly flew into one of my eyes mid-swing.

By the end of the third week I had twelve logs in place on the cabin walls. That my skill was improving was evidenced by corners that grew tighter as the walls grew higher, and chinking gaps that grew narrower with each successive log. Problem was, the walls grew higher while the logs they were made from continued to weigh three-quarters of a ton apiece. Even using fulcrums, levers, and every trick of physics I could come up with, I'd reached the point where I couldn't lift them any higher. It didn't escape me that a trapper of old would have had the advantage of a horse or mule to do the work that I'd been performing with my back.

It was time to go to town **for** more tools—I definitely needed a stout come-along winch. I also wanted another handsaw, a case of 10-inch lag screws with ⅜-inch heads, and another box of 3-inch spiral deck nails. Might as well pick up a dozen **boxes** of snack cakes and a couple of pounds of chocolate, too.

I hit the trail with a mostly **empty** pack at 7 A.M. the next morning. To help keep it from being vandalized, I moved the van to a different location every few days, and this time it **was** at the Carp River, 3.5 miles away. I broke out onto the North Country Trail under a dark, rumbling sky that suddenly burst open with torrential rains before I'd reached halfway. I didn't know it at the time, but this rain **was** just the first sign of things to come.

THE MONSOON SEASON

M y first trip to town was a short one. I arrived in Petoskey at about 9 A.M. My first stop was at Big John's apartment to have coffee and catch up on what had been happening in civilization during my absence. As I listened to the local gossip, I realized that what I'd been missing back here in civilization had been worth missing. My God, but the people who lived out here were vicious to one another.

Maybe it was because I'd been so long in the woods, where the things that were important were the things that directly affected comfort and survival. Who was screwing whose wife was of no consequence, and was in fact a distasteful topic to me. It simply didn't concern me that people whose existence didn't have a direct impact on my life were buying new cars, having babies, filing for divorces, or getting busted for drunk driving. I didn't care that an irate ex-employee had burned down the Arby's restaurant in Petoskey, or that local business owners were screaming bloody murder over plans to build a beltway that would route traffic away from their establishments. That these happenings provoked such animated discussions among people who weren't directly involved with them seemed superficial and unimportant to me.

In their turn, none of the several friends and acquaintances I met in town wanted to hear about what I'd been doing in the wilderness. Probably most of them still didn't comprehend that I'd actually moved to the woods to build a homestead. Those who did couldn't relate to any of the experiences I'd had, or to the tasks I still had left to accomplish. The events in my life had become as unimportant to them as theirs were to me. It was still raining when I left for the Home Depot store in Petoskey to pick up the tools I needed, but even the prospect of hypothermia was preferable to subjecting myself to more local news.

By 1 P.M. I'd finished with my supply run, and was almost in a state of anxiety from my need to flee the savagery of civilization. In the short time I'd been in town I'd been cursed at and given the finger by motorists, treated rudely by shoppers in Wal-Mart, and blown off by store clerks who apparently regarded my questions as an interruption of their lives. I loaded the stuff I'd bought into the van, filled the backpack I'd brought with munchies and smaller items, and was headed back toward French Farm Lake by 3 P.M.

Intermittent sunlight broke through the rain as I drove, and the rutted two-track leading to the dam felt like it was leading me home. I could hardly wait to feel the weight of a backpack on my shoulders and a trail under my boots. There was a feeling almost like urgency in my belly as I locked the van and hurried into the shadowed woods beyond French Farm Creek.

When I'm hiking I have a habit of suddenly spinning around and looking behind me to see if I'm being followed. My friends usually attribute this idiosyncrasy to a sense of paranoia, but I've learned that animals will often take cover when they scent an approaching human, waiting until he's passed, then resuming their travels. Most of the time this "Crazy Ivan" habit reveals nothing, but I figure you can't know what might be there if you don't look.

This time it paid off. I was in the deep woods, about a quarter mile from the cabin, when I turned just in time to see a timber wolf break from the woods on the west side of the trail and bound across to the opposite side, crossing not 50 feet from where I stood. I'd been seeing 4-inch canid tracks pressed into the trail for more than a week, and this large animal, whose weight I estimated at 90 pounds, confirmed what I already knew.

I dropped the winch I carried right there to mark the point where I'd turned, then walked back to study the tracks left by the wolf's crossing. The tape measure I carry clipped to my pack measured the tracks at 4 inches, just like before, and I deduced that this was the same individual whose sign I'd been seeing. Probably a two year old whiling away the day until the nightly reunion with its parents and their new litter of pups.

I'd been tracking wolves in this area for nearly four years, logging hundreds of miles with the Northern Michigan Wolf Detection and Habitat Survey Team, and had seen only two prior to this one. I felt privileged as I continued toward the cabin, the angst created by my visit to town all but forgotten. It was hard for me to stay uptight when I knew there was a wolf in my neighborhood.

The next morning dawned rainy and cold. I could hear the moan of foghorns out on the straits as I broke out my new winch. It had only 7 feet of pull before its cable was fully wound onto the reel, but in that distance it was capable of exerting 2 tons of pulling power. I was feeling almost vengeful as I clipped the come-along to the drag cable already hitched around a monster log that had been defying my best efforts with pry bar and rollers. I extended the winch cable and tied off the static hook to a stout pine with a doubled 50-foot length of nylon marine rope, and started cranking the winch's handle.

The rope stretched a few inches as the log dug into the earth under its own weight, then the big section of tree sprang forward, furrowing the humus beneath it as it came. Oh yeah, this was going to work. I extended the winch cable, took up the slack in the rope, tied it off again, and pulled the log another 7 feet. It was still slow going, but not nearly as taxing to my muscles as it had been with the pry bar and rollers. In fact, I made a picnic of sorts of the job, kneeling in front of the winch, a hot cup of fresh coffee and my radio beside me while I cranked the big log toward the cabin.

Next I applied my newfound muscle to a 60-foot "hanger" that leaned over the path leading to the camp like a giant wooden Sword of Damocles. As the cabin walls grew, I was forced to go farther into the forest to cut suitable trees, which increased the danger of a falling tree getting hung up in the branches of one or more other trees. This one was wedged firmly in the crotch of a large birch, but only by its thin top, which was bowed as though it might suddenly snap in half at any moment. Being right across the path, I walked under it several times each day, always expecting that my luck would cause it to come crashing down on my head like a massive fly swatter.

So far this hanger had defied my every effort to bring it to earth, while the constant threat it posed was wearing on my nerves. This time I was openly vindictive as I wrapped a choker around the tree's butt end, muttering promises that it would now see who was boss here.

I winched the cable to its end, until the butt was actually suspended 3 feet off the ground, but still the tree refused to fall. Cussing out loud at that point, I roped the tree off, still suspended against the laws of physics, and reset the winch for another try.

This time the giant poplar pulled free of the birch with a loud crack. I jumped back as its massive weight came crashing down, narrowly escaping being hit by the wildly whipping winch handle. "Hah!" I yelled, kicking the prone trunk hard enough to hurt my toes. Normal folks would probably have thought me fit for a padded cell, but I took real satisfaction from cutting that tree up and forcing it to become a log in the wall of my cabin.

In the next three days I added four more logs to the cabin walls. At this point the corner notches were all tight and the cabin was beginning to look pretty good to me. The problem now was that the walls were 4 feet high, and I couldn't lift the ends up onto them any more. I'd pulled the last two into place by tying the winch rope across the cabin walls, anchoring it to a strong hemlock on the other side of the cabin, and sliding one end of the logs upward on my white ash pry bar, which I'd leaned against the cabin's outside corner to form a ramp of sorts. As I pulled horizontally across the walls, the log end was forced to slide upward over the pry bar. I still had to get a shoulder under it to boost its butt over the wall, but the winch held most of its weight.

The tricky part was making sure the log was leaning solidly against the corner where adjacent walls intersected before I released tension on the winch to get a new purchase. After that it was a matter of pulling the log across until either end was supported atop opposite walls, where it was notched and rolled into place.

It didn't escape me that being in the path of an 800-pound log when it slipped in an unintended direction could easily crush any part of my body

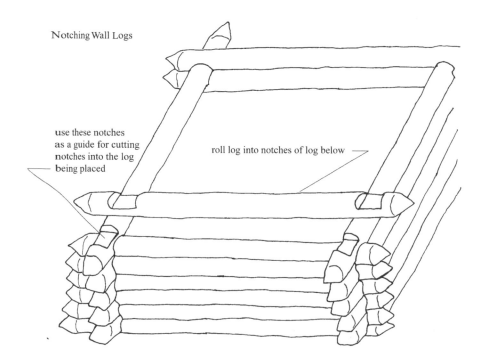

Notching Wall Logs

use these notches as a guide for cutting notches into the log being placed

roll log into notches of log below

that was in the way. I got a warning when one of them slid unexpectedly and pinned my left forearm between itself and the wall. I felt my radial and ulna bones bend under the force, but quickly got a shoulder under the log and was able to apply enough upward strength to pull my arm free with no more than a large purplish bruise. I cursed myself for being in that situation in the first place, and resolved to never let such a thing happen again. I'd laughed when Cheanne expressed concern that I might lie out here for days with a log across my crushed spine before one of my friends found me, but after that little incident it didn't seem quite so impossible or humorous.

What I needed was an overhead anchor from which to winch the logs upward. The most efficient way to accomplish that was to mount the ridgepole, which would form the roof's peak when the cabin was finished. I hadn't intended to mount that piece until the walls were finished, but now it seemed necessary. That meant further construction of the walls had to wait until the ridgepole was in place.

First, I had to mount center posts at the cabin's front and rear for the ridgepole to sit on top of. I'd already determined that these needed to extend 10 feet from the ground to give the roof a 12/12 (45-degree) pitch that would shed snow. It wasn't really necessary, but I decided to make the center posts 12 feet long, then sink them 2 feet below ground—I've always have a tendency to build everything heavier than it actually needs to be, mostly because I detest the idea of doing the same job twice in my lifetime.

There were plenty of poplar treetops lying around, so I sawed off a couple of 12-inch-diameter sections at 12 feet, making the tops as flat as possible to give the ridgepole ends a secure platform. After delimbing them with my axe so they'd fit flush against the cabin walls, I measured 6 feet from the side walls and dug a hole on the inside of either end wall to plant the posts. I actually dug about 28 inches, then placed one of the larger stones I'd excavated from the well at the bottom of each hole to further support the posts.

When both center posts were planted so they sat as vertically straight and flush with the walls as I could make them, I used my brace-and-bit to drill a 1-inch-diameter perpendicular hole about 1 inch deep into them at every point where they made contact with a wall log. Using these holes as countersinks, I then fastened each wall log to the center post using a 10-inch lag screw over which I'd slid a 1-inch-diameter steel washer. I'd originally intended to peg all these joints together, but considering how much sweat it took to drive home all those lag screws using a ⅝ socket on a 10-inch breaker bar, I was glad I hadn't.

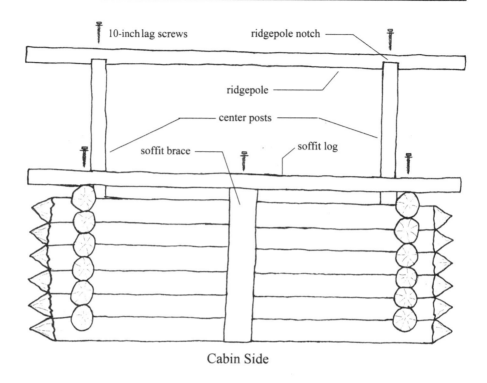

Cabin Side

When the center posts were almost ridiculously solid, I went shopping for a ridgepole. None of the treetops I'd left lying around were suitable, so I had to cut down another 12-inch-diameter poplar to get the 18-foot length that was needed to insure a 1-foot overhang at the front and rear. It's important that a cabin's roof extend beyond its walls on all sides to keep rain and snow from collecting on and eventually rotting the logs below. I purposely made my overhang a bit excessive to allow the door and windows to be left open without fear that rain or snow might come inside.

Next came the task of mounting the roughly 200-pound ridgepole on top of the center posts. Cheanne, who had been coming out to visit every few days, had expressed doubts that this could be accomplished by one man, but I had a few tricks up my sleeve. Although I hadn't figured on using them for that purpose, I'd brought with me three very cool telescoping ladders made by the Ol' Man treestand company. Designed to be an environmentally friendly alternative to the crude screw-in tree steps used by bow hunters, the ladders strapped securely to the side of any tree or pole that was at least 8 inches in diameter, and could be extended, then locked on place,

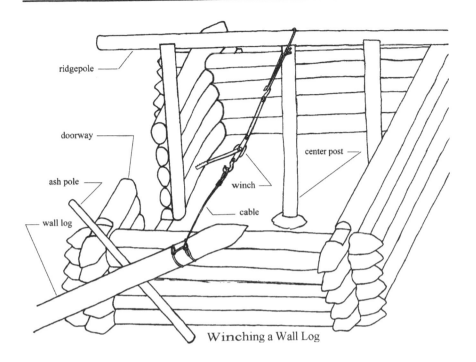

ridgepole

doorway

ash pole

wall log

center post

winch

cable

Winching a Wall Log

to a length of 4 feet. With a single section of ladder strapped to the inside of each centerpost 3 feet off the ground, I could easily reach their tops to mount the ridgepole.

With the ridgepole laying across the front and rear walls, I tied a timber hitch around one end and hoisted it as high as I could, fastening it in place at that point with another timber hitch tied around the center post. Then I climbed down and did the same with the opposite end. After repeating this procedure twice on either end, I had the ridgepole tied at the top of both center posts. Using the center-post tops as a location guide—because I'd learned that trying to precisely measure and precut logs was futile—I cut shallow, flat-bottomed notches into the top side of the ridgepole at either end with my SP-8 machete. When I twisted one end of the ridgepole hard, both ends rolled squarely on top of the center posts, settling nicely into the notches. Finally, I drove a lag screw down through the ridgepole and center post at both ends.

With the ridgepole mounted, I set another vertical center post under its center, then secured it with another 10-inch lag screw driven downward through both of them. Now the ridgepole was supported at either end and in the center. I had my overhead winch point; getting the rest of the wall logs into place would be comparatively easy.

I'd been eating double the recommended number of daily calories since I'd started this homestead, and apparently burned them all, but I was getting a little bored with dried foods. I suddenly had an intense craving for fresh meat. There were lots of edible animals living in the forest around the cabin, but it was the quacking of ducks on the beaver pond that had been getting my juices flowing these past few days.

I shouldered my .22 rifle and walked out to the pond, where there were dozens of black ducks swimming in circles and bobbing tails-up as they fed from the bottom. I hunkered down next to a fast flowing runoff stream and lay prone within the concealment of tall sawgrass while I waited for one of them to wander close to my position. It wasn't a problem to kill one, but I didn't want to go swimming in the still-cold water to retrieve my dinner after I'd shot it. If I could take one close to the flowing current, all I had to do was wait for it to bring the duck to me, then grab the carcass before it was washed downstream.

The busy ducks gave no sign that they'd seen me, and after just a few minutes there were a half-dozen of them circling on the water less than 10 yards from my hide. I flipped open the scope caps and picked a fat one. The crosshairs settled rock-steady on the feeding duck as I slipped the safety to fire and took up the trigger slack.

Oddly, I hesitated for a long while, watching my victim make its living in the shallow water. Maybe I'd just taken too many lives in my years as a hunter, but I felt a real reluctance to take this one. I could actually feel tears welling up in my eyes as I watched this beautiful bird, and I wondered at my own reaction. Even as my finger tightened against the trigger, I hoped that I'd miss, knowing that was unlikely with this well-seasoned rifle.

I didn't miss. The .22 cracked, and the powerful little Yellow Jacket bullet struck the duck at the base of its neck, just above its breast. It died instantly, its spine severed by a wound that nearly removed the neck from its body. There were hot tears on my cheek as I hung my head and said a prayer of thanks to the duck's spirit and to its Creator. The people who knew me wouldn't believe I was acting like this over a duck.

Back at camp I skinned the duck and boiled it until the meat separated easily from bone. I mixed the tender meat with a pot of boiled rice and fiddleheads, and ate the dish with relish. Still, I had a nagging worry that I'd developed an allergy of sorts to killing, and I hoped it wouldn't prove to be a liability to feeding myself in months to come.

With the coming of warmer weather it had begun to rain almost every day, especially from early morning to afternoon. Most of the time it was just a gray, misty drizzle that made working miserable but didn't seem to hamper the blackflies in the slightest. Frequently, though, the sky growled as if it were pissed off at me personally, and opened to pour out a torrent of water that drove me to take refuge in my tent while raindrops pounded off its rain-fly with such force that I couldn't hear my radio clearly from mere inches away. An added curse was that fly and mosquito eggs that should have dried up and died in a normal spring received enough moisture to hatch twice over.

The day my friends arrived coincided with a cold front that kept the sky sunny and the bugs to a minimum. I heard them coming down the trail at about noon, their approach sounding noisy after having spent so much time in the quiet company of animals. Cheanne and Pete led the way, followed by Al Colby. Behind them were Kathy and Cheanne's son, Jerod, a tribal police officer who often backpacked with me.

This time everyone was suitably impressed by the obvious labor that had gone into the cabin and well. Al was itching to get to work, and after they'd all toured the construction site, he wiped his palms against his jeans and asked me where they should get started.

The truth was that there was really little they could do to help. I'd learned through doing it that everything had a method, and it just wasn't possible to transfer the experience I'd gained the hard way to these well-intentioned friends in a single afternoon. Although just nineteen years old, Pete was the only person to acknowledge that fact; he kicked back in the hammock I'd strung between a couple of large birches and watched the proceedings with veiled amusement. I knew that he wasn't lazy, as Al inferred with a sideways comment from time to time, he was just smart enough to know that he didn't know how to do what needed doing.

Al and Jerod, on the other hand, seemed to believe we could finish the entire cabin that day. Jerod was twenty-four and a giant of a man, while Al was my age and reasonably fit, but I couldn't hide a grin when they suggested we just pick up the logs and carry them to the cabin. Instead of arguing the point, I countered with a suggestion that they might first try to lift one end of a smaller log. They did, and immediately came to the conclusion that it couldn't be done.

Instead, I put them to work chopping a wall log from one of the four trees I'd already downed in preparation for their arrival. I started the cut to show them the finer points of axe work, but they were both a little intimidated by the unfamiliar instrument, choking up on its handle and pulling their swings so that its razor-sharp edge removed far less wood than it might have, while at the same time wearing them to a frazzle. They were going to be busy for a while, so I left them with a warning to be careful, and turned my attention to Cheanne and Kathy, who were equally anxious to do something productive.

To the ladies I assigned the task of sawing a fireplace hole through the cabin's back wall, a job that was every bit as tiring as chopping wood, but required less brute strength. I'd already sawed out the top log to give them a guide for cutting the three logs below, but I really doubted they'd get through more than one of them.

They surprised me. Both women were in their forties and fit from backpacking and kayaking, and Cheanne's dad had been a carpenter. They had the first log cut free at both ends before the men had gotten through the one they were chopping with an axe. In fact, the fireplace was ready to be built by the time they left. I couldn't have done the job any better than they did.

By the time Jerod and Al had parted the first log, neither wanted any more to do with an axe. Now they wanted to try their hand at getting the log they'd cut to the cabin, 50 yards away. The problem was that neither knew how to tie a timber hitch or a quick-release double half-hitch, and neither wanted to learn the mechanics of using a come-along. I think they were a little embarrassed that everything about cabin construction was harder, heavier, and more complicated than they'd anticipated. They needn't have felt that way, because I'd been learning the very same lesson for a month.

Since they were still of a mind to manhandle a log to the cabin, I turned my attention from the ladies, who were doing fine without assistance, and set them up with the pry bar, cable, and rollers I'd first used. The log they'd cut was too big to be dragged that way, so I hitched the cable around a smaller log and demonstrated the proper technique for moving it the hard way.

It didn't go well. Maybe it was a desire to prove to themselves they could do the job, but neither wanted my help. I stood obligingly to one side while they wrestled the 500-pound log onto three rollers placed under its front, center, and rear, and began levering it forward inches at a time.

Basic Lumberjacking Knots

Square Knot — Fastens two ends together.

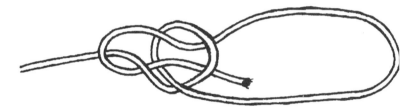

Bowline — Nontightening loop.

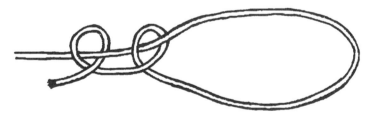

Double Half-Hitch Slipknot—
Noose tightens when pulled.

They'd dragged the log about 30 feet when the first injury occurred. Jerod had the white ash pry bar wedged behind a tree and was pulling hard with all the considerable strength his 225-pound frame could exert, but the log was stuck, it's nose dug into a mound of earth. He relaxed to get a more solid point to lever against, then heaved back mightily just as Al, who was straddling the log's fore end, yanked upward on the log's nose with all his strength. The log shot forward and the hardwood pry bar smashed Jerod across the mouth with all the force he'd exerted against it, bloodying his lips and loosening several front teeth. I didn't say a word, but the look in my eyes told them that there would be no more helping me today. I was grateful for the attempt, but watching my friends try to do potentially dangerous things in ways I'd already learned wouldn't work was making me so anxious that I just wanted them to stop, before someone really got hurt. We all decided that a picnic on the shore of Lake Michigan was a better way to spend the remainder of the afternoon.

After my friends left, I went back to work. If nothing else, they'd showed me what a difficult task I'd set before myself, so I poured it on, chopping, sawing, winching, and cussing from the time I could get my abused body moving in the morning until darkness and exhaustion made me actually grateful to crawl into my sleeping bag.

I'd been at it for more than a week when Cheanne came out to see if I'd done real harm to myself yet. I was never surprised to see her, but this time she wore a troubled expression. I asked her what was wrong, and she hesitantly said, "Don't lose your cool, but someone smashed out your van window."

I didn't lose my cool, but a feeling colder than the well settled into my gut. Although I suffer from a penchant for calling out rude people that more often than not makes me look foolish, I had no enemies except for the off-roaders who refused to stop destroying French Farm Creek. Despite the DNR having specifically made this area off-limits to motorized vehicles, despite the fact that it's universally illegal to drive through a streambed, and in disdain of Michigan's off-road vehicle law prohibiting off-road operation on any trail not clearly marked for such use, every fish in French Farm Creek had twice been killed by malicious drivers. Once one of the best brook trout streams in Emmet County, it had never recovered from the silt and destruction inflicted at this delicate headwater in the early '90s, when a few impotents on machines turned the clay banks to a pudding that suffocated any aquatic life unable to flee downstream to Lake Michigan.

What made the off-roaders hate me was the deal I made with conservation officers from the Indian River DNR field office in '97 to cement log posts across the shoreline of French Farm Creek, thus preventing vehicles from reaching the stream. In exchange for looking after the creek, DNR officials agreed to leave the big steel gate at the start of this two-track, nearly 3 miles distant, unlocked and open. The public at large appreciated free access to a great bass fishing hole, but ORVers were incensed that there should be even one place where hikers and animals didn't have to endure the stench, noise, and environmental damage created by their machines. To further block vehicle access to the delicate streambanks I'd always made a point of parking my vehicle parallel with the poles, and this wasn't the first time some sociopath had crawled from under a rock to vandalize my property.

I walked out to the dam with Cheanne and surveyed the damage. Sometime in the past three days since I'd last been out here, someone armed with what looked to be a baseball bat had felt the need to deliberately smash one of the large, expensive tinted glass windows that separated conversion vans from delivery vans. They'd done a thorough job; one blow to smash the large upper pane, two more to be certain that the slider window and its aluminum frame were beyond repair. Then, the vandals had fled, not stealing anything, or even looking inside, judging from the way the glass lay undisturbed on the folded-down back seat. The disturbing part to me was that if I'd been sleeping inside the van when either blow was struck, the bludgeon would have come down across my skull—I'm still not so sure that wasn't the original intent.

Because it was a crime scene, I left the van where it was, then rode to town with Cheanne to call the Emmet County Sheriff Department. The patrol deputy who responded refused to drive to the dam, claiming his car couldn't get through the two-track (I'm told local police avoid the area because it's a geographic dead zone where radios and cell phones don't work). The deputy suggested I drive the van to the sheriff department in Petoskey to let them have a look at it. I thanked him and concluded that there was no point in making further contact; these guys didn't care. In fact, the deputy inferred that vagrants who park the vehicles they live out of on public land should expect locals to vandalize them. Crackerville counties in the Deep South had nothing on Emmet County.

Because the Scottish side of me hadn't purchased glass coverage with my insurance, I ended up replacing the window myself, cutting a new pane from a large sheet of Plexiglas that big John had lying around. It required bringing the van to town so I'd have access to power tools, but after a day of cutting and fitting, I had the new window installed. I put a sign on the Plexiglas pane that offered a $100 reward for information leading to the arrest of the vandals, but nothing ever came of that.

Aside from the vandalism, everything was coming along well at the homestead. I was feeling stronger and more confident with each passing day, and I was fit enough to tackle the biggest chores. I was continually learning new ways to get hard jobs done with a minimum of exertion, and life was treating me okay.

Then one day I was crunching a mouthful of honey-roasted peanuts when the rearmost bottom molar on my left side just split in two. This really sucked, because I knew what was coming. The journalist in me understood that dental problems were a part of the homesteader's life that had to be dealt with without outside help, while insufficient funds in my savings account prohibited going to a dentist in any case.

After four days the broken molar had begun to ache from its roots. The pain was tolerable with an assist from ibuprofen at bedtime, but then the gum began to swell. I continued to chew with the broken tooth, hoping to loosen it from its moorings, and kept it brushed clean, but after a week my entire jaw became swollen from an infection at the molar's roots.

Here's where it got a little scary for me. Having grown up under conditions that would be described as abusive today, I'd nearly died when I was twelve when an abscessed tooth had eaten clear through my lower jawbone on the right side. My parents, fearing only that they'd face explaining why their oldest kid had died of neglect, had finally driven me to what was then Little Traverse Hospital in Petoskey. I recall the doctor who took my temperature exclaiming "Jesus Christ!" when he looked at the reading of 107 degrees. A thousand milligrams of penicillin shot into my buttocks had me feeling good the next day, when the foul abscess drained through the bottom of my jaw. I came close to death that time, and I had no desire to repeat the experience in a wilderness setting.

Most critical, I figured, was preventing the abscess from being a closed infection. If pressure were allowed to build under the molar, the trapped sepsis might be forced into my bloodstream, where it would likely cause a systemic reaction with a debilitating and potentially fatal fever. If that happened, death would come slowly and almost certainly.

First I needed to localize the infection. I soaked a washcloth in boiling hot water, placed it into a zipper-lock bag, and wrapped them both inside a dry towel. Then I held the makeshift heat pack against my jaw, directly on top of the abscessed molar, where it created an artificial fever to bring the poison to a head at the gum, thus preventing the infection from getting into my bloodstream.

When the applied heat had caused a blister of sorts on the outside of my gum, making the skin there taut like the skin of a balloon, I took a large-gauge carpet needle from my sewing kit. With an index finger crooked into the side of my mouth to expose the gum, I felt around for the most swollen spot with the middle finger of my other hand, which held the needle pinched between thumb and forefinger. I didn't bother to sterilize the needle, because it couldn't have carried anything worse than the germs that were already there. Regrettably, I didn't have a mirror either, because that might have made the operation less hit-and-miss than it was.

Predictably, the most blistered spot was directly over a root, very close to my jawbone. That was good. I steeled myself for the pain, then shoved the carpet needle directly into that spot, perpendicular to the gum. Tears came to my eyes as I drove the needle inward until I felt the tip scrape solidly against a root. I wiggled the needle in a circular motion and felt the electric shock of a pus sac bursting from around its still living nerve, followed by an immediate relief as pressure was released from that sensitive area.

With thumb and forefinger, I squeezed the infected gum around the hole I'd lanced. I wiped away a copious amount of yellowish pus with tissue paper, reducing the size of the swelling considerably as I did so. When the tissue came away bloody, I figured the infection had been purged—for now at least. I hadn't solved the problem, but by lancing the gum I'd insured that the molar wouldn't become more than a painful distraction.

Now came the hard part. The abscess had killed the tooth, and the socket would keep infecting, trying to push it upward, as long as the molar was left in place. I had no choice but to pull it.

Oral surgery wasn't one of the contingencies I'd prepared for, so I didn't have much in the way of dental tools. I took the big lineman's pliers from my tool bag and wiped them clean with alcohol pads. I snapped the disinfected jaws open and closed a few times; I doubted a dentist would approve, but it would have to do.

By feel alone I managed to get the pliers jaws locked around the molar. Tooth material is hard, and the pliers slipped a couple of times before I got a grip strong enough to twist against. When I did get a solid lock, I rocked the molar back and forth with the steel jaws. The pain was almost blinding as I heard the cracking sounds of flesh tearing away from tooth. My vision narrowed to a black tunnel and bright spots danced in front of me as I channeled the energy of this powerful stimulus to rock the molar even harder.

It came free with a cracking sound, and I was holding the dead tooth before me, still gripped in the pliers jaws. The good news was that I'd extracted the roots completely on one side. The bad news was that the other two roots had broken off below the gum line. I rinsed my mouth with salt water and spat blood until the hemorrhaging stopped. With my tongue I could feel the remainder of the tooth still embedded just below the gum, where I couldn't get at it with tools.

The dead root wasn't a danger to my health, but it was a constant irritation. The gum tissue healed nicely around what was now essentially a foreign object, a sliver that was no longer part of my body. There was an occasional jolt of pain when I was chewing, and if I ignored the pain I'd awaken the next morning with the gum around it feeling tender and swollen. The root had to be extracted too.

With some trepidation of the unknown, I honed my Spyderco folding knife to shaving sharpness and prepared to perform oral surgery on myself. I laid the tip against the outer gum, directly over where the dead root lay trapped, and pushed the cutting edge inward through the soft tissue until it stopped against the harder root. I could only imagine what was happening as I operated by feel alone, but I felt the gum separate from around the embedded root. I used the knife to pry tissue away from tooth until the root lay exposed.

Then I went to work with the big lineman's pliers. Blood was flowing, causing me to spit bright red from time to time as I felt around for a grip with the pliers, but my endorphins were apparently working because the pain was negligible. When I felt the jaws close securely onto the broken root, I gripped the pliers handles firmly and twisted hard. A bright spot of pain formed in front of my vision as the root rocked free of my jaw, finally coming free in the jaws of my pliers.

Like an iceberg, the extracted root was larger than it had seemed from the surface, measuring roughly half an inch square by a quarter-inch thick. I rinsed my mouth with salt water to help stop the bleeding, glad to have that irritating chunk of bone removed, but a little concerned that the incision I'd made to get at it might not heal properly. A dentist would have stitched the severed gum together, but I doubted I could perform that operation by feel alone, so I left it to heal on its own.

As it turned out, I needn't have worried. The incision and empty socket healed quickly and without secondary infection. I kept the damaged gum brushed regularly to keep out food particles and to toughen it, and in two weeks I was healed enough to chew on that side.

Maybe I am masochistic, but I enjoyed the experience for the insight it gave me. I had a new empathy for a part of life that had been endured by all trappers of old, and by every animal unlucky enough to survive past its prime. I could imagine what an aging bear must go through as every tooth in its mouth progressively became the same problem I'd had with just one molar. I'd known from books that dental troubles become a real health issue in older animals, but now I understood why that was so from a personal perspective.

COPING WITH CRITTERS

O ne problem that has faced every person who ever tried to settle in a wilderness is coping with the animals that already make the place their home. A raccoon can't understand that chickens in a coop aren't there for it to eat, and mountain lions know only that sheep are easy prey. A pack of wolves sees no difference between a Hereford calf and a moose calf, nor can they comprehend that a dog shouldn't be killed for being a competitor, then eaten as food.

I've always felt that any wilderness belongs to those animals able to make a living there; we humans might possess the power to displace or destroy them, but the forest is their birthright, not ours. We self-righteously cry foul when one segment of humanity attempts to kill off another segment that it perceives as a threat, yet our kind has been committing those very same atrocities against every wild species that has offended us since the beginning of history.

Still, a settler in any wilderness must of necessity learn to deal with animals that consider the place their home, and my experience was no exception. Few wild animals pose a physical danger to people, and fewer still consider us edible, even when dead, but most denizens of the forest are territorial, as they must be. To expect any of them to stop frequenting the places where they eat, breed, and bear young just because a human has taken up residence there is unjustifiably arrogant.

It's no less unreasonable to expect that they won't take your food and anything else that appeals to them should an opportunity present itself. That's where troubles begin, because wild animals that raid the food stores of a homesteader may put him in genuine danger of starvation and sickness, especially through the long months of winter.

The most contentious challenge I faced in my own struggle to stake out a small bit of wilderness as home was from a three-year-old black bear.

Mature enough to survive on his own, he'd been ejected from cubhood by his mother during the previous summer. She, like all grown sow bears, came into heat every two years, which meant she had forcibly abandoned her grown offspring in his second year to find another mate.

It was a story as old as bears themselves. The newly emancipated cub had been forced away from his mother and her new mate to prevent any possibility of inbreeding. Alone and confused, the adolescent bear had nonetheless survived quite well by following a trail of seasonal foods that his mother had shown him, growing to about 200 pounds in the first full year he'd spent on his own. Barely half his adult weight, the young bruin already possessed twice my physical strength, and he proved to be very territorial, which made him a powerful and potentially dangerous competitor to me at the personal level.

My troubles with this bear started the first week of June, when the cabin had grown to become a box of logs, but didn't yet have a roof. Access into the box was through a 3-foot square fireplace hole in the left side of the rear wall. The doorway, which was to be more than 3 feet across and ten logs high, hadn't yet been cut out when the bear began making trouble.

Our dispute centered around my food barrel, the 55-gallon plastic open head drum with a snap-down plastic lid and a steel cam-locked retaining ring that prevented the lid from being popped off. I'd reasoned that the lid also couldn't be pulled open from the outside, while thick high-density polyethylene construction would resist even the most determined animal from chewing through to its contents.

The bear's first raid came during one of my trips to town. Big John had found a large pile of used roofing steel lying at the Emmet County fairgrounds, and the manager there had consented to let us have it if we hauled the entire bunch away—as well as all the cable, pipes, and other discarded metal lying about. It was a lot of work, but I ended up with more than enough steel to cover a cabin roof, even if it did have nail holes through it already, and John made a few dollars by selling the rest of the scrap metal to a local junkyard. I loaded sixteen sheets on top of the Indian van and tied it down in preparation for my return to the dam at French Farm Creek.

I'd been gone two days, and when I returned to the cabin carrying four bundled sheets of steel balanced on my head, the first thing I noticed was that my supply barrel wasn't where I'd left it. In fact, the 200-pound container had been wrestled free of its chocks and rolled 50 feet from its original location. Large powerful claws and teeth had left deep gouges in the barrel's thick walls, and its surface was covered by muddy paw prints that clearly identified the marauder as a black bear. I was glad to see that, despite being knocked about, the drum had withstood an apparently persistent assault without opening. I dragged the heavy container back onto its moorings, while making a mental note that it was requiring considerable effort to do so.

The bruin made his next raid within a week, again while no one was in camp. Pete and I hiked in from the dam carrying six more sheets of steel on our heads to find the barrel still chocked in place, but opened, its lid and ring lying off to either side. Empty packets of powdered cheese, raisins, and chocolate bar wrappers littered the ground immediately in front of the open barrel, as if the brazen bear had plopped down right there to feast. A plastic screw-top bottle of vanilla extract had been carefully uncapped, then guzzled dry without leaving so much as a drop spilled. Most insulting was the large, awful-smelling scat left deliberately on top of my hardwood cutting board—a clear and somewhat ominous challenge to my claim on this particular piece of forest.

After that, the bear prowled the perimeter of my camp every evening, usually keeping out of sight in the underbrush, but huffing loudly and purposely clacking its teeth together in an attempt to frighten me away from my food. Pete questioned my sanity one night when I took up a flashlight and a stout white ash sapling in either hand, and ran toward the bear that stood grunting at us from the shadows, merely 50 feet to the rear of the cabin. Taken by surprise, the bear wheeled and ran from my approach. The ash stave whooshed past its rump, and the animal broke into full retreat, easily outdistancing me. I continued pursuit through the darkened woods for better than a hundred yards to show it that my intentions were serious, stopping when I realized that I didn't know where the big animal had gone. I felt considerably less brave as I played the Maglite's beam over dense forest and realized that there might well be an angry bear with good night vision behind me in the shadows.

When I returned to camp, muttering and cursing, Pete looked at me as though I'd just sprouted a second head. "Len," he said, "what would you have done if that bear hadn't run away?"

I explained to my young friend that black bears are by nature unwilling to fight if they can flee, and that if this one had stood its ground, a couple of thumps from my hardwood bludgeon would have convinced the animal to head for safer ground. The look on Pete's face said that although he respected my judgment about most things, he wasn't too sure about it this time. I hid my grin and changed the subject, because I wasn't too damned sure that I was right, either.

Whether I was right or wrong was a moot point, because the bear was back again the following night, having learned only that I couldn't run fast enough to catch him, and that I couldn't see in the dark. I chased him through the woods again, this time backing up the flashlight with my .308 Winchester rifle. But even the roar made by this respectable caliber when I fired it into the air didn't keep the overly bold bruin from returning. It was obvious that this bear had acquired a taste for human food—for all he knew, the cabin was a wonderful place where chocolate and cheese simply sprouted from big plastic barrels. The animal was only following an instinct to put on 50 pounds of fat in preparation for the coming winter, but I could no more allow his larceny to continue than could my musket-toting predecessors.

Frontiersmen of old were known to resolve such maraudings by lying in wait for a troublesome bear, sometimes over a baited leghold trap, then killing it on sight with a bullet. I didn't think so lethal a solution would be necessary for a twenty-first-century frontiersman. Savvy as they'd had to be, the sourdoughs of old didn't have access to the half millennium of scientific data about black bears that I had at my disposal, nor had they possessed the modern materials I did.

Cutting out the cabin's doorway, a daunting bit of hard labor that I'd been putting off, now became an imperative. Because I intended to build my own door from rough lumber I'd split off full logs, the height and width of the opening was at my discretion. I decided to go with a 4-foot opening that was 7 feet from threshold to top, a fairly standard size doorway.

With those dimensions in mind, I framed in what would become the opening, measuring from the cabin's front center post. To allow room for error, I mounted a 10-inch-diameter framing log vertically at 4.5 feet from the center post, angling its top to correspond with the end rafter above. The door frame would actually mount flush to the cut ends of the wall logs, but this framing log was needed to hold the corners tightly in place while I cut through them. Once the framing log had been fitted, I secured it to each wall log with a countersunk lag screw.

That was the easy part; now I had to remove a 4-foot section from eight wall logs to create the doorway opening. I set to work with axe and saw in the morning, cutting, chopping, and sweating all day until a door-size hole had been made through the cabin's front wall. Then I set to work flattening the top of the foundation log with axe and hatchet to form a threshold.

It was in the middle of this chore that I felt the head of my axe loosen. Before it went flying off into the woods mid-swing, I stopped work and used the hammer side of my roofer's hatchet to separate handle from head. The fiberglass handle had indeed broken from the abuse I'd inflicted, and the only reason the head hadn't flown off was because I'd previously drilled a hole through both sides and driven a pan-head metal screw through head and handle to prevent that from happening.

I couldn't continue without an axe, so I sawed down a 6-inch white ash sapling from the adjacent marsh and started whittling a 4-foot section of it into the shape of an axe handle using my Ka-Bar survival knife. It took about two hours to complete the job, but when I'd finished I had a pretty darned good axe handle made from the toughest tree in the forest. I twisted the pan-head screw back into place to lock the two components together and went back to work.

Fastening Axe Head to Handle with a Screw

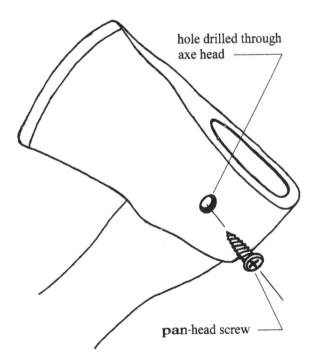

hole drilled through axe head

pan-head screw

When the doorway was finished, I tugged and cussed the heavy blue container inside the cabin walls, chocking it on place over the fireplace hole to prevent entry from that avenue. There, within an enclosure too tall for a bear to see over from all fours, I hoped my food cache would be protected by the marauder's own sense of claustrophobia.

To further bolster the bear's reluctance to raid my cache, I left the campfire burning and a radio playing whenever I left the cabin site for even a short time. If it was dark outside, or would be by the time I figured to return, I left a lighted kerosene hurricane lantern secured to the cabin's centerpost, 7 feet off the ground. In front of the doorway outside, a candle lantern burned atop a section of sawn log that I'd upended to serve as a small table. There was no danger of fire on the cleared dirt and sand of the cabin site, and the cabin wall logs were too large and too green to be ignited by a half pint of kerosene should the lamp be knocked down.

One morning in the middle of this contest between man and beast, Cheanne came into camp while I was cutting out the cabin's back window. I was expecting her, so I barely glanced up from my work when I heard her coming down the trail toward the cabin.

But I was more than a little surprised at the way she made her appearance. In her hand, pointed skyward at shoulder height, was the Glock .40-caliber pistol she prudently carried with her whenever she came to see me. There was an excited look in her bright blue eyes. I pointed my fingertips at the clouds and said half seriously, "What?"

She holstered the Glock, and with a huge smile told me how a large, brazen bear had shadowed her, making no attempt to remain unseen, for the last few hundred yards before she turned off the main trail toward the cabin. She and the 200-pound bear had walked virtually side by side in the same direction for the last hundred yards before it deliberately crossed her path no more than 50 feet ahead, then disappeared into dense woods on the opposite side of the trail.

It was pretty clear that the bruin had known she was there, and was testing her courage. When she'd drawn her sidearm and continued along her way, regardless of the big bear's presence, it had doubtless concluded that her lack of fear meant she was a potentially dangerous opponent and best left unmolested. I was glad for her courage, because if she had retreated, or worse, fled, there was a better than even chance that the animal would have regarded her as prey and given chase. I didn't want to even imagine how that chain of events would likely have concluded if she'd backed down.

Placing the food barrel inside the cabin walls seemed to be working for about a week. Then one especially warm evening just after dark, Pete, Jerod, and I returned from a swim at the beaver pond to find the bear feeding leisurely outside the cabin doorway. The marauder heard us coming toward the cabin, and for just a moment stood his ground, as if to defend the rich goodies he had plundered from our mutual food stores. Without pausing or saying a word, I slid the .308 off my shoulder as we came within sight of one another at a distance of less than 30 feet, intending to kill this bear right there in front of the doorway if it didn't immediately retreat. As he had with Cheanne, the bruin sensed from my demeanor that he was overmatched and in imminent danger. He wheeled and ran off, taking with him a stuff-sack containing 2 pounds of chocolate bars and other candies.

Inside the cabin walls, the now lidless barrel lay still chocked in its original position, its retaining ring and lid removed as deftly as I could have done it. Cheese, raisin, and candy wrappers were strewn everywhere on the ground just outside the doorway, carried there one item at a time so the animal wouldn't be caught by surprise inside the cabin's confining walls. I couldn't escape the irony that I had provided this marauder with music and dinner by candlelight.

Pete, who had until then thought my bear problem was humorous, suddenly became more sympathetic. The stuff sack of chocolate bars had been his, and his furnacelike metabolism made him take the theft of precious calories more seriously than most would have. He said it was pretty clear that this bear had to be terminated, but his extreme prejudice turned to a grin when he noticed that Jerod and I were getting a laugh from his sudden change of heart.

I was heartened to see that the critter still feared a confrontation with humans. Still, it was asking for trouble on several fronts to let this bold young bear get away with such larceny. Since it had apparently figured out the barrel ring's latch, I further secured its shipping lock with a bent nail that required fingers to remove it.

Then I enlisted Jerod, who can bench-press a small truck, to help me hoist the still very heavy barrel up to the cabin's ridgepole, 10 feet overhead, and hang it suspended from the groove around its mouth using my logging rope and a timber hitch knot. I later gave up this strategy after the bear learned to bounce the barrel violently enough from below to slip its noose. I'd already tried laying four set leghold traps across the threshold, placing them upside-down so they'd snap shut when disturbed, without actually catching the critter that set them off. Nothing seemed to discourage this bear.

Pete left the following night. Jerod and I walked him to where his Bronco was parked at the dam, 1.5 miles from the cabin, and we returned to camp just after dark. Jerod was standing in front of the cabin's doorway, examining it by lantern light while I rebuilt the fire to provide more light. Just then a low prolonged growl issued from the shadows immediately to Jerod's left, no more than 10 yards from where he stood.

Eyes wide, he looked at me and asked, more or less rhetorically, "What was that?"

I answered, also more or less rhetorically, "What do you think it was?" His reply was to walk quickly over to the safety of the crackling fire.

Jerod left the following day, and I went back to work on the cabin. I spent the next week on the roof, lag-screwing rafter poles between soffit logs and the ridgepole. Next came the process of fitting and nailing down sheets of metal roofing to provide a shield from the pounding rains that fell in sheets whenever air temperatures dropped enough to allow condensation. I was getting incredibly tired of living in a tent.

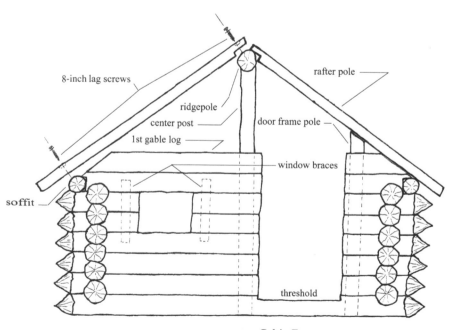

Cabin Front

Surprisingly, my tents, the 3-man Moss Olympic that was my home and the 2-man Starlet that served as my clothing storage, never caught the interest of any wild animal. I worried that a bear powerful enough to bounce a 200-pound barrel through the forest would have no trouble shredding these vital pieces of equipment, but neither received so much as a tear in their screen doors during the entire six months they remained in service. I believe that was due to the combination of strong human odors emanating from a small enclosure into which they couldn't see, but animals of all types shunned the tents.

The food barrel, however, remained irresistible. The bear took to circling the cabin every day just after noon, undeterred by the noise my hammer made against steel. I could see his big coal-black body clearly from my elevated position on the cabin's roof as he prowled the perimeter of the camp, and I knew damned well that he could see me too. A showdown was coming, that much seemed inevitable, because this bear was losing more respect for me with each passing day. It pissed me off having to do it, but I made a loaded pistol part of my daily attire from then on, even when I was on the roof. I didn't even take a crap without the gun strapped to my hip, and whenever I left camp there was a rifle in my hand.

I rehearsed our final encounter in my mind a hundred times, trying hard to envision every possible scenario. The bear wasn't bad, and to kill him merely for stealing food would twist my conscience in a very uncomfortable way. I obviously couldn't beat him hand-to-hand, but shooting the animal meant that I would be forced to kill him, because a wounded bear could be counted on to double back and jump me from hiding. Yet if I didn't instill a strong fear of humans into its psyche, this animal would then become a real danger, not only to me, but to every backpacker and mountain biker who was carrying food. The solution was to punish the bear enough to make my homestead an unpleasant place for him to visit, but not severely enough to provoke a retaliatory response. That was going to be tough, and very probably dangerous.

The showdown came one hot, sticky night in early July. I was trying to fall asleep in my tent, a few yards from the cabin's rear wall. The tent's front and rear doors were as open as the mosquitoes would allow, but the air was thick with humidity and not conducive to sleeping. As usual, I'd left two lanterns burning to illuminate the cabin, not so much to discourage the fearless bear as to provide me with sufficient light to get off an accurate shot.

I'd just dozed off when I heard the scratching of stout claws against plastic, followed by the distinctive sound of the heavy barrel being rocked on its moorings from inside the cabin walls. This was intolerable; it was one thing to raid my cache when I was gone, but to have this bold and powerful animal invade while I was sleeping crossed the line between annoying and dangerous.

My hand settled over the loaded .40-caliber automatic lying next to my head. I made no effort to be quiet as I zipped open the tent's net door and scrambled toward the cabin, pistol at the ready. I really had no desire to shoot this bear—in fact, I rather admired his pluck—but the situation had to be resolved, one way or another.

As I ran around the back corner of the cabin, I could see the bear over the wall, still near the barrel. He saw me and spun toward the doorway at a gallop. I couldn't get an accurate shot through the rafters, so I raced him to the doorway, coming around the front corner of the cabin as he was exiting the structure. If he so much as turned toward me, I intended to shoot him until he was dead. But the bear seemed panicked, wanting only to get away. Just before his furry black rear end disappeared from the circle of illumination cast by the door lantern, I squeezed off a round as near to his bouncing buttocks as I felt I could get without actually penetrating flesh.

The bullet didn't hit meat, else I would have found flesh and blood on the ground, but there was a small cluster of black fur lying on the leaves nearby, clipped free when the hollowpoint grazed the bear's wide ass. I listened intently for several long minutes, ready to fire another, killing, round if the bear turned, but the panicked bruin crashed headlong through trees and brush until it had traveled beyond my hearing.

Satisfied that I'd made my point, I crawled into my tent and tried to get back to sleep. No sooner had my eyes closed than once again I heard a rustling and scratching from inside the cabin walls. This was it, no more warning shots. I unzipped the tent's screen door slowly and, as quietly as if I were stalking a deer, I crawled on hands and knees to the rear wall of the cabin.

My palms were wet and sweat trickled down my forehead as I rose slowly to peer through the window hole in the cabin's back wall. The Glock's sights were in front of my eyes as both simultaneously cleared the uppermost log. My fingertip was lightly touching the gun's double trigger, depressing the safety so that only the slightest pressure would cause it to fire.

There, squared in my sights and sitting atop the front wall with a nearly empty powdered-cheese bag, was a fat raccoon weighing about 20 pounds. Maybe it was the noise made by the crinkling plastic wrapper, or maybe it was simply too involved with this delicacy to pay attention, but the raccoon hadn't noticed my approach.

There was no way I was going to kill this animal either; yet I couldn't allow it to consider my cabin site as a food source any more than the bear could. I held my finger firmly against the Glock's trigger, and when the raccoon raised its head to look about, I released the sear, sending a bullet between its ears and about 2 inches above its furry skull. It screeched and backflipped off its perch, hitting the ground outside the cabin with an audible thud. It scrambled away into the shadows with a rustling of leaves, uninjured except for the strong impression of terror I'd inflicted on its psyche.

I couldn't help but laugh as the 'coon's chattering headlong escape continued until it was out of earshot, even though my shot had also put a hole through the door rafter. I crawled back into my tent, sure that any animal even considering raiding my camp was long gone, but sleeping lightly and well armed, just in case I was wrong.

CHAPTER 5

HEAT, HUMIDITY, AND BUGS

July of 2001 was hot and extraordinarily humid. Farmers and meteorologists complained about having no rain, yet the humidity was always high enough to saturate the air; it was just too damned hot for water vapors to condense into precipitation. There was a constant haze in the air, despite sunny skies and daytime highs of 90 degrees or more. When air temperatures dropped a few degrees after sunset, a thick white fog settled over the lowlands to a depth of 20 feet or more. Walking through that earthbound cloud left one wet and feeling clammy, and if you wore glasses they were too fogged-up to see through.

Laundry wouldn't dry in air that was already saturated, and perspiration simply dripped off without cooling a body at all. I was wet all the time, and even clothing that hadn't been worn smelled musty. Made entirely from synthetics and treated with silicone, my tents and sleeping bags endured the onslaught of mold and mildew without damage, but any item of clothing made with cotton or wool had to be washed in hot water at least once a week, even if it hadn't been worn, to kill whatever spores had gotten a foothold.

Metal tools also took a beating. My carbon steel knives were powder coated but the sharpened edges rusted overnight and had to be honed clean on a daily basis. Even the stainless steel blades of my Gator belt folder and Spyderco clip knife were spotted with rust. The winch was lubricated regularly, but shovels, axes, and hatchets were kept relatively rust free only through daily use.

Worst afflicted were my guns. Moisture vapors crept into their internal workings and stayed there, rusting chamber walls, trigger sears, and recoil springs. I've never felt that stereotypical relationship between my guns and my penis, but this humidity had me concerned because it could cause serious, permanent harm to both the function and accuracy of my firearms. Like a wristwatch, a gun that can't be depended on to work when you need it is useless, except that in the latter instance a failure could be downright life threatening. Out of necessity, I fired each of them once every few days, just to keep the bores clean, and wiped down the internal components with light oil. For years the outer surfaces of all my "working guns," that is, those shooting tools that must endure what I endure, have been weatherproofed with three coats of polyurethane over three coats of black primer, but keeping humidity and rust out of their internal workings was proving to be a never ending chore.

When air temperatures did drop enough for the humidity to condense, it poured the proverbial cats and dogs. Most times I found the warm rains refreshing, because they washed the sweat and grime from my clothes and body. They also turned the work site into mud, so I really didn't gain a thing as far as cleanliness was concerned. Other times it was like standing under a waterfall, with rain coming in such a volume that it could literally knock things out of my hand if I didn't keep a good grip on them.

The rains also made everything dangerously slippery, and I had to exercise real caution when walking over wet logs or swinging an axe. Wrapping my tool handles with safety tape helped to provide a more secure grip, but occasionally I still fell victim to an unforeseen accident.

One of the worst of the remarkably few injuries I inflicted on myself occurred during a hard rain, not from an axe or machete, but with a saw. I'd finished the walls, making each of them six logs high, and had lag-screwed a 10-inch-diameter white ash pole, 18 feet long, lengthwise along each side wall to serve as the soffit. The front and rear rafters were already in place, lag screwed to the soffit and ridgepole, and now I was cutting the angled-end logs that would fill in the gables between those rafters on the front and rear walls.

Because the gable logs were shorter than the wall logs, becoming shorter yet as they rose upward to the peak, they could be taken from the treetops that were lying all around the cabin. I was sawing through one of these with my left foot on top of the log to help steady it when my boot slid on the rain-slick bark. The slip knocked me off balance, throwing my body toward the log just as I was applying power to the saw's forward cutting stroke. The saw's teeth made a zipping sound as they ran across the inside of my left knee, shredding the ripstop fabric of my trousers and laying the skin beneath open to a width of more than an inch. I could see exposed muscle before bright blood started to flow. It reminded me of what a deer looked like when I was skinning it.

I dropped the saw and grabbed my knee, trying to squeeze the sides of the cut together as I applied pressure to lessen the flow of blood that was already spreading through the fabric of my wet trousers. I was feeling plenty stupid as I hobbled toward my tent, 50 yards away, to get the first-aid kit. I threw myself into the tent vestibule, landing hard on my butt, and leaned inside to drag the daypack containing medical supplies over to me. I never let pressure off the wound as I rummaged for a box of butterfly sutures to pull the skin back together.

When I found them, I released pressure on the wound and quickly pulled my pants leg up over the knee, immediately applying pressure again after the cut had been exposed. The jagged laceration was as long as my index finger, but although the skin had been cut clean through, the muscle beneath was barely scratched. All I really had to worry about was getting my hide pulled back together so the bleeding would stop and healing could commence.

With my leg extended to take some tension off the parted skin, I kept the cut pinched together between thumb and forefinger, and swabbed off most of the blood with alcohol pads. Next, I applied six butterfly sutures, starting in the middle and working toward either end, until the laceration had been completely closed. It looked pretty good, and I was just starting to compliment myself on a good job when the goddamned butterflies began pulling loose—all of them.

"Fuck Johnson & Johnson," I said aloud, slapping my right palm over the wound to keep it from separating any more. I reached for the roll of silver duct tape that lay in a corner of the tent, and tore off a 4-inch section with my teeth. I angrily stripped off all six butterfly sutures, then, squeezing the wound together yet again, I stuck the edges to one another with the strip of duct tape. The wound stayed put this time.

I'd had enough for the day. I was wet, angry, and wounded. I was going to town. I wound an Ace bandage around the damaged knee to further help keep the wound closed, and to limit how far I could bend it, and hiked out to the van.

I met Cheanne for coffee when I got to Petoskey, and I guess I forgot she made her living as a paramedic. Being a nice person, she didn't actually say so, but the look in her eyes said my first-aid methods were retarded. She was right, of course, but the knee healed well, and I have a great 4-inch scar to show off at parties.

Since I'd decided to come to town, I figured I'd also bring along the half-dozen 10-inch lag screws that had twisted in two while I was driving them into cabin logs. It probably wouldn't have been a big deal to most, but my grubstake was dwindling, and I'd paid more than a dollar apiece for them. Every one had sheared at the top thread, just below the shank, and it didn't seem right that a half inch of steel would break under the torque of a 10-inch breaker bar powered by only muscle. More than forty of them had been driven home without breaking, so I concluded that these must be defective.

The thirty-something clerk who worked in the hardware department at Home Depot didn't agree, and said there were no refunds or exchanges given for broken lag screws. Further, he told me, he broke them off all the time. I looked at his 5-foot-4-inch frame and slight musculature and doubted the veracity of that claim. He further convinced me that he didn't know what he was talking about when he stated, "After all, they're only made out of zinc." The store's customer service manager agreed with me, however, and replaced the broken screws.

I returned to the cabin site after a particularly productive four days in civilization. Big John had scavenged a couple of windows for me, a small single-pane crank-open type that had been removed intact from the bathroom of a mobile home he was junking out, and a smaller double-pane slide-open window that some clown had shot a hole through for no apparent reason. I could use them both, although several strips of duct tape were needed to make the vandalized sliding window intact again.

A carpenter friend had also donated a full-size insulated steel door with a large double-pane window, locking doorknob and key, and a prehung frame. A few macho guys gave me grief about using a manufactured door and windows, but none of them would accept my invitation to come out to the cabin and show me the right way to do things. Considering that I only made 300 yards carrying the white 100-pound metal door atop my head before stashing and camouflaging it in the woods, I wasn't too sure that this was doing it the easy way. I did separate the door from its wooden frame, though, and I hauled that back to the cabin so I could at least get it hung in readiness for when the door made it there.

It was late afternoon when I finally arrived at the homestead, my Peak 1 daypack loaded with nails and granola bars, and a window under each arm. The sun already had dropped below the treeline, even though it wouldn't actually get dark for another three hours. This was bear time, so the first thing

I did after dropping my pack was to check the barrel. It was intact, and there was no sign of any animal having come near the site during my absence. The bear had apparently gotten the message. Too bad I couldn't do the same with the swarms of mosquitoes that seemed to have no victim other than me.

It wasn't until an hour or so after I arrived home that I unzipped the rainfly vestibule of my tent to retrieve my Grundig TRII shortwave receiver. I'd left the radio lying in its case under the vestibule, out of the elements, but outside the tent's inner screen door.

When I pushed the receiver's slide switch to its ON position, nothing happened. I'd put in new batteries before I left, and humidity couldn't have corroded its electrical connections in so short a time. Only then did I actually look at the unit. The case was intact and appeared undamaged, but when I looked at the window that housed the dial indicator, the frequency scale was mostly obscured by a large number of tiny white egg shapes. As I handled the radio, the eggs' owners became agitated, and soon there were tiny brown pismire ants scurrying all over the inside of the tuner window, grabbing up the little ova and shuttling them off to the Grundig's inner recesses.

I actually felt a little guilty about evicting the tiny insects from what they had probably perceived as luxury accommodations, clean and safe from predators. But this was no less a matter of territorial claim than I'd experienced with larger animals, and I couldn't let the little buggers turn my source of news and entertainment into an ant farm. I opened the battery compartment and removed the three AA cells inside it to provide the minuscule invaders with an easy escape route. For the next few minutes a steady stream of ants ran from the battery compartment, many tirelessly carrying eggs larger than themselves in their mandibles. I watched this exodus until each of the hundreds of them had disappeared into the forest, where they would find a more suitable and natural home within the softened core of a rotting stump or log. It would be a long journey, perhaps as far as 20 yards, and there would be predators to contend with along the way, but God had not intended these creatures to make their home within a shortwave receiver.

Surprisingly, the TRII recovered in fair condition after I'd disassembled its case to let the innards dry thoroughly, then cleaned the connections and electromechanical components with a cotton swab soaked in rubbing alcohol. The only trouble spot I couldn't eradicate lay in the radio's 7-band tuning capacitor, probably the most delicate of its components. It worked more or less normally in the FM and shortwave bands, but AM—the band to which it had been set during the pismire invasion—was scratchy or nonfunctional over the higher half of its frequency range. Too bad, because I really enjoyed listening to AM talk shows; I guess I derived some sort of humor from listening to others get all heated up over mostly urban topics that meant nothing in the wilderness environment where I lived.

When I walked to the well to draw cooking water, I was dismayed to see that it had nearly gone dry; only a small puddle of water remained in its bottom. It was still 7 feet deep, but the water table had dropped drastically in the short time I'd been away. I reasoned that it would need to be excavated to 10 feet to insure a year-round supply of water. That task would require a full day of hard labor, and I wasn't going to do it until I had at least half of the cabin's roof covered with sheet metal to provide protection from the rain.

Jerod came hiking into camp a few days later, intending to spend the next two days. I told him he could feel free to dig the well deeper, but that didn't appeal to him at all. He pitched his tent in a small opening 50 feet north of the cabin, next to a majestic 60-foot spruce, and rekindled the campfire. Then we caught one another up on the current events of our two worlds while I fitted and screwed more rafters in place to provide solid nailing where the edges of the sheet metal came together.

I did convince him to help me haul the steel door I'd left trailside back to the cabin. I'd already tacked the frame in place inside the doorway, and I was getting anxious to have a door that could be closed. We set out at 7:30 P.M., with more than two hours of daylight left. The woods were hazy with evaporated moisture under a still-hot sun as we hiked toward where the white door lay well camouflaged under grass and bracken ferns just 10 feet off trail. It was still a hazy 80 degrees throughout the forest, but swarms of humming mosquitoes forced us to wear head nets and our sleeves rolled down.

We, of course, found the door where I'd left it. Its big window, which I'd feared might be broken by animals walking over it, was still intact under a layer of damp vegetation. Even with two of us the door seemed ungainly and overly heavy, but we hoisted it onto our heads and headed back to the cabin. We got it to the camp without resting, but both of us were happy to finally lean it against the cabin's front wall.

Only then did I notice that the door was 4 inches wider than the frame. That meant I had to take the frame back out, cut each of the doorway logs back that amount, then split the frame to fit against either side before I could mount the door. I'd anticipated having to do no more than slip the door onto its hinges and square up the frame. Now I was faced with another half day of labor before I could even get to that point. I was not happy.

The weather matched my mood. Here in the deep woods the junglelike heat and humidity hadn't eased up at all. It was still around 80 degrees after sunset, with a sky full of black roiling clouds that thundered almost angrily, and frequent flashes of heat lightning that would blind you for a few seconds if you were looking at them. There was no rain, though, because it was too damned hot, and the air was still as death at ground level. Neither of us had ever seen weather quite like this. We retired to our tents some time before midnight, not so much because we were tired, but because it was nearly impossible to carry on a conversation in such loud weather.

I slept naked atop my sleeping bag, as I had for the past month, with both front and rear doors open to the screens. I generally like sleeping in thunderstorms, but the oppressive humidity made me sweat profusely, and I tossed from one perspiration-soaked side to the other all night long. There was no air movement inside the tent, and even the screen doors held in heat, but there was no opening them to the hordes of mosquitoes that crawled over their outsides, searching for a way in.

I awoke just after 4 A.M., when Jerod called my name.

"Hey, Len" he said, "I'm gettin' outta here."

With eyes that hadn't slept enough, I looked out the screen toward his voice. I could see in the predawn twilight that he had his backpack on and was facing the trail out.

"What's the problem?" I asked groggily.

He cited a litany of complaints. "It's these goddamn mosquitoes. And it's too fuckin' hot. And we don't have any water. And . . .," he paused, as if unsure about saying it, "I think I got hit by lightning."

He looked pretty good for a guy who'd been hit by lightning. I guess I didn't take his claim too seriously because, although taking shelter under a tree in the middle of a field is never a good idea, dense forest like the one we were in is one of the safest places for avoiding static discharges. He was determined to leave, though, so I told him to be careful on the trail out, then went back to sleep.

I crawled out of my tent at about 8 A.M. to bright sunlight and the promise of a blistering day to come. I truly doubted that Jerod had been hit by lightning, but I walked to where his tent had been and looked around for signs of a lightning strike nearby. I'd seen a few trees stuck by lightning—once from less than 50 feet—and they typically exploded dramatically near their bases. The giant spruce Jerod's tent had been next to seemed untouched, and there was no evidence of a lightning strike anywhere in the area. I concluded that his experience had been just the product of a bad dream induced by real lightning.

As days passed, however, I noticed that the big spruce in question was dying slowly from the top down. The needles of its uppermost branches turned brown, followed by the next tier of branches, and the next, until the upper half of the tree was completely dead. As the cancer progressed downward over the next several weeks, it became obvious that the tree had sustained serious internal damage. Maybe it was because its roots were making contact with the water table, but the tree had apparently been grounded well enough to channel that huge static energy to the earth without bursting its trunk. That was lucky for Jerod, who would have certainly been injured if the trunk had exploded the way I have seen others do, and maybe even killed if the tree had fallen on top of his tent. Probably his nonconductive tent floor and synthetic sleeping bag had afforded him a measure of protection, as well.

When I pointed out the dying tree to Jerod later, he beamed, feeling more vindicated than fortunate. "See," he said, "Maybe next time I tell you I was hit by lightning you'll believe me." I hoped there would never be a next time.

I still needed to dig out the well. Being without it for a few days had showed me just how much I'd come to rely on this hole filled with water. Without it, the place really was nearly as intolerable as Jerod had described. It wasn't a job I was looking forward to, but comfort, if not survival, depended on having a permanent, readily accessible source of water.

I started in the morning. I was wearing my Teva water shoes that were actually made for kayaking and rafting, but water is water, I figured. Besides, I didn't like getting wet, abrasive sand inside my boots, the way I had when I'd first dug the well. I lowered myself to the bottom of the 7-foot hole by placing my soles against one side, my shoulders against the other, and wriggling downward. I couldn't help a sharp intake of air through pursed lips when my feet hit the few inches of frigid water laying in the bottom. It wasn't going to feel better when that water was knee deep; I understood why the proverbial well-digger's ass was so cold.

I noted a stench of decay as soon as I'd lowered myself into the hole, and it became fouler as I dug, flinging shovelfuls of wet sand and rocks out of a hole that was already a foot taller than me. The source of the smell became apparent as I removed the upper layer of sand, tossing three drowned mice and a dozen bloated frogs out of the well. Drawn to the odor of fresh, clean water, the little animals had fallen into an inescapable pit, where they died of hypothermia and drowning. The well definitely needed a cover to prevent that from happening, and I made a mental note to get it done before winter.

I stopped digging when the well was 10 feet deep and smelled of clean earth. There was enough water in the bottom to make my feet numb, but I knew it would take a day or so for the bottom to refill with fresh water. I estimated the depth of that water would reach a minimum of 3 feet, and remain at that depth or more year-round. I got out of the well the same way I'd gotten in, only in reverse, and with a little more effort.

The well never again went dry, and for all but the driest months it had a full 4 feet of water. I learned to empty it periodically by dropping a 5-gallon bucket with a rope attached to its handle to the bottom, dragging it up after it had filled, and dumping the water onto a slope that ran away from the well pit. It was hard, tedious work, but the bucket suctioned in any dead or living critters that had fallen in, and it proved surprisingly effective for removing all but a tiny puddle of water at the hole's center. When the well refilled a day later, it was with pure, cold spring water that was a pleasure to drink without filtering or boiling it.

By this time I had most of the roof covered with sheet metal, but I had to leave the end rafters open until I could get the gable logs in place up to the peak, or else I wouldn't be able to lag-screw them to the wall rafters. The gable logs were proving to be a particularly sharp pain in my butt, because any rules I'd learned about carpentering with processed lumber didn't apply to working with heavy, bumpy, crooked logs. The end rafters provided an angled guide for fitting them, but even though they were themselves more or less straight, it was tough to consider and compensate for irregularities between the log I was trying to fit and the one directly below.

I finally ended up hoisting the gable logs into position and tying them off to the center post inside at the desired height while I hand-fitted either end with my big roofer's hatchet. This was a dangerous proposition, hanging a 500-pound, 10-foot log 6 feet above the ground by a rope around its balance point while I chopped angles at both ends, but aberrations in the wood made cutting them to fit beforehand almost impossible. It seemed ironic to think that I'd once made my living working with machine tolerances in ten-thousandths of an inch.

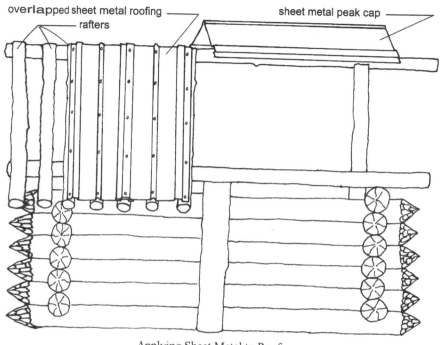

overlapped sheet metal roofing — rafters   sheet metal peak cap —

Applying Sheet Metal to Roof

When I had one end chopped to fit, I'd tie it in place as securely as I could with a rope, then start on the other end. When both ends could be fitted between the rafters, I tied the log in place, then went inside to secure it by driving a countersunk 10-inch lag screw through the center post and into the gable log. With the lag screw drawn down tightly and the gable log secured, I then drove another lag screw through the rafter and into the center of the gable log from either end. All this was probably overkill, but it was comforting to know that the strength of this cabin made a stick-built house look like a cardboard box by comparison. I needed to know that the construction was stout enough to snap a falling tree trunk in half without sustaining any serious structural damage.

July turned into August, and the temperatures began to cool a bit. The blackflies were gone, and the swarms of mosquitoes had lessened to being a mere annoyance. The only downside was that cooler temperatures allowed the tropical humidity that had existed all summer to turn into precipitation, and the rain came down in buckets. There were nice days, too, but it seemed the more I needed to get something done, the harder it rained. I cursed the cabin, I cursed myself for taking on such an impossible task, and I cursed God for making this the most miserable year I'd ever seen. I believe God was listening, but I think He just laughed at me and made it rain that much harder.

It was in the middle of one of those really pounding rains that I injured myself, almost seriously. I'd nearly finished filling in the front wall, and now I was cutting the 12-foot gable log that would form the top of the cabin's rear window when it was placed. Because I didn't want to drop any more trees, I'd been taking the gable logs from the tops of trees whose trunks had been used to build the cabin walls, the pickings were getting slimmer the nearer I came to completion.

I winched and lashed the big log into position 4 feet up on the back side of the cabin, nearly drowning in the pouring rain as I did so. Only then did I finally see that it had a serious dogleg that not only made it very tough to fit at the ends, but left a 4-inch gap between itself and the log below about halfway along its length. That of course meant that an equal gap would exist between this log and the one I placed on top of it, but at the opposite end.

Disgusted, I untied the log, letting it fall heavily onto the saturated ground. There was another candidate for this position on a treetop lying about 75 yards distant, so I chopped it free, de-limbed it, and winched it over to the cabin. After a lot of wet, muddy labor, it was up on the rear wall where the rejected log had been.

This log was worse than the first. I hadn't noticed, but it had a definite bow in its center, and one end wouldn't go into place against the rafter at all. I went into a rage, dropping it back to the ground, then jumping down from the wall after it. I grabbed the first log I'd rejected and rolled its center up my forearms to the inside of my elbows. Then, with a heave powered by the adrenalin of fury, I lifted the log up and jammed it into the same place it had been.

The log went into position between the rafters and against the center post, but I felt the ligaments in both my shoulder joints stretch beyond their limits. My arms didn't quite pull from their sockets, but I knew I'd injured myself. In great pain I tied the log to the center post, then grabbed my pack from the tent. It hurt like hell as I shrugged the pack onto my shoulders, but I'd had enough of building a cabin for the next couple of days. I hiked out to the van and drove to Petoskey.

When I returned two days later, accompanied by Pete, the sky was sunny and things didn't seem quite so terrible. I made the doglegged log fit rather well, then determined to use the bowed log in the place above it. I winched it up, tied it off, and chopped its straightest end to fit against the rafter. Then I lag-screwed it in place at that end and through the center post.

The opposite end bowed outward from the other rafter by a good foot, but I wasn't taking no for an answer. With the straight end and center anchored securely with lag screws, I wrapped a cable around the warped end and took the winch inside the cabin, tying off to the front center post. I pulled the 2-ton come-along to its limit, I think, but the 11-inch-diameter log slowly bent toward the rafter. Pete stayed far away, just in case those tons of force came suddenly free.

When it was against the rafter, I climbed up and chopped the end until it would fit flush, then finished winching it into position. When it was where I wanted it, I left the winch holding it there under tremendous strain, while I drove a 10-inch lag screw through the rafter and deep into its center. I released the winch and it held. After a few days, the green wood had succumbed to the hundreds of pounds of pressure restraining it, and it conformed to its mount until almost no pressure was needed to hold it in place.

The gable logs that came after were progressively shorter and lighter, and less length meant that it was easier to cut one that was straight over its span. The problem now was that the logs had to be placed higher than I could reach. I needed a ladder.

The treestand ladders wouldn't work—there was nothing vertical to fasten them to on the outside of the cabin wall, only horizontal logs. Pete volunteered to make a ladder from ash saplings, the strongest wood in the forest. He got it about half done before he had to leave, so I finished the job.

The completed ladder was a monstrosity, standing 9 feet tall with rungs and uprights that were 4 inches in diameter, and a finished weight of about 75 pounds. Each rung was notched at both ends to fit flush against the uprights, then held in place with three 3-inch galvanized deck nails. The uprights were both bowed inward, but there was 2 feet of stepping surface at its narrowest point. It took muscle to move it from one place to another, but it would support more weight than I could carry up its rungs, and I figured it was at least up to OSHA standards.

Now that I had the tools and the know-how to get the gables done, I tackled the doorway yet again. The rafter angle prevented me from cutting any more from the direction of the side wall, but there was just enough room to gain the space needed by cutting back toward the center post.

There was no room to use a saw, as I had on the opposite side, but I figured that once I had one log cut back the desired distance with my axe, I could get the saw blade inside to make nice flat cuts that would insure the door frame mounted as straight as possible. As it turned out, I did the whole job with axe, hatchet, and my SP-8 machete. Even I was a little surprised at how evenly I could face the log ends by chopping alone, but in about four hours the job was done.

Next came the door frame. First I mounted the hinge side toward the outside of the cabin with 3.5-inch drywall screws—I was getting pretty comfortable driving these with a hand screwdriver. I had to mount and dismount the door on its hinges a few times before I got them in just the right spot, but once the frame was shimmed straight and the door slid easily over the threshold, I screwed that side down tight, leaving the door hanging.

That left the latch side of the door frame hanging in space, with a 4-inch gap between it and the logs I'd just cut. I took a bit more pleasure than I should have in smacking it hard once at the top and bottom to separate it from the wire staples that held it together. Then I repeated the fitting process until the door latch lined up with the plate on that side of the frame, and the door clicked shut smoothly. When it did, I secured the split frame permanently with a dozen more long drywall screws.

Now there was a 4-inch gap between the threshold and header on the hinge side of the frame and the latch vertical. I filled those in by fashioning filler pieces from two of the thousands of wood chips lying around the work site. When I was finished, the door swung smoothly shut with only tiny cracks of daylight where I'd modified the frame.

Finally, with the door closed, I hacksawed a length of metal carpet strip that I'd brought for that purpose to fit across the threshold. I pushed the beveled edge of the strip snugly under the door's bottom edge, so that the two parts would seal tightly against one another when the door was latched closed. The metal strip worked well for sealing out drafts, and it helped to hide the filled gap where I'd split the door frame. The job wasn't as pretty as I would have liked, but it was functional, and it seemed nice just to go inside the cabin and shut the door behind me.

PETE AND NOKI

August turned to September, and the hard labor portion of my cabin's construction began drawing to a close. Aided by the heavy ladder Pete and I had made, I was able to carry the shorter gable logs up to where they were needed, then chop and screw them into place with a minimum of cussing. When the gables were filled, I was finally able to finish covering the roof overhangs with sheet metal. As soon as the roof was finished, I was going to move in, and I was very much looking forward to taking down the tent that had been my home since I'd started this project in April.

Based on years of harsh conditions under which I'd used the Olympic that was my house and the smaller Starlet that served as a warehouse out here, I can unreservedly claim that Moss makes the finest tents in the world. But I'd had my fill of living in a tent, no matter how good it was. I wanted to sleep in a room that I didn't need to crawl in and out of, and I craved the luxury of being able to stand up. Strange how one's values change after a few months of life in the woods.

I was wrapping up the gables when Pete came out with his dog Noki and announced his intention to stay with me for the next month. He was just twenty now, with an extremely good head on his shoulders and better intellect than most men twice his age. I considered Pete to be one of the most trustworthy friends I'd ever had. He was, of course, welcome.

I asked him why he'd decided to make his family doubt his sanity by spending a month in the boondocks. He said it was an experience he wanted to have, and that he might never again have the freedom to get it. I could certainly understand that motivation. He pitched his tent to one side of the cabin—well away from the lightning-struck spruce, I noticed—and set up housekeeping.

I was equally happy to have Noki, because a dog in camp not only provides a warning about animal intruders before our comparatively useless human senses can detect their presence, but usually keeps even the largest species from approaching in the first place. Noki was half gray wolf, half malamute, five years old, and weighed 90 pounds, all of which helped to make him a useful animal companion in the woods. Pete had adopted him from Cheanne a few months earlier, while she in turn had rescued him from being destroyed by his overwhelmed owners two years prior to that. Noki was a terrific companion for someone who understood his lineage, but he'd been bred in the era when people with no knowledge of wolves had foolishly tried to turn a wild canid that kills only to eat into a guard dog.

Contrary to fairy tales and movies, a wolf won't attack a human, nor will it defend one. Mixing its wild blood with that of a dog that will do both those things only creates an animal that can never be fully trained, and is more likely to bite its owner than an intruder. Owning a wolf hybrid, which can't live on just dog food, but requires frequent meals of raw meat (and will readily kill other animals to get it) proved to be more than a typical pet owner could handle, which led to the wholesale abandonment of these unfortunate animals. Cheanne had made certain that Pete understood and accepted this responsibility before allowing him to adopt Noki, and from what I'd seen, she'd made a good choice. There was real love between these two.

Like Noki, Pete seemed to be in his natural environment here in the woods, and he'd already become a fairly proficient all-around woodsman. He was well read—including my books—and he possessed an unusual capacity for logic that allowed him to think his way out of tough situations. But, as I once told him, "Pete, you're really smart, but you don't know every damn thing." I felt qualified to tell him that because, even though I was older than his father, I didn't know every damn thing about the woods, either.

Pete got a valuable lesson in humility in his first week with me. I was on the cabin roof, mounting the last sheets of metal that would finish closing its roof out to the overhang at front and rear, when he announced that he wanted to scout a hunting territory along the ridges west of there. He clipped Noki to a 25-foot steel cable anchored to the cabin wall and asked if I would keep an eye on him. I agreed, barely glancing up from my work as he crossed through marsh to the next ridge carrying his daypack and the customized SKS rifle I'd sold him before I left civilization. I knew he had no intention of shooting an animal, but he'd learned from my example that a firearm completed the survival gear we all carried whenever we were away from camp.

Pete had been gone for about three hours when I began wondering where he'd gotten to. I wasn't really worried—he had the tools needed to survive almost anything—but the sun was setting below the treeline, and no one was immune from injury in the treacherous terrain he was exploring. It was a catch-22 of sorts: If he didn't get back by nightfall I'd have to assume he was in trouble, but there was no way I could track him down through such tangled country until morning, after his trail was cold and faded.

It was about then that I heard a single rifle shot, identifiable as an SKS by its distinctive two-stage report. I stopped banging with my hammer and listened. A few minutes passed and I heard another shot. I fixed its position at about 400 yards southwest of the cabin.

The first thing to cross my mind was that Pete had missed the ridge leading home, an easy problem to have in this country of broken concentric glacial dunes. But he hadn't fired the international distress signal of three consecutive rounds, which I knew that he knew, and that threw me. Conjecture was pointless, so I went back to work, figuring that if Pete was lost, he'd hear my hammer banging against the metal roof.

Pete walked in from the main trail about two hours later, when it was almost too dark to see. He was grinning broadly (partly from relief, I suspect) as he told me how he had indeed missed the cabin's ridge at one of the swampy breaks that dotted its length. Finding himself in unfamiliar terrain with darkness coming on, he'd made the deer hunter's mistake of just pressing on blindly, hoping to see something he recognized. Like me, he'd figured on being able to hear me pounding nails into the cabin roof, but for some reason the sound didn't carry to him.

That's when little things began to go wrong. The poppet top on his water bottle fell apart, he ran out of water and couldn't find more, and the mosquitoes were thick enough to require a head net. With sunset it had gotten dark quickly under the canopy, and he began tripping over forest debris that lay thick on the forest floor. Being tired, thirsty, and hot added to his sense of impending doom, and he began to panic. The more he panicked, the faster he traveled, the more he stumbled, the thirstier he got.

This is precisely the formula for disaster that has killed many a woodsman, but Pete had enough wilderness experience and self-control to get hold of it before it progressed to the point of mindless terror. After firing the two shots I'd heard, which had indeed been meant to alert me, he felt a little foolish, so he stopped to take a deep breath and assess the situation from a logical standpoint. He had a compass and flashlight, and he couldn't be more than a mile from the North Country Trail; he was still in control of his destiny. He forced himself to remain calm, took a bearing, and fought back the all too common suspicion that his compass was lying. Within half an hour he broke out onto the North Country Trail and was headed back to the cabin.

Pete was justifiably proud to have extricated himself from a dilemma that many others had not, and I congratulated him for having passed a critical test that every woodsman must face on the journey to proficiency. He'd learned that the ability to survive is more attitude than skill, and even the best equipment means little if you don't maintain the presence of mind to use it effectively. Humans aren't equipped to operate from instinct, but from intellect; the fight-or-flight instinct can get a woodsman killed, but knowing how to play chess might well save his life.

Noki too learned a few lessons about the woods. He'd been raised like an ordinary dog, and the latter half of his almost six years had been spent in a large kennel, so he'd never had a chance to discover his wilder side. Now that he was in the deep woods and able to run as he pleased (never too far from his beloved Pete, though), he was like a kid in a toy store. Like every dog, he tried chasing deer a few times, and like all dogs, he soon discovered that they could easily outdistance him, so he gave up on that pastime.

One of Noki's more valuable lessons came from a porcupine. I was awakened at 8:00 one morning by Pete calling to me for help from the front of the cabin, where I couldn't see him from the door of my tent. I rose quickly and slipped on my sneakers, grabbing my leather work gloves as I exited the tent, because I knew what the problem was even before I saw him; it was one that I'd been anticipating since Noki arrived.

Sure enough, I rounded the front corner of the cabin to find him holding a struggling Noki by his collar. A half dozen quills bristled from the poor wolf dog's muzzle as he wriggled in pain and confusion, convinced by his master's anxiety that he must have done something wrong. I sighed and cautioned Pete to stay calm while I retrieved a heavy lineman's pliers from the cabin.

Like a child with a sliver, Noki was frightened, afraid that I was going to inflict more pain by touching his injuries. But I'd done this only too many times before, and like every task I really hate to perform, I'd become fairly proficient at de-quilling dogs. I wrapped both arms around his torso, pressed my chest against his shoulder from a position where he couldn't bite me, and bore him to the ground under my weight, all the while speaking to him in soothing tones and calling him a good boy. Then I scissor-locked the base of his neck between my thighs from behind and pulled his head up by cupping one palm under his jaw. Forced to submit, the dog settled down a bit and stopped struggling.

The quills were fresh, their hollow airtight interiors hadn't yet expanded from their victim's body heat and fluids, so it wasn't necessary to snip their ends. Noki winced and struggled a little as I quickly grasped each one in the pliers' jaws and extracted it straight outward with a single hard yank, but he seemed resigned to the fact that this was going to be done.

In less than three minutes Noki's muzzle was quill free. Now came the hard, and potentially hazardous, part—I had to pry open his powerful wolflike jaws and pull several quills, some of them broken, from his tongue and gums. With leather gloves protecting my skin, I pulled his mouth open and shoved my open hand back to his molars, where it would both hold down his tongue and keep him from biting down as hard as he might. Noki struggled and whined a little as I pulled the barbs free of tender tissue that had already become swollen, and I, too, winced as molars designed to crush bone closed painfully on my hand, but all in all the operation went smoothly. There have been times when I emerged from this procedure bloodier and more injured than the dog.

Noki recovered almost immediately. He chewed his dry food gingerly that first day, but there were no secondary infections. He forgave Pete and me for holding him down and torturing him, and he apparently understood what had happened, because he never again fooled with a porcupine.

There wasn't much Pete could do to help me with the many small tasks that needed to be done on the cabin, largely because the project was still a learning experience, and I was deciding how best to do things as I came to them. The well, however, was in dire need of a cover to keep out the small animals that persisted in falling into the pit and drowning. I'd tied a large conical strainer onto a long pole to make it possible to scoop out frogs and salamanders that kept falling in there at night, but the mice were usually drowned by the time we found them, and a few critters always sunk to the bottom and fouled the entire well. It cleaned up nicely after being emptied, but that was a lot of work, and then we had to wait a day for it to refill and settle before drawing water.

While Pete set to work building a well cover from what was left of the trees I'd felled for the cabin, I installed the cabin's windows. I'd decided to mount the smaller slide-open window with the patched bullet hole in front, facing east, where the small amount of light it allowed in would be augmented by the large door window that also faced east. There was already a hole for the window there, kept purposely small so that it could be enlarged to fit whatever window I ended up with. The bigger crank-open mobile home window would go in the rear wall to catch light from the setting sun, next to where the fireplace would be.

Fitting the windows was easy compared to the job I'd faced with fitting and mounting the door. I set to work with my big roofer's hatchet, and by nightfall the front window was mounted snugly and squarely in its sill. It seems silly, but I took great pleasure in going outside and sticking my head through the open window to look inside. There was still a hole in the rear wall—two, if you counted the fireplace hole—but the cabin was starting to look like a log house.

With the experience of mounting the door and front window in a log wall, setting the rear window in place was simple. Unlike the front window, this trailer window had a flange around its perimeter, which left a bit more latitude for error. Being larger with a split pane of frosted and clear glass, both of which opened, I had to enlarge the window hole more, but in about three hours I had the second window fitted, nailed in tight, and working the way it was intended. There were still plenty of spots around the door, win-

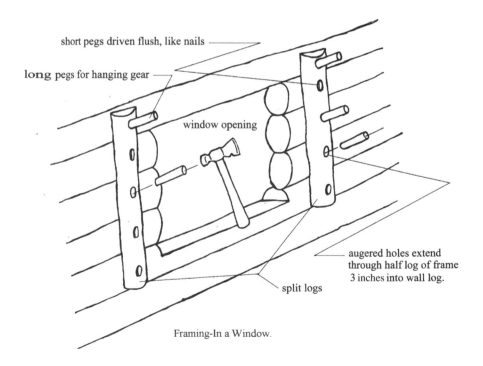

short pegs driven flush, like nails

long pegs for hanging gear

window opening

augered holes extend through half log of frame 3 inches into wall log.

split logs

Framing-In a Window.

dows, and in the walls where daylight came through, but chinking would take care of that problem. At least everything was in place, and it looked pretty darned good to me.

The roof was covered to its ends on both sides from eaves to ridgepole, but there was still a gap at the peak where the two sides met, and that was my next project. But first I needed more steel to fashion a peak cap. There were a dozen more sheets stashed in the woods at the dam, so after a supper of au gratin potatoes with tuna, Pete and I set off toward the beaver flooding. Night had fallen by the time we left, and despite a rising moon visible through the trees, it was dark on the trail. No matter, both of us knew the trail well, and both of us had hiked it in the dark more times than I could recall.

We'd traveled about a quarter mile when we heard the distinctive howling of at least three timber wolves roughly a half mile east of where we were. It wasn't the first time either of us had heard wolves howling in this place where DNR biologists claimed they didn't exist, but we stopped to listen anyway.

Noki's wolf side heard them, too, and it was like the song of a siren to him. He suddenly bolted off the trail and into the woods toward the howls. Pete and I both tried to call him back, but the call of the wild was stronger than his training. Noki looked like a wolf to the untrained eye, but I feared that if he met up with even one wild wolf, it would see him as a dog and try to kill him. And if a wolf tried to kill Noki, it would almost certainly succeed within seconds, because a dog fighting a wolf is like a barroom brawler fighting a trained assassin.

Pete was only too aware of the animosity wolves felt for their domesticated cousins, and he began to get anxious. There was no way we could follow and catch Noki in these shadowed woods, so I told Pete we'd just have to trust that he had sense enough not to make contact.

There was real concern in Pete's eyes when he said, "Len, I don't want to lose my dog." But he knew I was right, there was nothing we could do.

Fortunately, I was right about Noki, too. He apparently approached the wolves just close enough to get a better look, then headed back to us. He met us again on the trail ten minutes later. Pete and I both breathed a sigh of relief, because neither of us harbored any illusions about what would have happened if he'd met with a pack of hunting wolves.

The moon was full and bright when we crossed the dam. No one was there, although fresh tire tracks in the sand told us the place had been visited by more than a dozen vehicles in the few days we'd been in the woods. Both our vehicles were intact, parked directly in front of French Farm Creek to further reinforce the poles planted there to keep idiots with ORVs from ripping up the banks again.

Both of us had become a lot more paranoid about vandalism since my van window had been smashed in five months earlier. But there is indeed safety in numbers, and the gangs of drunks who came to this remote place to raise hell and tear up the forest seemed intimidated by a second vehicle whose owner couldn't be located. Pete and I had both experienced unmitigated animosity from men who hated us simply because we went into the deep woods where they feared to go. One guy had even stolen Pete's compass while he was swimming in the beaver pond to cool off on a hot day last July.

Aside from the half dozen sheets of steel I'd carried to the cabin by myself, Pete had helped me haul the entire roof, up to six 3 x 10-foot pieces at a time, and we had it down to a science. I lashed four sheets together at both ends using a single piece of rope tied with a timber hitch, and we simultaneously lifted both ends of the bundle, setting its center onto our heads. A folded handkerchief under our ball caps provided padding, not so much from the steel, but from that damned button that's in the center of every ball cap I've ever seen. Without a pad, the button dug painfully into our skulls, and by the time we reached the cabin there'd be a bruised bump on top of our heads.

When we had the load balanced, we set off walking in step across the dam and into the woods. The trip went smoothly and nonstop. As usual, Pete led the way, which was illuminated for both of us by the Mini Mag flashlight I held between my teeth as we hiked. It struck me that we'd become used to working together when he said "Log dip," and I knew that he meant we were about to step into a washout that somebody from the North Country Trail Association had tried to fill with sections of ash sapling.

After coffee the next morning, I finished the roof. The monster ladder we'd collaborated on was proving handy; I leaned it against the eave and clambered up to the peak, hauling a sheet of steel behind me. The sheets had a strongback, or fuller, groove running lengthwise along their centers to help stiffen them, and it was an ideal place to bend them along the roof peak so they overlapped the steel covering the roof from either side. A single sheet wasn't long enough to cap the 18 feet from one end of the ridge to the other, so I used two sheets, overlapping them in the center. When both cap sheets were formed and in place, I nailed them down at the edges. Except for the tarpaper that would cover the steel and make it watertight, the roof was finished, and it looked pretty good.

Pete was nearly finished with the well cover. He'd started with four heavy logs, a foot in diameter and 7 feet long, laid across the well pit with a 4-foot gap between them in the center of the well. Across these framing logs he nailed a platform of smaller 8-inch logs, again leaving a 4-foot gap in the center. When he'd finished there was a platform over the well that would have supported a loaded truck, with a nicely squared four-foot-square hole in its center through which a 5-gallon bucket could be dropped and drawn back up without hitting the sides. Sod placed around the outside edges of the platform sealed it against small animals that might get under it. It was a good job.

That afternoon I took down my tents, feeling almost like celebrating as I transferred all my belongings into the cabin. There was some trepidation as I turned the empty tents upside down to dry their floors before stuffing them into their bags. No tent was warranted to withstand the kind of long-term abuse I'd subjected both of these to, but when I inspected their floors I was pleasantly surprised to see that neither of them had suffered the least amount of damage. After half a year of being pressed directly against the earth I'd expected at the very least to find mildew and some degree of rot, but both looked as good as the day I'd put them there.

The fireplace wasn't ready, but I still used it, digging a shallow pit just outside and building a small fire in its bottom. Neither Pete nor I were quite ready to abandon the fire pit around which so many great conversations had taken place, but it was very cool to be inside while I made coffee and cooked supper. We felt even better about that when the sky darkened that afternoon and let loose with one of those torrential rains I'd become accustomed to.

I didn't expect the roof to be watertight, what with used steel covering it, but the pitch was steep enough to make rain run off without leaking through the nail holes. There were more than a dozen places where you could see daylight from inside, but the roof actually leaked in just three spots, and not very much at that. Hell, I knew people who lived in houses that leaked worse than this.

I doubt Bob Vila would recommend this practice, but while it was still raining, and we could locate the worst leaks, Pete and I set to work sticking patches of duct tape over the holes from inside. We soon had all the leaks patched and were snug and dry. There was nothing to done about the noise, though; the steel roof reverberated from the pounding rain, making it necessary to raise our voices to be heard by one another. Tar paper would take care of that problem.

It now became imperative to construct a proper fireplace. The fire I'd built outside the fireplace opening was quickly doused by rain, and not having it enclosed meant that whatever heat it did generate was lost to the open air. I didn't know how to build a fireplace, never having done it before, but I'd have to figure it out before cold weather hit.

My grubstake was almost depleted, and being out here meant that I wasn't in a place where I could make money writing magazine articles—or doing anything else, for that matter. I had plenty of food to make it through the winter, even if most of it was in the form of beans, rice, and other dried goods, and I could always hunt, trap, or fish if I had to, so there was no danger of starvation. But it was nice to have a few bucks to take in a movie or buy munchies while I was in town. I was down to $300, and there were still a few building supplies to purchase.

That first night in the cabin also convinced me that a real floor was needed. It was nice to be inside a place that was dry and large enough to move around in, but the romantic notion of a dirt-floor cabin wasn't so attractive in the sand country of northern Michigan. I'd read about the concretelike floors of pioneers' cabins in Southern states, but those were built on clay. All of the 1700s-style cabins that had been reconstructed at Fort Michilimackinac in Mackinaw City had rough-hewn plank floors, but I'd always thought they were there to provide insulation from the earth during winter. Now I could see that a raised floor was needed in my cabin too, not just to keep out the cold, but to keep grit from getting into everything from food to bedding.

It occurred to me to make a clay floor, along the same lines as the small experimental clay and stone hearth I'd laid in front of the fireplace. But the only real source of clay in this area was in the well, at a level 5 feet below ground. I didn't think I could excavate enough from there to cover even half of the floor without turning the well into a pond, and I didn't care for the idea of digging another deep hole just to get a questionable amount of clay. There was a small pile of the stuff that I'd at least had the foresight to toss aside for later use while I was excavating the well, but it was reserved for the fireplace, and there wasn't enough to do even that much properly.

I didn't have a sawmill to rip floor planks, either. As far back as the 1700s, settlers around here had had access to the sawmill at Mill Creek, about 10 miles west of here, and virtually every town in northern Michigan had grown up around a river for that reason. I looked at the insulated steel door I'd just installed, and thought that there was something really ironic about that.

I considered splitting planks from whole logs using wedges and the back of my big axe as a sledge, but dismissed that notion as too impractical. I knew it could be done, because I'd already fashioned a few short boards that way, but that experience had also shown that the results would be extremely uneven, splintered, and of varying thickness along the plank's entire length.

I even thought about laying straight wall-length spruce and hemlock saplings side by side onto the floor to cover it that way. But even my best ef-

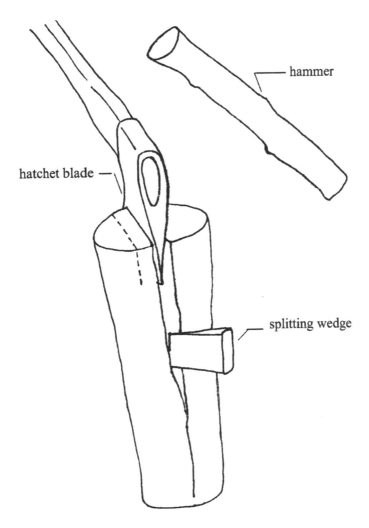

Splitting a Log into Usable Lumber.

forts would result in a platform of rounded surfaces that was uneven and gapped enough to trap almost any small object I might drop there, and I couldn't tolerate the sticky sap that would be exuded from those saplings until the wood dried.

After considering every method for using natural materials that I could think of, I decided that the only good solution was to haul in enough 4 x 8 sheets of OSB (Oriented Strand Board) or chip board, to cover the floor, then mount them atop a lattice of joists cut from saplings. It was hardly traditional, but the result would be a raised floor that was insulated from the earth, as flat as the joists allowed, and without gaps that would steal small items if you dropped them.

But first I needed to create a fireplace. The hole where it should be was defeating the purpose of having a door and windows as far as keeping out animals was concerned, and it was a matter of time before some bear or raccoon came in across the cold ashes of the fire just outside to raid my stores. I figured to do the job with conventional stovepipe, which I'd have to go to town to get.

Pete opted to stay at the cabin while I was away. I think he wanted a little real solitude to ponder his future in the only place he could find it. Noki, of course, preferred to be with his master, especially if they were both in the woods. I'd grown to love the big silly wolf dog and the amusement he provided us as he explored long-dormant instincts that had never surfaced during his life in civilization. I could relate.

I shouldered my pack and hiked to the dam, where I was glad to find our vehicles still unmolested. As usual, the Indian van started right up—funny how the vehicles I like the least always seemed to run the best—and I bounced along the two-track leading out to the main road.

My first stop in Petoskey was Big John's place, where I got yet another earful of gossip about people and events I didn't care about. Several of John's friends stopped by while I was there, and they, too, seemed to have a fixation over what other people were doing with their lives. I knew most of these people to varying degrees, and I had to grin when they inquired about what I'd been up to. When I told them, most just stared at me blankly, as though I'd just spun some incredible yarn that couldn't possibly be true.

My next stop was Home Depot, where I hoped to pick up a couple lengths of stovepipe for the fireplace project. I walked in the front door with Cheanne and looked up and down the main aisle, muttering that I wasn't quite sure where we'd find it. Cheanne immediately called to a passing employee, and asked the nice lady where we might find stovepipe.

"All our pipe is in plumbing supplies," she said, pointing to the other end of the store.

Thinking she must have misunderstood, I said, "No, I'm looking for stovepipe, not water pipe."

This time she gave me an outright sneer, and repeated slowly, as if speaking to a child, "All our pipe is in plumbing supplies." She stabbed her forefinger toward the opposite end of the store again.

"Thank you," I said with enough sarcasm to make her hear the word "bitch" in there as well. I turned and walked in the opposite direction from where she'd tried to send me, and found stovepipe in the second aisle I looked at. Christ, but I was starting to dislike civilized people.

The price of stovepipe there took my breath away, and to this day I think someone had mismarked them. I left without buying anything and went back to Big John's. A true scavenger, he made a couple of phone calls and got me three 4-foot sections for free, one with a damper already installed.

Having learned by necessity to do a little scavenging myself, I called a carpenter friend to see if he might know where I could get some "blueboard" Styrofoam insulation. I'd worked with this stuff before, and it seemed nearly ideal for use in the cabin. It was easy to transport, easy to cut and fit, and had very good insulation properties. I didn't get all I needed, but I got enough to get started.

Since it was the weekend, I spent the next couple of days in town, living out of my van, which was better appointed than a motel room. I spent most of my time with Cheanne, walking along the shore of Lake Michigan, chatting in a local coffeehouse, or just strolling among the tourists on Petoskey's streets. Since my divorce in 1999 I'd had no interest in taking up with another woman, but the barriers I put up weren't holding where Cheanne was concerned. I found myself telling her things that I didn't talk about with anyone else, and what had begun as a close friendship three years earlier was starting to evolve into something even stronger.

CHAPTER

BUILDING A FIREPLACE

When I arrived back at the cabin carrying the stovepipe with which I intended to make a fireplace chimney tied onto my backpack, Pete told me there'd been a little excitement at the homestead during my absence. He'd risen early the morning before and was making coffee at the fire pit when he caught a movement out of the corner of his eye. There, coming down the wooded back trail, an alternate footpath that led to the cabin from a different point off the main trail, was a very large raccoon. It was an old grizzled male, weighing more than 60 pounds—huge, but not at all unusual in northern Michigan—and it was heading straight for the cabin. The 'coon had already seen Pete, and it must have scented Noki, but it didn't seem the least deterred by the presence of either.

I can only surmise that the raccoon was bent on raiding the camp for food, although it didn't appear to be the least bit starved. Nor was it rabid, as rabies occurs almost exclusively during March and April in northern Michigan. Maybe it was feeling overly territorial and wanted to see if this unfamiliar human being would stand his ground. This 'coon was much larger than the one I'd chased off with a pistol shot in July, and it seemed to have an almost unnatural lack of fear. It was pretty obvious that this animal had already learned to associate humans with food, and that it had never learned fear from them.

Pete rose from his seat on the log bench by the fire pit, hoping that by standing upright he could frighten the animal into backing down. A normal raccoon would have retreated up one of the many nearby trees, but this one kept right on coming.

Alerted by his master's actions, Noki jumped up from where he'd been lying near the fire. As soon as he discovered the cause of Pete's sudden concern, he attacked without hesitation, catching the big 'coon by surprise with a swift charge. Noki's reaction also took Pete by surprise; he barked a command for his dog to return, but there was no stopping him. The wolf half of Noki considered raccoons to be both natural prey and a competitor for food, while the dog half was bent on protecting its territory.

With less than a hundred feet separating them, Noki covered the distance before Pete's shout had stopped echoing through the woods. The two animals came together with an audible thud of flesh hitting flesh, and a battle to the death began. Noki had never tangled with a raccoon before, much less one that was two-thirds his own size, and by that virtue alone, a seasoned veteran of many life or death battles. He quickly discovered what every experienced human 'coon hunter knows: that a raccoon in fighting mode is ferocious, strong, and a capable fighter. Only a few of the largest predators would have considered tackling one this size, and the wolf dog found himself in the battle of his life.

Pete have never seen a raccoon fight, either, but he'd heard my hunting stories about their ferocity, and now he could see for himself that I hadn't exaggerated. Despite having the better weapons and a size advantage, Noki's muzzle was bleeding from numerous small wounds, and a copious amount of blood was streaming from his right eye, effectively blinding him on that side. The raccoon had its share of injuries, too, but an ample layer of fat prevented Noki's sharp canines from inflicting more than superficial wounds. Human-like hands found good purchase in the dog's thick fur, while sharply pointed canines insured that every thrust Noki made resulted in an injury to himself.

From Pete's perspective, the action was a blur of snapping teeth, claws, and fur, but he could tell that Noki was getting as good as he gave. He didn't remember grabbing it, but the rifle he kept close by and loaded, after my own example, was in his hands. He snapped the safety catch to Fire and sighted through the scope, but there was no way to insure that the decidedly lethal 7x39 hunting bullet wouldn't hit his dog.

Fearing that Noki would be grievously injured if he didn't somehow end this bloody war, Pete ran toward the combatants, stopping within 10 feet of the melee and shouting loudly. It wasn't a strategy I'd recommend, but in this case it worked. The big 'coon turned instinctively to face this new threat, sending a chill of fear down the man's spine as he saw close up how one of these cuddly animals can transform into a demon from Hell.

Noki exploited his adversary's distraction without hesitation, diving in low and clamping his strong jaws onto the 'coon's vulnerable underbelly. Then, with a powerful upward yank that was pure timber wolf, he threw it into the air, tearing its abdominal wall and exposing the animal's entrails when it tore free of his grasp.

Despite having inflicted the first serious wound of the fight, Noki had had enough. He withdrew and literally ran behind Pete. This caused Pete considerable consternation as the mortally wounded but now insanely aggressive raccoon rolled back onto its feet within arm's length of where the man stood with his big dog cowering behind him. The 'coon charged at the same instant Pete pulled the trigger, firing from the hip. The softnose Remington bullet struck the enraged animal between its shoulders at an angle, traveling through its innards and turning its organs to jelly, exactly as it had been engineered to do. The raccoon died instantly, its carcass rolling to a stop just inches from Pete's slightly quaking boots.

Pete stood motionless for a few moments, forcing himself to stop hyperventilating while his eyes went back to their proper size and adrenalin levels fell back to normal. The raccoon was definitely dead, but it took several seconds for the level of terror he'd just experienced to subside. He'd taken a wagonload of crap from sporthunters who derided him for electing to take a so-called assault rifle for his survival gun, but at this particular moment he felt like that old SKS was his best friend in the world.

Noki recovered from his wounds, but he'll always carry a long scar from the inside corner of his right eye to the top of his muzzle to remind him that raccoons are not to be trifled with. His only other lasting scar is psychological, a deep-seated hatred of raccoons makes him attack them on sight. He never again took any of them lightly, but that didn't work to the benefit of the 'coons. Fortunately, he also never again found a raccoon that didn't immediately withdraw from conflict by climbing a tree.

I finished filling in the gables up to the peak in the next few days. There was a 6-inch gap over the door frame where it didn't quite reach up to the next horizontal log, and Pete, who had done some work as a carpenter, inquired whether I was going to mount a header strong enough to support the weight of snow on the roof. I chuckled and just looked at him while it slowly dawned on him that the question was a dumb one.

A conventional house with vertical wall studs does indeed require a reinforced header over the doorway to prevent the frame from being warped by heavy snow. But this was a log cabin, with walls made entirely from horizontally mounted logs stacked atop one another. It could be buried under rock, and still not flex enough to affect the doorframe. I filled in the gap with a log cut to fit, then nailed it tightly in place from under the top of the door frame with 8-inch spiral pole barn nails that essentially made both frame and filler log an integral part of the full-length wall log above them.

There was still a lot of chinking to be done between the logs before the walls were sealed, but I'd have those filled before snow came. My most urgent project now was to construct a fireplace. It was just too disturbing an irony to go inside and shut the door behind you with that big hole in the back wall.

With all the other aspects of cabin building occupying me, I hadn't given construction of a fireplace much thought. But now that the task was at hand, I began to consider a number of potential problem areas that hadn't occurred to me. Not the least of those was how to build and mount a hot-burning firebox into walls that were made entirely from wood.

Ideally, I would have joined fireplace to walls with an insulating barrier of rocks mortared in place against the log butts with wet clay, but there just wasn't enough of either of those to be had. The only suitable materials I had available in any quantity were sand and sheet metal. I'd have to get creative, but I'd spent five years in metal stamping and fabrication prior to choosing to live the impoverished life of an outdoor writer. With a little imagination, I knew I could make the same sheet steel I'd used on the roof serve as a firebox.

For the firebox walls I used a single 12-foot sheet of metal bent into a square-cornered U. The fireplace portal was 3 feet wide, so I laid the sheet flat against the ground, measured 4 feet 6 inches from either side, and formed a crease across the steel at those points using light blows from my axe. Stood on its edge, the narrow end of the U formed the back wall of the firebox, and the longer sections paralleled the side walls that mounted firebox to cabin wall.

It appeared that this design would work, but the sheet metal was too thin to be nailed directly to wood. The solution was as simple as folding a 2-foot cross section cut from leftover sheets into thirds, again using light blows from the axe blade to crease the folds, and nailing one of these to the log butts on either side of the fireplace portal. The folds were purposely rounded to maintain a gap of about 1 inch between the sides, thereby creating an air space that would inhibit the transfer of heat. I inserted the sides of the firebox through the fireplace opening, then nailed the ends in place through these folded parallels and into the logs.

I used the same folded steel method to prevent heat from getting to the flattened top of the foundation log at the bottom of the fireplace mouth. In this instance, the folded piece was made long enough to span the fireplace

The **Basic** Fireplace

Formed or **rolled** from roofing steel,
nailed or **screwed** in place, then
insulated on **the** outside with a
covering of **mud**, clay, or sand.

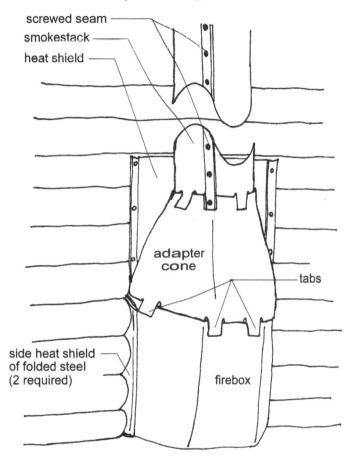

screwed seam

smokestack

heat shield

adapter cone

tabs

side heat shield
of folded steel
(2 required)

firebox

from one side to the other when laid flat on the foundation log, but was a
full 6 inches wider than the log it would insulate. I placed one folded edge
flush with the inside of the foundation log and nailed it in place. The overlapping steel, which extended into the fireplace, was hammered downward
to form a ramp from the top of the foundation to the earthen floor of the
firebox.

Next came the wall log that formed the top of the fireplace opening.
Once again I nailed a piece of folded steel in place to insulate the wood, then
mounted a flat sheet to that to form a roof of sorts over the firebox. I left

2 feet at the rear of the firebox uncovered to let smoke escape, and a 6-inch overlap inside, which I bent upward and nailed flush against the topmost log's face.

The firebox was finished, but now I had to make an adapter piece that would reduce the big hole at the top of the firebox's rear to accommodate the smaller-diameter stovepipe I intended to use as a chimney. That task was accomplished by rolling a cone from a 5-foot section of metal and mounting its narrow end up atop the opening at the rear of the firebox. It amused me to think that in my past life as a quality control manager this operation would have required a blueprint and precision measuring instruments; here I just rolled and hammered the damn thing until it fit.

When I had the cone the way I wanted it, I drove drywall screws through its edges to make it hold that shape. Mounting it atop the firebox was equally complex: I made a half dozen perpendicular cuts around the wider bottom of the cone using tin snips, then fitted those cuts over the edges of the firebox wall to hold it in position. To seal the joints where the pieces met, I squished wet clay into the gaps between them with my palms. The first fire I laid would harden the clay like a kiln, stiffening the assembly and sealing it against sparks that might escape to the outside.

Next came a covering of sand piled around the outside to prevent heat from escaping in that direction, and to further seal the firebox assembly. A small hand-dug gravel pit at the rear of the cabin provided all the sand I needed, while the red plastic kid's sliding saucer I used for hauling equipment in winter worked well enough for transporting loads of the heavy stuff.

When the firebox and cone were covered by an insulating layer of sand that was simply piled against their outsides, I mounted the stovepipe into the top of the cone. It fit loosely, with an inch of space all around between pipe and cone. That was okay—better too loose than too tight. I used the tip of my survival knife to drill small holes around the perimeters of both pieces, then screwed them together using drywall screws. The gap that remained I filled with clay, then finished the completed fireplace off with another layer of sand piled up to the stovepipe.

I stood back to admire my work, feeling pretty good about it until Pete walked up to where I was standing and said, "You know, Len, that looks like something a derelict would build." I was slightly offended, but when I looked at it again, I decided that he was probably right. No matter, if it worked properly I could live with it.

Pete left the day I finished, his own need for a homesteading experience at least partially satisfied. He and Noki had been my good companions for nearly six weeks, and I was going to miss them both. But Pete was young and his life was just starting; he had his own adventures to live, and I believed he had a chance to achieve the greatness I had only aspired to. He had the fundamental tools needed to become a trailblazer, but he'd never realize his potential by following the path I'd already laid.

There was a sadness between us as I walked with him to his Bronco. Even Noki was a bit subdued, not bounding off down the trail as he did normally, but staying close, as if savoring our time together. At the dam, Pete threw his pack into the truck and we shook hands. A wagonload of hugs, tears, and powerful friendship was contained in the grip of that handshake, but both of us were too reserved for such displays of affection. I knew that a single word from me would have caused him to unload his gear and stay the winter with me, but I didn't say it. An October darkness was settling over the beaver pond as I watched his taillights get smaller, then disappear down the two-track.

I hiked back to the cabin in darkness, feeling very much alone, and yet chiding myself for being overemotional. It wasn't like Pete was going far away—I'd still see him when I went to town, and there was no doubt that he'd be showing up to stay a night or two at the cabin as often as he could. Despite my best efforts at logic, the sense of loss persisted. There was an autumn chill in the air as I opened the cabin door, but the cold that surrounded this place now came from more than air temperature. I went to bed early that night.

Things were brighter in the morning, although I still found myself expecting to see Pete or Noki at every turn. I busied myself working on the inside of the cabin. The soffits, the space between the eaves and the side walls, were still open to the outside, and I'd been contemplating how best to seal these 12-feet-long-by-1-foot-wide gaps.

I'd considered just plugging them with sections of the blueboard I'd brought from town, but decided that I wanted a more solid filler that would actually contribute to the strength of the cabin's roof. Then it hit me: I'd use logs. If I rolled a log whose diameter was larger than the gap was wide over the wall from inside, it would fall into and fill the soffit gap like a wedge.

This turned out to be one of my better ideas. I didn't have any big logs left over from the poplars I'd felled that were long enough to span the entire 12-foot gap, but that was good, because I didn't relish the idea of wrestling a quarter-ton log into the cabin any way. Instead I used cut-off sections, three on one side, two on the other. Being of slightly different diameters, the logs made the resulting span a bit stepped where one section met another, but they all filled the gaps nicely. The logs were heavy enough to hold in place under their own weight, but I made sure they'd never move by nailing them to both the soffit poles and the wall logs. The final result was that the eaves, which had been the weakest portions of the structure, now had the same massive strength and support as the walls themselves.

There still remained a 6-inch gap between where the soffit logs pressed against the insides of the rafters and metal roofing. Because it was such a small gap, and because the filler needed to be cut to fit between rafters, I opted to do that job with blueboard. With no more tools than my Spyderco folding knife, I cut the Styrofoam to fit between rafters, soffit log, and roof, purposely making each piece slightly larger than the gap it was intended to fill, then just pressed it into place with my fingers. The blueboard was great to work with; it cut easily, didn't crumble like conventional bead Styrofoam, and it could be forced to fit and seal around bumps or into irregular shapes. Once pressed in place, it held there under its own pressure.

When the soffits were sealed, I went to work insulating the ceiling using the same pressure-fit technique. Because the rafters were round, they formed a groove of sorts where they met the roofing, so sections of blueboard pressed between them expanded tightly into those grooves, creating an airtight seal between metal and wood. Because I was working with cutoff pieces of the insulation that had been discarded from construction sites, I didn't have the option of filling between rafters with single full-length strips, but the sections I cut fit tightly enough to seal against one another. Considering that most of the rafters were both crooked and bumpy, with no two having the same space between, blueboard was an ideal insulating material.

I was still working on the ceiling when darkness fell. There was a chill in the air that reminded me summer was over, so I lit a fire in the fireplace—the first since I'd finished it—and lighted the place brightly enough to work with three kerosene lamps and a candle lantern. The fireplace smoked when I lit it, but I figured it would stop once the fire had a hot bed of coals under it.

But it didn't stop smoking. I kept throwing dry wood on the coals to keep the fireplace burning hot, hoping to force the smoke out the stovepipe, but as soon as it burned down smoke would seep into the small room. I opened the door several times to air the place out, but it was chilly outside, and as soon as I closed it again, smoke began to fill the cabin.

Years of sitting around a campfire has given me a kind of resistance to wood smoke, so finally I just ignored the problem, focusing on cutting and fitting the blueboard. I got it all up at about 2 A.M., and went to bed. As I lay there on my sleeping pad, I could see by the flickering firelight that a cloud of smoke had gathered against the roof. My eyes were burning when I closed them to sleep.

I awoke in the morning at about 8:00, having gotten my required six hours of sleep. My eyes were puffy and they felt scratchy, but I foolishly denied that there was a problem with the fireplace. I spent the day fitting small scraps of blueboard into the remaining cracks with the door open while the fire burned, refusing to believe that my fireplace design wasn't going to work.

By afternoon I was nearly blind. My eyes felt as if there were sand under their lids, and they were swollen to the point of being mere slits. Finally I was worried, but it was too late. I could barely see as I shouldered my backpack and headed for my van, anxious to get there before I went completely blind.

The trail was a blur as I hiked, and my eyes had begun to hurt like hell. I put my mosquito net on, even though there weren't any mosquitoes left, because sunlight increased my discomfort. I breathed a sigh of relief when I crossed the dam. At least I wouldn't be stuck out there in the deep woods if I lost my eyesight altogether.

My vision had improved by the next morning, and my eyes felt better. They still looked red and puffy in the van's visor mirror, but I hoped they would recover without permanent damage. I felt like a damned fool for causing myself to have a potentially life-threatening problem.

Jerod and Cheanne drove in to visit that afternoon while I was still at the van. Cheanne looked at my eyes with the concern of a paramedic, while Jerod, who held a degree in fire safety, worried that I might have done real damage to myself. Me, I just felt stupid, and it was a feeling I wasn't used to having—after all, I was supposed to be the expert out here. None of us went back to the cabin that day, deciding instead to go into Mackinaw City for a hot meal.

They dropped me back at the van just before dark, and I spent another night there. By the next morning my eyes were almost back to normal, and I headed for the cabin. I really hate doing anything twice, but there was no denying that my fireplace design didn't work. I'd have to tear it all down and come up with something better. The nights were already dropping below the freezing mark, and I really needed to have that thing working properly before it started to snow.

As if to remind me, a mix of snow and rain had begun to fall by the time I dropped my pack at the cabin. I went to work right away, disassembling the top of the fireplace while there was still daylight. I'd had a couple of days to ponder the problem while my eyeballs healed, and I'd concluded that the firebox was okay, but the stovepipe chimney was too narrow and restrictive to conduct the amount of smoke generated by what was essentially an enclosed campfire.

I could double the stovepipe, placing two of them side by side, but then they wouldn't reach above the roof. Jerod had cited case histories of houses that had burned down because their chimneys were lower than the roof, and I believed him. I needed a long, big-barreled smokestack, and I needed to construct it from the limited materials here at the homestead.

The answer came to me as I was studying the construction of a section of stovepipe and musing over how a piece of rolled and crimped thin-gauge sheet metal could be so expensive. My swollen eyes unconsciously shifted to where the leftover roofing steel leaned against a cabin wall, and it hit me that the only differences between those and the stovepipe in my hand were shape and size. If I fastened two of those 32-inch sheets together at the edges and rolled them into a tube, I'd have a smokestack that was 10 feet long and approximately 20 inches in diameter. I could do that.

I laid the two remaining full sheets parallel on the ground, edges overlapping, and lightly hammered 1-inch drywall screws through the doubled steel until just the tip of each screw penetrated the bottom sheet. I didn't want to drive the screws in completely because the screws would hold more tightly if they were forced to cut their own threads when I drove them home with a screwdriver. In all, I used ten screws, one at each corner and eight more spaced equidistantly between at intervals of 1 foot.

When the two sheets were joined securely at the edges, I rolled them lengthwise into a tube, screwpoints facing inward. When the tube was formed the way I wanted it, I held it in that shape with a length of cord tied around either end. Placing a section of heavy log inside the tube to provide something solid to pound against, I repeated the process of lightly driving screws into the overlapped edges on the opposite side. When the screws had been driven home, I untied the cord and inspected the finished smokestack. If anything, it was too big in diameter, but it was going to work.

I mounted the smokestack upright on the firebox cone by making small lengthwise cuts around its bottom edge with tin snips and fitting those over the top edge of the firebox, letting the weight of the smokestack lean against the roof overhang until I could secure it permanently. Then I leaned the homemade ladder against the cabin wall, climbed up, and fastened the smokestack to the cabin roof by wrapping a length of perforated steel strapping—the stuff shade-tree mechanics use to hang car mufflers—around its outside and nailing either end of the strap to the overhang rafter.

With the smokestack in place, I filled the gaps between it and the firebox cone with wet clay and covered the outside with sand piled around the perimeter. Now it really looked like the work of a derelict. To check its draft, I went inside the cabin, closed the door, and held a lighted candle in front of the fireplace. The flame was immediately drawn toward the firebox, which indicated that it was sucking air from inside to the outside.

The final test was to lay a fire inside the firebox. I built the fire with damp wood, making it purposely smoky, and the revamped fireplace worked like a charm, sucking every wisp of smoke up the chimney the way it was supposed to. The fireplace was fixed, and I never again had a problem with smoke in the cabin, or with rain dousing the fire.

Another problem that needed to be addressed before winter arrived was the lack of an outhouse. It hadn't been a problem yet because everyone who came to the cabin had simply used the surrounding woods all summer. We guys had a designated pee tree a few yards from the front of the cabin, and none of us was shy about whipping it out and urinating while carrying on an over-the-shoulder conversation. If ladies were present—and Cheanne was just about the only woman who ever came out here—we discreetly walked off into the woods.

The procedure that everyone who came to my homestead followed for the proverbial number two was a bit more complex, because human feces are among the foulest on the planet. When that particular call of nature came up, we grabbed one of the pointed shovels that were always leaning against a tree and walked to a secluded spot a hundred yards or so from the camp, and at least 50 yards from any water.

After cutting out and removing a square of sod that averaged about 1 foot with the shovel, we'd just squat and deposit whatever we needed to get rid of in the hole. Used toilet paper was left in the hole, as well. On completion the sod was replaced into the hole like a plug, sealing the waste against flies that might find it attractive and then carry contamination back to camp.

Although this practice causes some civilized folk to wrinkle their noses in disgust, it worked out very well in a wilderness setting, and I dare say it's more hygienic than using a toilet. There was never a trace of waste near the homestead, and, despite concerns that I might run out of unused square footage, there was always a clean space available for my visitors and me. Not only did this method negate the risk of being poisoned by my own offal, it actually contributed to the health of the surrounding forest. It wasn't much fun in a pouring rain, but that kind of went with the turf.

An added benefit is that pooping from a squatting position is easier on the colon. Doctors have long recognized that defecating from a sitting position causes undue strain on that delicate portion of our anatomy, while squatting with knees fully bent and buttocks resting on the heels results in a straighter shot, so to speak. The difference was so remarkable that I frequently heard visitors say, "Y' know, I shit good out here." Folks who found it necessary to use a toilet several times a day at home were pleasantly surprised to discover that they typically needed to go just once a day in the woods.

The problem was that the snow and frozen ground of winter would make digging a hole impractical, while crapping in a snowbank was just asking for trouble when the spring thaw came and washed ground contaminants—including animal feces—into the water supply. From winter till spring it would be necessary to confine my waste in a single isolated location that was as hygienic as possible, conveniently located, and out of the weather.

I don't like outhouses. I'd had to use them as a kid, and I recalled too well the natural revulsion and reluctance they generate in people who know at an instinctive level that this is a bad place to hang out. Adding to the problem was a tendency to make the pothole below large and deep to extend the outhouse's useful life, which in fact created a huge breeding ground for disease-carrying flies, and often poisoned the well from which families drew drinking water. I was determined to avoid those mistakes.

My solution was to use a folding deer blind that I'd field-tested for Viking Industries several years earlier. It weighed 16 pounds, folded to a rather inconvenient 2 x 5-foot carrying size, and its large zipper-and-Velcro windows were sure to alert every animal within a quarter mile. In its favor was sturdy construction that had proved able to withstand the snows of a northern Michigan winter, a spacious 5 x 5 interior, and a camouflaged exterior that made it inconspicuous in a woodland setting. It may have failed as a deer blind, but it would work great as an easily movable outhouse.

The blind had been in storage at Big John's place since I left, so I made a trip into town to retrieve it, along with a supply of munchies and whatever blueboard I could scavenge. I actually spent the next four days in town, partly because archery deer season had made the forest edges around my homestead a popular place for hunters, and largely because the coming of whitetail gun season kept me busy sighting-in rifles and mounting scopes.

Big John's girlfriend, Robin, had determined that she was going to deer hunt this year for the first time. John agreed to help set her up in the woods, which virtually guaranteed she'd at least see several deer. The marksmanship portion of her training he left to me, so we threw our cased rifles and a few boxes of shells into the truck one sunny afternoon and headed for an abandoned apple orchard north of town where locals had been shooting for years. Cheanne went with us, bringing the customized Marlin bolt-action "squirrel sniper" I'd given her when I left for the woods. Next to her gun behind the truck seats lay my Thompson/Center .308. John's truck carried a Savage 110 bolt-action in .243 caliber, an excellent choice for the lady deer hunter.

Predictably, the Savage was way off, probably having never been zeroed over several years of knocking about. Before shooting, I tightened the scope's mounting screws, about half of which were loose, to eliminate the fairly common problem of a scope that moves during recoil. Then I focused and sighted in the rifle's nice Bushnell scope until three consecutive shots fired across the truck's hood landed center of a 3-inch bull's-eye at 100 yards. At that point I turned the Savage over to the others and assumed the role of range instructor, offering tips about sight alignment and trigger pull especially to the ladies, neither of whom had ever fired a centerfire rifle before. At the end of two boxes of cartridges, John, Robin, and Cheanne were all printing 3-inch groups at 100 yards, which is more than adequate for taking whitetails in the northern Michigan woods.

Then I broke out the .308 with a box of old-fashioned softnose cartridges and set up a broken concrete block that had been abandoned at the end of the 2-track, offering John the rifle when I returned. When his first shot went high and wide he looked at me and complained, "I wasn't ready." I stifled a laugh, admonished him not to touch the trigger until he was ready to fire, and told him to try again. This time he demolished the middle of the cinder block in a cloud of concrete bits and dust.

As usual, changing to a target that was dramatically destroyed when you hit it appealed to everybody. I spent the next half hour running downrange and back to set up increasingly smaller bits of concrete block so my three companions could blow them to bits. It was a fun way to focus them on using the skills they'd just learned with paper targets, while blasting bits of concrete into gravel gave them an idea of how much power they wielded.

When the box of ammo I'd brought to shoot was empty, everyone was grinning at having just demonstrated shooting skills beyond what they'd thought they were capable of. Made me feel pretty good, too.

I returned to the cabin the following night, arriving in darkness, when I could be certain that there'd be no hunters parked at French Farm Creek. I hadn't purchased any flooring material, but tied between the luggage racks on top of my van were two dozen 2 x 4-foot blueboard cutoffs, an assortment of plywood pieces for shelving, and the hunting blind outhouse. I took the blind first, remembering why I'd rejected it for hunting as I lugged the cumbersome package down the trail by flashlight.

Cheanne and Jerod came out to visit the following day as I was setting up the blind on a small knoll about 20 yards southeast of the cabin. Jerod excavated the 2 x 2 x 2-foot hole I'd specified while I cussed and tried to remember how this Chinese puzzle went together. When it looked right, we moved the erected blind over the hole so that it was located near the back wall opposite the zippered door, and staked it in position.

Inside the outhouse I placed two large coffee cans, one containing a roll of toilet paper under its snap-down lid, the other left open and filled with wood ashes from the fireplace. The wood ashes, which are essentially lye, would be sprinkled into the latrine pit each time after it had been used to speed decomposition and to keep flies from landing on the waste it contained. The ashes also kept odors to a fraction of what they would have been in a conventional outhouse.

The pothole was made small and shallow on purpose. Having already dug a well, I knew where the water table lay, and I made certain the hole was shallow enough to insure that there was no danger of contaminating it. The hole's small volume meant that it would fill more quickly, but I preferred smaller concentrations of waste; it would be no problem to fill it in with soil, then move the portable outhouse to a freshly dug hole.

The final step in turning the log cabin into a house fit to spend a winter in was chinking the walls and any other gaps through which heat could escape to the outside. In the 1800s, that chinking medium would have been a mortar made from wet clay mixed with grass, but I wanted something better and more permanent. I'd already experimented with filling in some of the cracks using wood chips and blueboard for the larger spaces and Great Stuff brand expanding spray foam for the smaller ones. All of them worked, but blueboard and spray foam were the easiest to work with, so I mostly used those as chinking.

First I cut and pressed sections of fitted blueboard wherever the gaps were large, making them slightly oversize, then tapping them snugly into place with the back of my roofer's hatchet. The blue Styrofoam looked a little out of place contrasted against the cabin logs, but the seal was good and tight. I could have filled all the cracks with spray foam, but I'd need a lot less of the stuff if the wider spaces were already filled with blueboard.

When the big cracks were filled, I set to work with the spray foam. The air was cold, with a sky full of black clouds and temperatures that promised snow, so I'd set the pressurized cans in a row 5 feet from the fireplace, which was now burning beautifully smoke free.

The foam worked even better than I'd anticipated. I laid the strawlike delivery tube atop the bottom log where a crack needed filling, pressed down on the top, and smoothly drew the tube along the gap as it filled with the viscous liquid. Within seconds the foam had expanded to completely fill and seal any spots that I couldn't get to. An added benefit was that this Great Stuff, which appeared to live up to its name, was also an adhesive, so I was literally gluing the logs together, as well as chinking them.

When the walls and gables had been sealed, I foamed in the window frames, doorframe, and whatever cracks still existed around the soffits. A bead of foam laid into the gaps between roof and gable rafters closed any cracks there, and I even foamed between the corner notches to eliminate drafts from those.

Although it needed about five hours to cure completely, the foam set to a tough, Styrofoam-like consistency that couldn't be pulled from the logs without tearing it off in pieces. I even tried to kick free one of the wood-chip fillers I'd foamed in place, just to see how strong the bond was, and it splintered without having budged. I also liked that the foam wouldn't break down, shrink, or dry out like conventional chinking materials, and this job would never need to be done again.

When I'd finished, there were nineteen empty cans to haul out, and all the blueboard had been used. At $7 a can, chinking the cabin had proved to be a fairly considerable investment, but I was pleased with the results.

I was just finishing the chinking when Pete showed up. He'd been camping with a friend a few miles away, in an area of shallow glacial ponds known among those familiar with the area as "the potholes." They'd decided to spend the last night of their trip camped on French Farm Creek, and since they were in the neighborhood, Pete had hiked back alone to see if I'd consent to his friend coming back to the cabin. I told him it was okay with me, then walked with him to the dam where our vehicles were parked because I needed the rest of the blueboard that I'd left lashed to the top of my van for insulating the cabin ceiling.

The day had turned gray and cold when I met Pete's friend, with precipitation that alternated between drizzling rain and snow. He seemed a nice enough young man, and I told him he was welcome to visit the cabin, but that he'd have to help me carry some of this blueboard back there.

Only then did I look at the roof of the Indian van, where I'd tied the materials I scavenged from town into a neat plastic-wrapped package. The rear of the Varathane tarp I'd wrapped the stacks with had been ripped loose and lay pushed toward the front of the van.

Every piece of blueboard had been stolen, as well as a couple of the larger pieces of plywood. I almost couldn't believe it; some trailer trash sons of bitches had actually stooped to stealing scraps of Styrofoam. They'd committed a crime punishable by jail time to get a few discarded materials that had no value except to someone who was insulating a cabin—or a deer blind. It seemed pretty obvious that the thieves had been deer hunters, and I was genuinely disturbed to realize that people of such low intellect would be carrying a loaded firearm into the woods.

CHAPTER 8

DEER SEASON

November is a month of some excitement in northern Michigan. Not only does it herald the first snowfall in most years, but also the hairy-man sport of whitetail deer hunting, when unshaven men wear the bright orange hooded sweatshirt and ball cap of a hunter with pride. Hunting season in Michigan actually starts in mid-September for small game, followed in October by the archery season for whitetails, cresting with the two-week firearm deer season in November, and finally ending in December with muzzle-loader deer season. Some small game seasons run until March, and for a few critters, like porcupines and red squirrels, there's no closed season.

I harbor a little fear of gun hunters, even though I've defended their right to hunt in print numerous times. Many of those who travel to northern Michigan each November haven't had a firearm in their hands since the previous hunting season, so neither the rules of proper gun handling nor the idiosyncrasies of their own guns are ingrained habits. Dwindling numbers of so-called accidental shootings indicate that sport hunters are at least handling their firearms more responsibly, but too many in the most recent generations didn't have the benefit of someone like my Uncle Alvin, who had me bull's-eyeing a Winchester 30—30 at 100 yards before I was twelve years old.

The biggest problem, I think, is that too many deer slayers don't truly comprehend the killing power they carry in almost any centerfire rifle loaded with hunting cartridges. The .308 I'd selected for my homesteading experience could punch clean through a 15-inch green poplar at 100 yards, and still remain lethal for another 200 yards beyond. It consistently left fist-size holes on the exit side of whitetails it hit, which was just what a deer hunter wanted, but to imagine a human suffering that much trauma is horrifying. My paramedic friend, Cheanne, tells me that most people shot with a hunting rifle through any part of the body are dead before the ambulance arrives, which only confirms what I've seen with whitetails. I think if every deer hunter understood the power he carries, there'd be more sharpshooters, more dead deer retrieved by guys who shrug their shoulders and say, "It ran off," and no more "accidental" shootings.

The second week of November found me in Petoskey, parked in Big John's back yard. I was in town to spend my last few dollars on four sheets of 4 x 8-foot flooring with which to fashion a raised floor over the sandy ground inside the cabin. I also wanted to buy or scavenge roofing paper, preferably the expensive self-adhesive "bitch-o-thane" used by professional roofers. I'd calculated that two rolls would cover the roof. It just happened that my nephew Josh was working as a roofer then, so I had two of the 85-pound rolls in cardboard boxes almost as soon as I got to Petoskey.

The four half-inch sheets of OSB chipboard I picked up at Home Depot for a fair $12 per sheet. In fact, I actually only bought three and a half sheets—exactly what I needed—because I found a 4-foot cut-off for $4 on the lumber department's scrap cart. I loaded the OSB underneath the tarpaper on top of my van, and lashed it all in place under a large sheet of Varathane plastic. I couldn't help but wonder how I'd get those very heavy rolls to the cabin, but I'd come up with something when the time came.

In the meantime I found lots of entertainment listening to hunters get revved up for Michigan's gun deer season. Groups of men huddled together in restaurants, bars, and kitchens all over Michigan, discussing guns, bullets, and whitetail habits as they thumbed through the deer hunting annual of *Field & Stream* magazine. One needed rubber boots to wade through the bullshit of some of these testosterone-building sessions, but I got a tremendous kick out of listening to seasonal good ol' boys trying to top each other with stories of high adventures in the deep woods. Some claimed they could kill deer at 500 yards, by God, while nearly everyone's caliber could knock the tracks off a battle tank, and whatever rifle a hunter was using was among the most reliable and accurate ever crafted.

With two days to go before opening morning, Howard, the upstairs neighbor who'd adopted my cat, suggested that we go to the cabin for a couple of days. He hadn't seen the place yet, so I agreed, but only on condition that he drive. My van was loaded and ready to go, but I didn't want to make a round-trip with that gas hog unless I had to.

We got to the dam at French Farm Creek early in the afternoon. Howard parked his Volkswagen bus where I usually parked my Indian van and we unloaded our gear. There was a new maroon Chevy pickup parked there with an ORV trailer attached, and I knew damn well that I'd find the owner riding a quad-runner back on these obviously restricted hiking-only trails. I'd had enough run-ins with off-roaders who felt they possessed some divine right to ride anywhere they pleased, regardless of laws or the rights of others, to have lost all patience with this one.

Sure enough, the driver's tracks squeezed between the posts along the bank of French Farm Creek, crossed the stream, and went up the opposite bank toward the woods. As we followed the machine's tracks, I could see that it was loaded heavily and traveling slowly, no doubt loaded down with bags of corn and carrots.

When we found the red 4-wheeler parked in the middle of the trail a mile in, I couldn't maintain any longer. I was overcome by the surprising amount of anger that seeing that stinking trail-wrecker out here generated; I couldn't have been more offended if the guy had pissed on my cabin's floor. I could see tracks where the driver had gotten off his machine and walked onto a ridge, though I couldn't see anyone through the trees.

"Who owns this fuckin' machine?" I bellowed into the woods. "Get your ass out here and get this piece of shit outta here before I take it to the DNR."

There was silence from the forest. Howard said quietly, "Hey, don't piss this guy off or he'll do something to my bus."

"No he won't," I said. Then I yelled into the woods, "I've got your license plate number. If this piece of junk is here when I get back, it won't be when I leave."

Howard and I continued down the trail, cutting off onto a secondary trail well before we reached the intersection so as not to leave obvious tracks. As soon as were out of sight of the machine, we heard it start and pull away quietly, its operator trying to make as little noise as possible. Howard was his usual nonconfrontational self, but I reckoned I'd gotten the point across that this area was closed to machines to yet another cavalier off-roader. Since he probably believed I'd taken down his license number, I doubted he'd make any trouble.

We got to the cabin with plenty of daylight to spare. I lit the fireplace and put on a pot of coffee, but the evening was so nice that we elected to sit outside in front of the cabin. Howard really liked the place, I think, despite the sandy floor. He was reluctant to use the open-pit outhouse, though, and he all but refused to ingest any water from the well because it was "frogwater."

It probably didn't help that Howard had suffered a fairly severe bout of intestinal parasites while camped with me on the Carp River a couple of summers before. All he'd done was rinse his toothbrush in the river, but his immune system was off enough that day to let a waterborne bug—cryptosporidium, I'd guess—get a foothold in his lower parts. We knocked the bug out of him in only three days using an old recipe for a rather toxic tansy tea, but the experience had left him a little paranoid about water.

We rose before daylight the second morning to gunshots echoing through the forest from every direction, same as they did every Opening Morning. It seemed improbable that each of those dozens of predawn rifle and shotgun reports had resulted in a dead whitetail, but they caused Howard and I both to shake our heads in dismay. We were glad to be far beyond the range of those trail hunters, where we, like the deer that hunkered down around us during daylight, understood that few humans would venture. Anyone could wander down a trail, but the area's terrain demanded map-and-compass orienteering if you went off trail, and not many hunters would even consider dragging a gutted whitetail more than a few hundred yards to their vehicle. I knew of only three hunters who'd ventured this far back in a decade, and none had left the main trail, so we were safe from the melee that was going on in the outer woods.

The problem was that we had to leave that afternoon, which, of course, meant running that gauntlet of pumpkin-looking people with guns. Howard had been looking pale and feeling nauseous since we'd risen. He started reloading his backpack while I made coffee, and I could see that he wasn't enjoying himself any more. I recognized the symptoms from past experience: He was dehydrated and constipated. I forced a big canteen cupful of coffee on him, and within an hour after finishing it he was headed for the outhouse. He returned from the outhouse feeling much better.

We took our time loading up, in no hurry to leave before the first wave of hunters had gone home for lunch. At 3 P.M., with the fireplace burned down to embers and the dishes done, we shouldered our packs and locked the cabin door behind us. Howard broke out an orange ball cap for the trip out, while I reversed my knit balaclava from camouflage to orange. I also set my radio to a strong FM music station and carried it playing in a pocket at full volume. The noise might irritate a few hunters, but they probably wouldn't mistake us for deer.

The trip out was nice and uneventful. I spotted four fluorescent hunters off in the woods as we walked, but they were well away from the trail. I'd expected more, but the four vehicles parked at the dam confirmed that there weren't many hunters here this afternoon. The same maroon Chevy pickup was there, but without an ORV trailer this time.

One of those vehicles was an '80s-model F-150 2-wheel-drive pickup that had been buried to its rear axles in loose sand at the side of the parking area. The two young men who'd arrived in it scurried back and forth and periodically spun the tires in complete confusion. We were situating our backpacks in Howard's Volkswagen when the pickup's desperate driver walked over to ask if we'd loan him a jack so he could raise the axle and put wood under the tire for traction.

Howard took his jack from inside the bus, and we walked 50 feet to where the pickup was buried to have a closer look. The driver had been backing up to get a straight shot at the two-track when his rear end dropped onto loose sand. Being from a place that's mostly paved, he wasn't sure how to react when the truck refused to roll, so he'd gunned it, burying the rear tires in holes of his own making.

"So what possessed you to bury it to the axles?" I asked. The driver just shrugged his shoulders and admitted he hadn't known what else to do.

The worst part was that his full-size truck extended clear across the trail leading out, which made his problem our problem too. We couldn't get around him through the mud on the pond side, or through the sand field he was already stuck in, so Howard and I were left with no option except to get these fellows unstuck and on their way.

The guys had the right idea; I'd jacked up a truck or two and filled the holes under its tires with pieces of wood, not so much for traction as to get the undercarriage off the ground. But the more I looked at this half-ton Ford with its 8-foot bed and long wheelbase, the more I was convinced that three of us had enough mass to rock it free if we worked in unison with the driver—and vice-versa.

Wearing gloves, we positioned ourselves along the truck's step bumper. Its bottom was sitting atop the sand, but we pushed our hands underneath enough to get a good grip. I yelled for the driver to hit it while we lifted weight off the axle and pushed forward with all we had. The truck rolled forward about 2 feet that first time, and we let it roll back as soon as it stopped moving. We repeated the process several more times, breaking down a ramp out of each hole that extended farther toward freedom with each push forward. Finally, the long but light truck broke away under its own power, spraying us with damp sand as the jubilant driver floored it. I yelled at him to ease off the gas pedal, afraid that he'd dig himself another hole before getting clear of the way out.

Both hunters were grateful for our assistance, but it was nearly dark and they were in a real hurry to leave this dreadful place. Two more hunters came out of the woods as we were pulling away, and I realized that I'd just as soon not be here myself until hunting season ended.

It was dark when we rolled into Petoskey, but Howard had the next couple of days off, so we picked up a fifth of Jack Daniels and went back to his apartment. Being a self-sufficient bachelor of twenty-seven, Howard more or less enjoyed a steady stream of young folks stopping by several times a day. Most of them saw a grizzled middle-aged man when they looked at me, but I like being around people who were excited about their futures. Most of my longtime friends had gotten old somewhere along the road.

Robin came home with John that evening looking glum. She said she'd shot a buck, but it had run off a quarter mile onto someone else's property. John and Robin arrived at the property line in time to see another hunter dragging the tagged buck across a field.

At 5:00 the next morning, after having been up all night with Howard and Jack Daniels, I handed Robin my .308 and a box of 180-grain Remington cartridges that I wanted to see in action. It was a pretty big deal for me to lend my precious Thompson/Center to anyone, but I felt obligated to see that Robin had sufficient power to go with her shooting skills. Then for some reason I went with them to the parcel of private woods where John had set up an almost cushy hunting spot for her.

I'd never been to the spot before, and we arrived in pitch blackness, so I was totally ignorant of the layout. Robin gave me pointed directions to where the scattered bait lay and from which direction the deer were likely to come, but I could see nothing in the darkness. We climbed into the hulk of an old motor home and John lit a kerosene heater to warm up the inside. It was a far cry from lying behind a log in the deep swamp until a deer came down the trail, but I probably could have gotten used to the bucket seats with armrests.

Big John went to sleep on a bed in the rear of the motor home within half an hour of our arrival. His snoring rattled the windows, but between snorts I could hear animals moving about near where Robin said the scattered bait lay. These deer had learned to identify humans with food, so they weren't the least deterred by our presence.

The window next to my seat was stuck, so I worked it, and even pried it in the darkness with my Ka-Bar survival knife. Robin was concerned about the noise I was making, but she didn't say anything. Me, I reckoned that if Big John's bearlike snoring didn't alarm these deer, they weren't very easily scared away. After a full ten minutes of prying and pushing by feel alone, the window slid back, and I could peer into the darkness through open air.

Daybreak found John still snoring, lying on his back on a motor home bed that had never been intended for a man of his mass. Robin was still alert at the big side window, clutching my Thompson/Center single shot almost lovingly in her hands. Since John was obviously not hunting, I picked up Robin's Savage and scoped out the slowly emerging bait. I had no intention of shooting a deer, but I wanted to look for myself at the underbrush where deer might come in to feed.

Like all good scopes, the Bushnell gathered more ambient light than the naked eye, presenting the shooter with a brighter, sharper sight picture. I could clearly make out pumpkins, apples, carrots, sugar beets—all the stuff a hungry mating doe wanted to eat at the start of winter. And where rutting does went, horny bucks were sure to follow.

It was 8:00 before the first deer stepped out into the open. The rising sun would have been directly in our faces if the forest hadn't been tall and thick, and I could see the baited area clearly enough to estimate its distance at 65 yards. There were no bucks among the group of five whitetails that stepped up to the bait, but Robin and I could both see movement in the brush beyond from at least one deer that was too educated to make a daylight appearance.

I waited for Robin to shoot. She had the Encore pressed snugly to her shoulder and was looking through the scope, but her thumb was on the cocked hammer and her trigger finger was extended along the trigger guard. She whispered that she wanted to wait for the buck to come in. I reminded her that 50 pounds of processed venison meat went a long way toward making ends meet, with or without antlers. But Robin was in the grip of buck fever.

I held the Savage's crosshairs tightly on the spine of the biggest deer I could see, ready to squeeze off an aimed round as soon as my .308 bellowed. I could hear the crunching of apples in the quiet morning air, but Robin didn't fire for ten minutes. Finally John woke up and stumbled over to assess the situation.

"You might as well shoot one, Bud," he said to me, "She ain't gonna shoot nothin' but a buck."

He'd barely finished saying it before I felt the trigger roll off its sear. The Savage barked and the deer I'd targeted hunched involuntarily, then took off in a low ground-hugging "death run" toward a thick cattail marsh. I unloaded the rifle and inserted it into its case while John walked over to find the downed animal. We both knew from its actions that it would be within a hundred yards of where I'd shot it.

In fact, John found it lying dead not 50 yards from the bait. The bullet had impacted within a half inch of where I'd aimed it, taking out the spine and inflicting maximum shock to both lungs. John gutted the deer more swiftly than I could have, and I dragged it 75 yards to where his truck was parked. We tossed the roughly 120-pound doe onto the tailgate and John wrapped one of the self-adhesive doe tags around its foreleg. There were venison steaks for dinner that evening.

Robin didn't need any prodding after that. We downed our limit over the next two weeks, including Robin's trophy-quality 6-point buck. Her kills were made using my rifle and whatever ammunition I wanted her to test for me. Every cartridge caused deer to go equally dead, and the only real problem was that Robin had fallen head over heels in love with my rifle, which meant she was no longer satisfied with her Savage.

We hung the deer Robin brought in under the deck off the rear of the apartment house. There was nothing wrong with doing that, but skinning and quartering a whitetail in the middle of town always attracts curiosity seekers. Men and women from around the neighborhood found reason to stop by and chat while John and I butchered, but I'm always happy to show anyone why safe gun handling is important, so I didn't mind.

When the deer was skinned, we quartered it into tenderloins, shoulders, haunches, and neck, removing one piece at a time and taking it into the apartment to be washed in the double sink in John's kitchen. Once washed, the larger pieces were boned and cut into steaks, roast, or stew meat. Finally, the cut meat was wrapped in freezer paper, identified and dated with grease pencil, and tossed into the freezer. Because we took only meat, we could get five butchered deer into Big John's average-size refrigerator freezer, and the sixth he had turned into summer sausage at a local butcher shop. Cheanne's three wolves enjoyed the rib cages, bones, and hide (wolves require hair in their diet, like people need fiber), so everything went to good use. Buddy-dog, who'd already become somewhat barrel-shaped in the care of John and Robin, ate like a furry black pig, feasting on lean, raw venison like a kid eats ice cream.

The rifle hunters left the woods November 30, but hard on their heels came the muzzleloading crowd, which had been growing steadily over the past decade. Smokepole shooters owned the deer woods for the first part of December, so Robin took a sudden interest in muzzle-loading that year, as well. She was a quick study, and in a couple of days she was a proficient black-powder rifle operator. We already knew she could shoot straight enough to get the job done with a single shot. She brought in one more deer that year, with her smokepole, before finally hanging up her guns until next autumn.

I went back to the cabin the first week of December, packing 7 pounds of summer sausage John and Robin had given me, cookies and fudge, and probably another pound or two under my belt. My roofing and flooring materials were tied on top of the van, under a protective plastic sheet, and they were all I needed to complete the cabin for winter.

It still hadn't snowed enough to say so, so I chanced driving back to the dam rather than parking at the more accessible—and shovel-able—seasonal two-track at the Carp River bridge. I was still wondering how I was going to lug those two very heavy rolls of roofing back to the cabin, so I figured I'd start by hauling the sheets of flooring first.

I didn't think there were many larcenous types who could lift a box of the roofing paper, let alone steal it, but I knew for sure that those sheets of flooring were very stealable. The first step was to get them across the dam and into the woods, where I could stash them almost in plain sight and not worry they might be found. When I had them all standing on edge between a small stand of spruces, I centered one of them on top of my head, the half sheet in the middle and held on either side by my fingers, and set off toward the cabin.

It was a little after midnight when I arrived at the cabin with the last two sheets of flooring. It was drizzling, so I leaned the floorboards on edge against the cabin's front wall, under the overhang. Rain was bad for OSB, which is really just a bunch of small wood chips glued together under pressure, but the sheets could withstand a light rain over a few hours without damage. With the materials for my next project at hand, I went to bed.

I awoke in the morning just itching to get a raised floor installed over the damned beach sand that found its way into everything. First I had to install the joists that would hold the flooring elevated off the ground and create an airspace below to prevent moisture from being trapped there. They needed to be 12 feet long to span the entire floor, about 4 inches in diameter, and as close to that thickness at both ends as possible.

The best candidates as floor joists were spruce and fir saplings whose typically arrow-straight trunks reached about 20 feet into the air. I didn't like cutting them because evergreens, especially white pines, are special trees to me. At a practical level, I don't like working with fresh pinesap because it's as sticky as honey, it won't wash out of clothing, and nothing short of a strong solvent will remove it from skin.

Despite those objections, conifers remained the straightest and best choice for floor joists. I calculated that I'd need 9 full-length joists to span the ground between walls at 1-foot intervals, stopping 4 feet from the fireplace hearth, which I was intentionally leaving uncovered. Then I'd need four 4-foot joists to support the 4 x 4-foot section that would border the hearth. I wanted a 4 x 8-foot area of bare ground in front of the fireplace, not just for reasons of fire safety, but to give me a place to break up, stack, and even chop a pile of dry firewood that would be nice to have close at hand on a cold night.

I set out with my tape measure, leather gloves, and Stanley SharpTooth handsaw under sunny blue skies that belied a temperature cold enough to freeze water. There was a very thick stand of spruces and hemlocks a hundred yards to the rear of the cabin where I'd been getting kindling wood from dead standing trees. Natural selection was forcing the healthiest trees there to grow tall and strong to take in more sunlight, while new saplings and trees that just couldn't keep up were slowly shaded out and died from lack of light. Despite a high rate of attrition, whenever one of the tall old trees was broken off by wind or killed by lightning, there were a dozen youngsters below just waiting for an opportunity to fight one another for its place.

I bowed my head and thanked the Creator and the trees for allowing me to deliberately kill some of their number to suit my own ends. Then I carefully selected and cut down ten suitable saplings from places where I judged their removal might actually contribute to the health of the surrounding forest. After de-limbing them with the SP-8 and sawing them to length, I had a pile of poles that looked like they'd work fine as floor joists.

That's where the leather work gloves came in, because I wanted to handle these really sticky lengths as little as possible. I dragged the poles inside, then, with everything that had been on the floor pushed into a corner at the back of the cabin, I laid the first joist parallel with the door threshold, and nailed it securely to the foundation log. I laid the remaining 8 full-length joists parallel to the first, spacing their centers at 12-inch intervals, until they extended 8 feet inward from the front wall.

There was a little shovel work needed to knock down high spots in the sand and humus, but soon I had the joists as even and level as they were likely to get. Except for the first joist below the door, I planned to leave them all free-floating, fastened to only the floorboards, which were themselves unattached from the cabin except at the threshold joist. The purpose was to circumvent any chance that the cabin's green wall logs might shift slightly as they seasoned and buckled the floor. It didn't look like the floor was going to turn out all that flat in any case, but at least it would be free to move as the cabin moved.

There were dozens of scraps of blueboard littering the sandy floor, all of them too small for use between the ceiling rafters. I threw these between the floor joists to add insulation, and used a few of the larger pieces to shim under them at low spots in the floor. Every scrap of blueboard went to good use.

I laid the first sheet of OSB along the cabin's side wall, its narrow end butting into the corner where it met the front wall. The corner wasn't square, but that was hardly unexpected. The front foundation log was straight, so I lined up off that, cutting small pieces from the board as I went to make it correspond to the crooked wall log. The foundation was sealed with sod around the outside, but I didn't want gaps that would almost certainly gobble up small items I dropped, and trap them under the floor.

With the first sheet of flooring situated, I secured it to the joists using four 3-inch drywall screws per joist. This tied all the joists together from that end. The next sheet I laid across the door, perpendicular to the one I'd just screwed down. With the edges of the sheets lined up to one another, I pushed the second one as far up to the doorway as it would go. It only went up to the center post and doorframe post. I left the sheet in place and used the posts to mark where it needed to be cut out to make the edge meet flush with the foundation log under the threshold. Using saw and machete, I cut squared notches just large enough to accommodate the posts, and slid the OSB up to match with the front wall. When it fit to my satisfaction, I screwed it to the joists beneath.

The third sheet I laid parallel to the second, its inside narrow edge butted against the inside edge of the first sheet. When it was screwed down, the floor was two-thirds completed from the front wall. I placed the half sheet in the back corner, where it fit and filled it in nicely after a little trimming. When it was screwed down, the cabin had a raised floor except for a 4 x 8-foot workspace in front of the fireplace.

I stepped back to admire the finished job, but even though I'd done my best, and even though the floor was a tremendous improvement over sand, there wasn't much call for patting my own back. True to the crooked nature of everything else this cabin was constructed from, the floor was uneven and a little wavy. I probably should have used ¾-inch OSB, I thought, but heavier sheets would have cost more at the store and on the trail. No matter, the edges of the flooring were tight to one another, and the menace of sand had been virtually eliminated.

Now I needed a broom. Having a floor soon made it apparent that I tracked a lot of mud in with my boots. It hadn't mattered with a dirt floor, but now a few trips in and out made the place look like hell. Here was a microcosm of the way civilization enslaves people with luxuries and comfort until they feel overwhelmed. It starts with a broom to sweep the floor, then escalates to a vacuum sweeper to clean the carpet, maybe a shampooer, and a shelf full of spot removers and pretty smells. I almost missed the dirt floor.

Because I was too lazy to walk a quarter mile to get sawgrass to fashion a proper broom head, I just stuck a half dozen evergreen branches trimmed from the floor joists into the hollow fiberglass handle I'd broke off my shovel the previous spring. The foliage extended outward from the tube like a fan—it looked like a broom all right. It didn't work as well as I might have wished, but the spruce broom was adequate for keeping the floor clean.

I had to admit, the floor really helped to make the little cabin look like a house inside, even if it did create another daily chore. Sleeping on it sucked, though. Maybe it was because I was past my prime, but even two closed-cell sleeping pads under me didn't prevent my hips from feeling bruised. Unlike the earth, where I could always find hollows that agreed with the contours of my body, the hard, flat floor forgave nothing. First a broom, and now I needed a bed; already the pressures of living in civilized fashion had begun eroding the purity of my homestead.

THE GALES OF
DECEMBER 2001

For a decade prior to the turn of the millennium I'd learned to worry for the state of our planet. New record temperatures had been established in both directions with disturbing regularity, growing seasons for plants and trees had shifted noticeably, and the habits of native fauna weren't nearly as predictable as they were supposed to be. Even the proverbial Gales of November, immortalized by Gordon Lightfoot's song "The Wreck of the Edmund Fitzgerald," hadn't materialized in 2001. It seemed that God's creatures, including one frequently surprised homesteader, no longer knew what to expect from an environment in chaos.

Because the abnormal had become expected, I wasn't too startled that the first week of December 2001 ended with really unseasonable temperatures that reached as high as 70 degrees, and even spawned a short-lived second blackfly hatch. My cabin should have been buried under a foot or more of snow by then, but the ground was totally bare and the insects were still active.

Jerod had come out to stay with me at the cabin for two days and nights during this freakish warm spell. I immediately enlisted his help in hauling the two 85-pound rolls of bitch-o-thane self-adhesive tarpaper still tied on top of my van back to the cabin. We first tried carrying the heavy cardboard-boxed rolls on our shoulders—one on his, one on mine—but their weight and ungainliness caused both of us to say "uncle" after about 300 yards.

Next, I lashed one of the boxes around its outside with rope to create handholds that would permit both of us to carry a single roll from either end. We stashed the other roll off trail under a camouflage layer of dead bracken ferns. We made it another half mile before deciding that even with two people the short, heavy roll was just too clumsy to carry. We abandoned that one in the middle of the trail, sure that no one would come along to find it so far back in the woods at this time of year, and certain no one was going to steal it if they did.

Late that night, while Jerod was asleep on the floor of the cabin, I took advantage of an apparent bout of insomnia—unusual for me—and went back to get the roofing paper we'd abandoned. I took the sliding saucer and 50 feet of parachute cord with me, reasoning that even without snow on the ground its slippery polyethylene surface should slide well enough to drag the boxes of roofing material.

It was after midnight when I left, having decided to tackle the roll that was farthest from the cabin first. A drizzle had been coming down all day, wetting the layers of fallen leaves and making the trail silent under my boots as I hiked. The rain had stopped now, and the air was almost disturbingly warm, with a temperature of at least 60 degrees. Within the lowland forest all was quiet, with not even a breeze. I could hear tiny tan tree frogs hopping about over the leaves, and occasionally I'd surprise a deer or raccoon that wasn't expecting me. Despite an occluded moon, the woods were bright enough for me to see clearly without a flashlight, so I did. I was a little surprised at how very much I was enjoying this solo midnight hike, in spite of weather that some might have described as clammy.

I reached the box we'd camouflaged after about twenty-five minutes, having walked past the other. I rolled the clumsy package from its hiding place and onto the saucer, then lashed it in place using the parachute cord threaded through holes I'd drilled around the saucer's perimeter. Disney characters smiled at me in the bloom of my Mini Mag flashlight as the saucer's rounded bottom squashed under a weight it had never been designed to bear. The saucer had served me well as a cargo transport for five winters, but I reckoned that the task I was using it for now might just be the end of it.

With the saucer's towing lanyard looped around the center of a stout section of dead wood that worked as a comfortable handle, I turned my back to the load, grasped an end of the wood in either hand, and leaned into it. Surprisingly, the load broke free and followed a lot more easily than I'd imagined. The chore certainly wasn't effortless, but neither was it strenuous enough to exhaust me. I had to readjust the lashings once after the roll shifted hard inside the box while I was dragging the saucer over a wind-downed tree, but aside from that minor inconvenience, the task was actually pleasant.

The roofing paper and I arrived at the cabin a little after 1 A.M. I could hear Jerod snoring peacefully through the closed cabin door, so I was careful not to wake him. I quietly left the loaded plastic saucer there in front of the cabin, then grabbed my spare aluminum saucer and went back to get the other box. By 2 A.M. I had both rolls of roofing at the cabin, and had tired myself sufficiently to join Jerod in a round of snoring.

We both rose at 10 A.M. to a sunny sky and 70 degrees. Mosquitoes were still humming about, although they really did appear to be confused and didn't bother us. Along with the mosquitoes, a new generation of blackflies had hatched again from eggs laid the previous spring—now that was unheard of in northern Michigan. I sat outside the cabin door on a bench, drinking coffee and thinking that it felt more like Memorial Day than Christmas. We were both enjoying the weather, but Jerod seemed troubled over this strange warm spell as much as I was.

We spent the day hammering down and nailing any loose spots on the sheet metal roof in preparation for applying the bitch-o-thane. I'd been a little concerned that cold temperatures would keep the tarpaper's adhesive backing from sticking to the metal as well as it should, but if the weather held, that wasn't going to be a problem.

We went to bed at 10 P.M. A stiff wind had begun to blow from the north, causing the treetops to sway, but temperatures remained warm enough to leave our sleeping bags unzipped. It felt good to be inside the cabin, safe from wind, rain, and falling tree limbs that occasionally bounced noisily off the little house's strong metal roof.

I slept soundly until about 4:00 the next morning, when I heard Jerod rustling around, trying to be quiet as he reloaded his bedroll and other gear into his backpack. When I rolled over to ask him what he was doing, he replied that he'd had enough sleep and had decided to get an early start for town. The truth was that he was in love, and he was missing his girlfriend. As he headed out the door wearing his pack, I mumbled that I hoped the wind hadn't knocked a tree across the two-track leading out. As he always did, he told me not to worry, he'd be okay. He closed the door behind him, and I went back to sleep.

I awoke an hour later to a wind that had increased to gale force. I wasn't sure that it hadn't been a dream, but I thought I'd heard my name being called over the howling trees. I heard it again, only faintly audible through the cabin's closed door. It had to be Jerod, and he must be having trouble.

I opened the door and yelled as loudly as I could into the blowing nor'wester. "Jerod, is that you?" It was a rhetorical question—who else could it be? It was then that I noticed the temperature had dropped about 30 degrees since he'd left, and a few flakes of snow were being driven before the wind.

Genuinely happy to hear my voice, my friend veered off the path he'd been taking into gnarly swamp and walked toward the cabin. He was shivering as he came inside, clad only in a perspiration-soaked cotton T-shirt. He didn't have his pack. I handed him the spare parka shell I always left hanging inside the door for just such emergencies, and he gratefully put it on. Being sized for me, it was tight on his large frame, but he could get it zipped. I built the fireplace embers back to a crackling blaze, and he sat in front of it, warming his hands as he related the events that had brought him back here.

I already knew what had happened, but I let him tell me anyway. He'd arrived at his 4 x 4 Ranger at about 5:00, still two hours before sunrise. The wind had been blowing hard on his trek out, but its real force was blocked by the forest, and the temperature was warm enough that he'd made the hike wearing only a T-shirt. He'd tossed his backpack into the truck and had driven a quarter mile from the dam when he found the road blocked by a 60-foot poplar tree that lay squarely across the two-track, its massive trunk suspended 3 feet above the ground by its own limbs.

Unable to get past the monster tree, he drove back to the dam in reverse, locked his truck for some reason, and headed back to the cabin to get my winch and axe. It was still warm, despite a gale force wind that was just a breeze inside the woods, and he was still sweating from the hike out, so he neglected to take a jacket with him on the return trip.

He'd made it about halfway back to the cabin when a cold front that had been pushing the warm front rushed in, causing temperatures to plummet from balmy to subfreezing in the space of ten minutes—now that wasn't at all unusual for the Straits of Mackinac. This sudden change blackened the sky, making the shadowed woods even darker. To make matters worse, heavy winds had shaken the trees hard enough to cover the entire forest with a thick layer of new-fallen leaves that obscured even well-traveled trails. Jerod had thought to bring his flashlight, but it didn't help much with the trail effectively erased.

With that combination of conditions working against him, Jerod had lost the trail a mere hundred feet from the cabin. To his credit, he'd been smart enough not to push on out of sheer macho, the way I'd seen other men do, and had stopped to bellow for help as soon as he realized he was off trail. He was lucky, and he knew it; any farther away and I couldn't have heard him shout over the wind, and he might easily have been dead from hypothermia in a few hours.

Because I'd taught him better than to take this area lightly, I made him wait until I'd had coffee before loading rope, cable, and winch into my Peak 1 Flex "working" backpack. I made him carry the axe and saw, so that I'd have both hands free to drink my coffee on the trail. I couldn't be too annoyed with him, though, because he looked really uncomfortable squeezed into my parka shell.

It was full daylight when we reached Jerod's Ranger. I laid my pack and tools in the truck's box, and we drove to where the tree lay across the trail. It was a big one all right, about 3 feet in diameter at is base. The wind had torn it loose by the roots, dropping it across the trail as squarely as I could have done it with an axe. I exhaled forcefully through pursed lips; this was going to take some time to clear.

A handsaw was useless against so large a tree, so we set to work with the axe, spelling one another as we chopped the narrower top end free of its thick trunk. My plan was to get the top free, which would still leave the road blocked by the trunk, then to pull the top away from it with my winch until a gap had been opened wide enough for Jerod to drive his truck through to the other side. He'd have to go through a low, muddy spot to get around the remaining trunk, but if he locked in the 4-wheel drive and kept his momentum, I figured he'd make it all right.

Nor could we just take our time. Jerod had to report to his job as an Odawa tribal police officer in Petoskey by 4 P.M., looking spiffy and smelling better than either one of us smelled right now. It was a twenty-five-minute drive from here to the nearest paved road, then another 45 miles to his house, so we needed to clear the road as expeditiously as possible.

After a half hour of hard labor, we had the poplar in two pieces. I hitched a choker around the butt end of the top with my cable and started winching. It was heavier than I'd hoped, and after pivoting the top about 4 feet, it hung up tightly enough to exceed my winch's 4,000-pound limit. Without releasing tension on the winch, I added Jerod's tow strap, hooking its opposite end to his truck's front tow hook. Even then the top was too heavy to move much, but between my straining come-along and his wheel-hopping Ranger, we managed to create a gap of about 7 feet between the sections.

It still wasn't enough. We needed to increase the gap by pulling the partly rooted trunk in the opposite direction to decrease the angle at which he had to drive between them. Otherwise he'd have to leave the road in an almost perpendicular direction before turning back, and the terrain wouldn't permit that from anything less than a bulldozer. That meant the heaviest, most anchored part of the tree had to be pulled from the side we were trying to get to, so there'd be no assistance from the truck. There was nothing else to do, so I transferred the winch and cable, and started cranking.

Amazingly, it worked. The monstrous trunk, whose weight alone was double the pulling capacity of the winch, twisted against its roots for a distance of about 3 feet. I yelled for Jerod to try it, but he was already moving, bouncing off the two-track's edge and accelerating between the cut ends with mere inches to spare. He wheeled hard back up onto the road on the other side of the tree with a war whoop.

My own enthusiasm was tempered by the fact that my van was still at the dam. It was too big, too heavy, and too 2-wheel drive to get through where Jerod's truck had gone, which left me with the somewhat Herculean task of chopping the barrel-size trunk in half, then pulling a 2-ton log to the side of the road. All of that had to be accomplished today, before the heavy snow that meteorologists were predicting would fall this evening trapped my vehicle there until next spring. My palms got blisters just thinking about it.

But first I thought it might be prudent if we both cruised the rest of the two-track to be sure there weren't any more trees blocking the way out. That question was answered after the first mile when we encountered a minivan headed in toward the dam. If that oatmeal box had made it this far, the road had to be clear.

We were about to turn around when the man driving the van pulled up to talk to us. Maybe it was one of those guy things that I hear women talking about, but I'd swear this fellow was fantasizing that he was Jungle Jim in a Land Rover, traveling through wild and dangerous country where ordinary men feared to venture. In fact, he was a fifty-year-old man wearing a white polo shirt that couldn't hide the 40 pounds of easy living that strained against his waistband. His right forearm was thrown jauntily across the top of the padded steering wheel as he lowered the electric window and said, "Hey, how're you guys doing?"

I just grinned as Jerod answered the man's rhetorical question, telling him about the monster poplar that still blocked the road ahead and what we'd done to get around it. The adventurous expression sort of drained from the man's face, especially after I told him that I was still stuck here until I could get the rest of that tree out of the road. He didn't offer any assistance, he just bid us a quick good-bye, backed into a nearby turnaround, and left in a hurry, before one of those big trees trapped him in here too.

Jerod drove me back to the downed tree. He told me he felt guilty about leaving me there alone with such a big job, but we both understood that God always intended for me to do everything the hard way. I assured him that I'd take advantage of his guilty conscience at a good restaurant when I went to town again.

I spent the rest of the day turning the huge still-rooted tree trunk into a log, then winching it off to the side of the two-track. It always kind of ground my ass to clear the way for others who wouldn't do the work themselves, or worse, for the few impotents who seemed obsessed with destroying this pristine environment with their repulsive machines. In this case, though, I had no choice. The snow was really coming down as I drove the Indian van out to Trailsend Road, then around to the Carp River bridge.

From Carp River I hiked 3.5 miles to the cabin over ground that was white with fallen snow, but as yet unfrozen. Temperatures were hovering around 30 degrees when I got to the cabin, wet, and feeling slightly chilled. This snow wasn't the one that stayed; that would come soon, almost certainly before Christmas.

I rose early the next morning and immediately set to attaching the bitch-o-thane to the cabin's steel roof. At first, when the rolls were heaviest, I just unrolled them on the ground and cut off sections at 17 feet using the cleaverlike SP-8 machete. Like gigantic shingles, I laid the first length of roofing I'd cut along the eaves, running from front to back of the cabin. I peeled away the blue plastic backing at one end, then stuck it and nailed it to the end rafter, through the roofing steel, with 1.5-inch roofing nails. With one end secured, I just peeled away the rest of the backing and stuck the roofing to the metal beneath, where it adhered well enough, in spite of a light snow that fell all day long. Three roofing nails at either end insured that the sheet couldn't slide, even under the weight of snow, until temperatures warmed enough for its adhesive backing to stick.

The next 17-foot strip overlapped the first by about 6 inches along its uppermost edge, and I applied it in the same way. The third strip was high enough to require tying myself off to a tree across the cabin's peak and to the safety belt of my treestand outfit, which allowed me to stand upright, leaning back against the belt, while I worked using both hands.

The fourth and last strips overlapped the peak from either side by 8 inches, making that critical ridge double thick. I also draped the remaining 4-foot sections from each roll over the peak, largely because I needed to do something with them. The finished roof was wavy, and not at all pretty, but it looked darned good to a guy who was about to spend a winter living under it.

I kept myself busy for the next several days cutting and hauling firewood for the cabin, but these were the shortest days of the year, when cool-

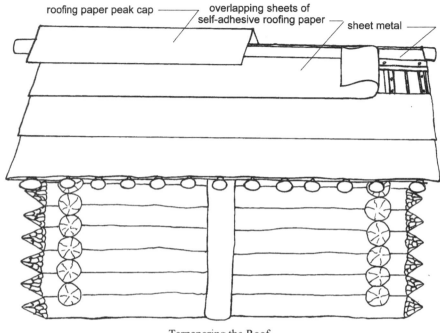

Tarpapering the Roof.

ing waters in the Great Lakes kept skies mostly overcast, and the woods always felt cold from lack of sunlight. I soon fell victim to that seasonal disor-
der psychologists say causes people to experience bouts of severe depression
near Christmas. There was no denying the boredom caused by short days
and long nights, but I also felt something I didn't recognize at first, because
I'd never felt it before: loneliness. Being a loner by nature, I've never minded
my own company, but being confined to the cabin for most of every day, not
by snow or cold but by darkness, made the homey little place feel like a
prison cell.

To make matters worse, the Grundig shortwave receiver that kept me in
touch with the world outside was broadcasting a steady stream of Christmas
songs intended to rip out the listener's heart. I cried at the one about a poor
little Mexican girl who released an injured bird she'd rehabilitated on Christmas Eve. Even the silly carol about Snoopy and the Red Baron seemed
poignant.

Between sad songs about the joys of Christmas there were news broadcasts about Americans murdered, bombing casualties in Afghanistan, and all

of the most horrifying events that could be gathered from around the globe using modern technology. I turned off the radio, but that left me sitting and staring almost entranced into the fireplace while the deepest recesses of my brain churned up memories of lost loves, dead people I wish I'd known better, and a longing for things that had never been.

I think it would have been easier if there had been snow on the ground, but the brown drooping foliage of ferns, grasses, and goldenrod gave the forest a dead look, covered with the decaying remains of beautiful things that I'd watched die. A winter forest isn't dead at all, just leaned down to its most capable residents, but without the cleansing and camouflaging effects of fresh snow this place looked and smelled of dead things.

I knew what was happening to my psyche at the conscious, logical level, but my most earnest attempt at pragmatism couldn't deny the fact that I was feeling unloved, that my life's best accomplishments had been woefully insignificant, and that I longed for someone to talk with. I tried to keep busy, driving more drywall screws into the flooring, turning what remained of fallen trees into firewood, and sealing drafty cracks in the cabin with wedges sliced from leftover scraps of blueboard foam insulation. Even cloudy days seemed fine, but the woods were dark by 5 P.M., making it impossible to work or travel without help of an artificial light, and I was effectively confined to the cabin area for fourteen hours out of every day.

Cheanne showed up a few days into the deep psychological funk that had gripped me, making me laugh out loud at the incongruity of her knocking on the cabin door. It was snowing when she came inside, but only a few flakes swirled on subfreezing air, and the ground was mostly bare. The cabin felt damp and cold, probably in part because it was constantly cooling as moisture from the green logs was forced outward by heat from inside. It would be warmer next winter, after the logs had dried.

Cheanne diagnosed my symptoms of depression almost immediately. She persisted in asking me to come to town for Christmas until I finally relented, a little surprised when I did that I'd reached a point where being lonely in the woods had become preferable to interacting with other people. No wonder the voyageurs and trappers of old Michigan had been a little odd when they came to spring rendezvous at the end of a long winter. I decided I'd better get to town before I became any more feral and antisocial than I'd already become.

Cheanne gave me a ride from the dam to where the Indian van sat on a concealed two-track a hundred yards from the Carp River bridge, driving

8 miles to save me a 3.5-mile hike. The ride was very much appreciated, more for the companionship than for the convenience, and I suddenly had a real craving for the company of other people.

The old Chevy fired right up. I warmed it up for a minute to get belts and hoses flexible before putting the engine under stress, then pulled out onto the asphalt, bouncing a bit on frozen tires that had gone flat on one side from sitting so long.

CHAPTER 10

THE BLIZZARD OF 2001

The streets were wet as I drove through Petoskey to Big John's place, where I'd park my rolling apartment until I left, sometime after Christmas. Street lamps were adorned with wreaths and ribbons, and there were messages of holiday cheer everywhere in town, but the place was barren of snow. It would have looked as dead as the woods had, except for throngs of shoppers, mostly tourists, who flowed in and out of the shops along Petoskey's main streets like one of the ribbons wrapping the packages they carried. It was really weird mentally shifting between two such extreme environments in the same day.

Big John has never been the type to celebrate just because someone said it was a holiday, but he enjoyed the feelings of goodwill that Christmas created in others. I had a good time visiting with him and Robin over the next few days, eating cookies and fudge, and generally maintaining a moderate buzz throughout. I was financially tapped out at that point, but I gave John a present of forgiving him a $400 loan he owed me from the previous summer.

Nearly everyone was lamenting the lack of snow for Christmas, including me. We should all have kept our collective mouths shut; the white Christmas started about midmorning on December 24, and by Christmas Day there was a full-grown blizzard blowing that shut down the entire northeast. Before the storm ended, Buffalo, New York, had asked for and was given federal disaster relief after being buried under 8 feet of snow. More than 9 feet had already fallen on northern Michigan by then, but as usual, the rest of the country just presumed we'd dig ourselves out okay. A blizzard here wouldn't cause wholesale panic and casualties, so it wasn't worthy of much attention among the national media.

I was mortified. I'd expected to spend the first winter storm of 2001 in the cabin, snug and secure against anything the elements could throw at me.

Instead I was stuck here, snowed-in inside the Petoskey city limits. Cheanne still got around in her F-150 4 x 4, but my van and John's 2-wheel-drive pickup were sealed into the driveway by a sea of chest-deep snow.

I hadn't seen such a storm in nearly a decade, and many of the people who'd migrated north to Petoskey in recent years had never seen a blizzard like this in their lives. Many of the recent immigrants were frightened, probably more by hyperbolic weathercasts of impending doom than by reality. They scurried around Petoskey's well-plowed city streets, huddled down into the collars of their coats, as they stocked up on milk, bread, and even video movies. Apparently some old-timer had been talking to them about what winters here had been like in the 70s, when snowdrifts frequently reached 14 feet in depth and rural residents were sometimes trapped for more than a week before the roads they lived on were cleared.

The truth was that a blizzard in 2001 bore less resemblance to a similar storm in 1977 than my homesteading experience did to that of an 1800s trapper. Commercial logistics and supply lines were more solidly established in the new millennium, with snow removal equipment that was more efficient and powerful than it had been a quarter century ago. More people had 4-wheel-drive vehicles, and snowmobilers kept regular trails packed down like highways from one town to the next all winter long. Getting snowed in for two weeks at a time was unlikely these days.

That was good; I recalled being buried for a full fourteen days in 1966, when I was just ten years old. By the time snowplows finally broke through to the rural dirt road we lived on, my mother, my five younger siblings, and I were down to eating rolled oats without milk or sugar. It was a turning point in my life, when I swore that such a thing would never happen to me or mine again. After that I became an avid woodsman—or, if you prefer, a survivalist—learning to fish, hunt, trap, snowshoe, and to stock up on and store foodstuffs that had long shelf lives every autumn.

The storm broke the day after Christmas, although weather reports claimed a second, perhaps worse, storm front was coming in from the northwest in a day or so. Big John supervised while Cheanne, Robin, and I shoveled away 20 yards of snow that had compressed under its own weight from 9 feet to a depth of less than 5 feet. It was dense and heavy, coming up on the shovel in great white chunks that were sometimes too heavy to throw. In a half hour the three of us had the driveway in front of John's truck cleared down to its surface, all the way out to the still snowy alley it intersected. The roads between towns were clear, so he and Robin drove off to find friends they could swap blizzard stories with. I dug out my van, but I wasn't going anywhere until that second front had passed.

That turned out to be wise, because it started to snow again almost immediately, and by the next morning our vehicles were buried again. A full 5 feet of compacted snow sat atop the roof of my van, adding several hundred pounds to its already burdened suspension and tires. I shoveled it off, then cleared the decks and sidewalks around John's house, but ignored the driveway. There was no place to pile any more shoveled snow; we needed the power of a snowplow to push the banks back.

It was New Year's Eve before that power arrived in the form of Little Purl, one of Big John's many nephews. His three-quarter-ton Chevy Suburban with Western plow had no trouble pushing the piled snow back into a hard, compressed wall. To everyone's amazement, including mine, the Indian van pulled out of the chest-deep snow bank that buried its sides and rear without spinning a tire. Purl plowed back the entire driveway, charged us a fair $20 for the service, and went home just in time to see the New Year arrive.

I left Petoskey for the cabin on New Year's Day. I got a late start, and the going was slow over icy back roads, but I arrived at the two-track near the Carp River bridge about an hour before sunset. I parked the van on the plowed shoulder and broke out a coal shovel John had loaned me (my snow shovel was at the cabin). Warming temperatures had already melted most of the ground snow, so all I really needed to do was clear the entrance of densely packed snow that had been pushed there by snowplows, then pounded down by snowmobiles. I made an earnest attempt not to remove all snow from the gravel shoulder, and to make the edges of the path I shoveled slope gently downward so they wouldn't come as a big surprise to snowmobilers who crossed there.

It was nearly dark when I backed the Chevy through the entrance I'd shoveled and down onto the two-track, easing it back 25 yards or so to insure that there were enough trees between it and the road to make the big gray van as inconspicuous as possible. A foot of wet snow covering the two-track compacted easily under the heavy vehicle's tires. I checked my tire prints, satisfied that if the cold spell I knew would come turned them to ice, there was sufficient sand around me to provide traction.

Although I'd walked the trails around here as many times in darkness as in daylight, I decided against snowshoeing the North Country by flashlight, especially since my backpack and saucer were both loaded. I made a small

fire in the existing fire pit and cooked a supper of dehydrated au gratin potatoes with a foil packet of tuna mixed in—the kind of stick-to-your ribs meal
a woodsman needs on a cold winter night. At about 10 P.M. I crawled into
the Indian van and slept well, despite being awakened a dozen times by
herds of whining snowmobiles flying past on the road. With the amount of
throttle most of them were using, I was glad I'd sloped the edges of the entrance I'd shoveled.

But recreational snowmobilers are sometimes a bitchy bunch, especially
a few visiting urbanites who think the sycophantic treatment they receive
from some local proprietors not only gives them unlimited right-of-way, but
must be representative of an unsophisticated local populace. I was only
mildly amused when an Emmet County Sheriff patrol car pulled up next to
the shoveled entrance of the two-track at 8:00 the next morning. I didn't
have to be clairvoyant to deduce that one of the snowmobilers had been annoyed by the sudden dip in his trail, and called them out of spite with a
made-up story about someone lost in the woods.

I'd just woken up, and I'm sure I looked it, but I had to grin when the
deputy walked around and actually knocked on the van's side door. I opened
the door and asked if I could help him with something. I'd already noticed
the second patrol car stopped a hundred yards behind the first, trying to remain hidden behind the trees.

"Oh," the deputy said, walking around to the Chevy's rear to see if my
license tag was current, "we got a call from a snowmobiler who said there
was an abandoned vehicle out here." He looked at me. "You look like you're
doing okay."

I told him I was fine, and he simply walked away toward his car. I was
expecting more.

"My name's Len McDougall," I said to his retreating back.

He waved a hand above his shoulder, never looking back. "I know who
you are," he said.

Somehow that didn't make me feel famous—at least not in a good way. I
watched the first deputy pull away, followed immediately by the second.
Both cars pulled off again when I was out of their sight (I could still see
them). The deputies got out of their cars and talked briefly, both casting in-
voluntary glances toward me as they spoke. They both drove off after a few
minutes, leaving me wondering why backup was needed to check out a supposedly abandoned vehicle.

I loaded my backpack and saucer, strapped on my big Atlas trail-break-
ing snowshoes, and headed across Carp River toward the cabin. Although

the night had been clear and cold, temperatures were already unseasonably warm, and the yards-deep snow that had fallen just days before had diminished to merely 8 inches. I broke the trail going in with snowshoes, but unless another heavy snowfall covered it again, I wouldn't need them on the way back.

A number of my friends had reasoned that with the coming of snow my cabin's location would no longer be a secret, because I was bound to leave tracks leading into and away from there. They were right, of course, but I relied on the examples of the deer and the hare to make it virtually impossible for anyone to follow my path to its end. Like the animals, I made no effort to conceal my trail, and like theirs, my course meandered constantly, more so the closer it got to my destination. In winter there's little difference between trail and woods, so long as you're wearing snowshoes, so I left the main trail about every hundred yards to break off into the forest on either side. After I'd traveled through the woods far enough to discourage anyone who might attempt to follow, I cut back to the main trail, only to leave it again on the opposite side after a hundred yards.

The purpose of this exercise was to make many obvious trails, just like the bunnies and the whitetails, to leave anyone behind me with a maze of zigzags and loops to sort through. After just two or three hikes along the same pathway, there were so many trails cutting off into the woods that I could take the most direct route without much fear that someone might follow my tracks to the cabin.

The cabin had survived being buried under what the media had taken to calling "The Blizzard of 2001." I wasn't surprised; I'd built it to withstand the force of a falling tree, so snow on its roof was insignificant to its structural integrity, no matter how much of it accumulated. A foot of hardpack still lay on the roof, but I had no intention of shoveling off the extra insulation.

There was definitely enough snow in the deep woods to require snowshoes, and until the area around the cabin had been packed down enough by my own tracks, I needed them to negotiate the swamps where I obtained firewood. I know that part of a homesteader's life is supposed to be laying in a supply of firewood sufficient to get through the winter, but that wasn't necessary in the first year, or probably the next. Not including the remnants of trees that had gone into building the place, there was enough dead wood lying and standing around to more than keep my fireplace stoked all winter. All I had to do was spend a half hour each day collecting enough to last until the next morning.

With snow on the ground and a new year under way, the homestead once again seemed a good place to be. Despite adventure novels that use terms like "barren" and "godforsaken," a winter woods is anything but dead, its wildlife has just been whittled down to the hardiest survivors. The cedar swamp next to the cabin was alive with browsing deer, porcupines, rabbits, and hares. Their tracks and scat were everywhere, and occasionally I'd see one of the animals, driven by hunger, come close to this human who had so far harmed none of them.

Every wild animal a person sees in the forest is like a gift, but some are more remarkable than others. One of the finest I've been blessed with was a snow-white ermine that seemed to be fascinated at finding a human in these woods. I first saw the beautiful little weasel at midday when I was splitting a log for the evening's firewood. I was working less than 10 feet from the front door when a flash of white against the cabin's wall caught my attention. I stopped swinging my oversize handmade splitting maul, wiped the sweat from my forehead, and studied the place where I'd seen movement. After a few moments, the ermine jumped up onto a log butt and studied me intently, its eyes looking coal black within the white fur of its face. The ermine remained on its perch for several minutes while I spoke to it softly, then its short weasel attention span and boundless energy sent it scampering off to find more interesting things.

I saw that ermine several times more, finally concluding that its real interest in the cabin was hunting for rodents. Whenever I left the cabin for more than a day, the mice did indeed play, leaving little mouse turds all over the shelves that held my clothing, dishes, and food, and causing me to scrub down everything with hot soapy water each time I returned. My foods were all repacked into hard plastic jars or in the barrel, where rodent teeth couldn't reach them, but I awoke almost every night to the scratching of tiny claws against metal pans and dishes. At first just yelling out in the darkness was sufficient to send the critters back into hiding under the floor, but after a while they just kept doing what they were doing, no matter how much I hollered.

I find it difficult to kill an animal that's just trying to survive, and never had that reluctance been stronger than it was here, deep in a winter woods so far off any track that no stranger had stumbled onto it in nearly ten months. Mice and voles didn't threaten my survival, and they had more right to live here than I did. In fact, I felt a closer kinship to these animals than I did to humans living in that other place called civilization. Besides, I couldn't help thinking that any mouse I killed might have been a critical meal in the diet of my ermine visitor.

Instead of setting traps, I fed the mice from my own table scraps, theorizing that a well-fed rodent would be less active, much like people. It worked like a charm. The mice no longer had to make a strenuous, noisy climb to find food—it was on a plate in front of the fireplace—so they no longer climbed onto and crapped on my shelves, and I was no longer awakened in the middle of the night by their meandering. Even better, the territorial instinct kicked in; within a week I had just one fat, healthy male mouse to feed, and it kept other mice away from the Eden it had found.

The next week was cold, with daytime highs in the single digits and nighttime temperatures well below zero. Little snow can fall in such cold temperatures, and soon what snow lay around the cabin had been packed to a sheet of ice by my boots, its surface turned a dirty gray by dirt and mud that I'd tracked over it.

Being spring fed and far below the frost line, the well never froze, but it did develop a skin of ice that I had to break through each morning. Usually the ice was thinner than a windowpane, shattering when I dropped the empty bucket onto its surface. Water drawn from it smelled and tasted clean, but although I drank straight from the well I suspected there were at least a few dead frogs lying at its bottom. That would doubtless become obvious when the weather warmed up enough for decay to resume.

While I never again experienced the severe depression that had gripped me in late December, after about a week I decided to head back to town, just to visit friends. It wasn't so much loneliness that took me back to civilization this time, but rather a vague boredom. There really wasn't a lot to do around the cabin. I took down a few notes for this book, but there was hardly enough snow to roam the back country on snowshoes. I didn't need to hunt, and I'd had my fill of listening to the radio, where country singers sniveled about being lonely, newscasters reveled in catastrophe and disaster, and talk show hosts complained about every damn thing. Whatever I'd needed to prove to myself had been proved; there was little doubt that virtually anyone could survive a whole winter in this well-stocked and heated cabin.

Now that there was nothing left to do except enjoy the fruits of my labors, I was bored. I loaded the saucer with tools and other items that were no longer needed at the cabin and towed it with me to the van. The trail was smooth and unbroken from cabin to van, so I didn't even bother to disguise my tracks, figuring that it was unlikely anyone would backtrack me 3.5 miles to the maze of trails that still protected the cabin.

Back in town I busied myself for a return to civilization in the following spring. Cheanne brought my desktop computer to Big John's, where he'd agreed to let me set up a temporary office in his spare bedroom. I tried breaking back into writing magazine articles, but the place was too noisy to get much done. I'd brought rope and climbing gear for shoveling off roofs, but it didn't snow much at all after that initial blow. I used the public library's computer to circulate my availability as a snowshoeing guide on the Internet as best I could, and I gave out a few flyers at the chamber of commerce and other offices, but there just wasn't enough snow to generate much interest. I spent a lot of time with Cheanne, though, and that was great.

After a week of fun in town, I went back to the cabin, accompanied by a twenty-two-year-old man named Steve, whom I'd known about four years. Now that the cabin was finished there were more people willing to spend an adventurous winter night at the homestead. I didn't really mind being a guide for free to folks I knew and liked, but I did nominate Steve to drive to save on the gas in my van. I had $10 left in my savings account, and a few coins in my pocket.

Steve and I dug out a parking spot for his Dodge Shadow at the Carp River access site at 3:30 P.M. on a Friday. A warming early spring sun shone down as we worked, and it was good to know that we had more than two hours of daylight left. It's generally thought that spring has arrived when the snow melts for good, but out here I could see nature's subtlest changes close up. Too-early hatches of gnats filled the air in spots, but none were biting yet. The river was high and open, rushing fast through a channel of crusted ice that bordered either side. If skies remained clear, everything would freeze tonight in temperatures that would probably be near zero, and even the river's currents would be hidden under a sheath of thin ice. It probably wasn't going to snow, though,

Enough snow had fallen while I was away to have erased the trail I broke just a week earlier, so we strapped on snowshoes before crossing the Carp River. About 4 inches of new snow had fallen on top of roughly 8 inches of hardpack snow over the past few days, and a day of sunshine had melted its uppermost layers. Now, with the setting sun, a clear sky, and overnight lows that would be at or below zero, that most recent accumulation had crusted with a hard shell of ice that broke like glass underfoot, even with the added flotation of snowshoes. There was frozen powder underneath, so once the trail was broken we were good, but that first trip was tough.

When Steve and I made the cabin it was past sunset, which comes early to the deep, shadowed woods, even without leaves on the deciduous trees. It was even darker inside the cabin, so I laid a warm fire in the hearth and we gathered a supply of wood for the night immediately after dropping our packs. The air was already still and cold, turning our exhalations to clouds of thin white vapor with every breath as we hauled in dead hemlocks, spruces, and poplars from the surrounding woods.

There were icicles in my beard and mustache when we finally went inside. I lit three kerosene lamps and a candle lantern to fully illuminate the place, and proceeded to make a fire that would throw as much heat into the cabin as possible. I did that by placing the ends of dead saplings we'd broken to 6-foot sections ends first into the firebox, which by now had a healthy glowing bed of coals. They were too long to fit into the fireplace, so I just left their ends lying on open sand in front of the fireplace while I stacked the parallel logs into a rough pyramid that maintained a wide bed of coals to throw maximum heat, but allowed a lot of wood to be placed into the fireplace at once. When the ends burned off each section of this "furnace pile," we slid the next unburned 2 feet forward and burned that.

I hung the kerosene hurricane lamp in front of the cabin to serve as a yard light so we wouldn't be stumbling past the outhouse in the middle of the night, and we settled in for the evening. Steve broke out a deck of cards and a pint of Jack Daniels and proceeded to create a card table from OSB cutoffs and an upturned 5-gallon bucket, while I made a supper of macaroni and cheese mixed with one of those new foil envelopes of canned chicken. It tasted good and we both ate until it was gone, washing the concoction down with strong swigs of bourbon and Coke.

Steve complained that he should have brought more whiskey as he looked mournfully at the upside-down bottle in his hand, but we'd been playing euchre for an hour without finishing a game, and most of the time neither of us could tell you which suit was trump. We called it a night at about 11:30. Steve, who hadn't been carrying much besides bourbon and Coca-Cola in his borrowed backpack, unpacked the military 15-degree bag that stayed in the cabin in my old ALICE (All-purpose Lightweight Individual Carrying Equipment) backpack. It was sort of a guest sleeping bag.

Steve only spent one night at the cabin. I think he liked the experience, but his feet got a little cold when the fireplace burned down in the middle of the night (I'd told him to wear his boot liners to bed), and he feared even boiled well water. By noon the next day he was dehydrated enough to be constipated, which was no doubt compounded by the natural instinct to conceal one's scent in an unfamiliar place. He'd come out to the deep winter woods as an adventure, and now that he'd seen for himself whatever it was he'd wanted to see, he was ready to go back to civilization and tell others of his exploits in this frozen wilderness. I was okay with that, because every guy needs a good hairy-man story about testing himself against the forces of nature.

A warm front had moved in early this morning, and with it another 3 inches of snow had fallen since we'd gone to bed. There were still a few fat featherlike flakes coming down when we hoisted our packs and hit the trail just after 5 P.M. The trail we'd broken coming in just the night before was almost entirely filled in, so we'd be breaking it again on the way back.

That usually meant I'd be breaking trail, because my Atlas 1033 snowshoes were nearly always the biggest present in any group, and they broke the widest trail. Having someone break trail with narrower 'shoes still left me with breaking down the sides of their prints to accommodate the greater width of my own.

Adding to the burden of humping a 50-pound pack while breaking trail was another 40 pounds of tools and gear I was removing from the cabin. I no longer needed a socket set to drive lag screws, or the multiple pliers, screwdrivers, and multitude of other tools that had accumulated at the cabin during its construction. It was almost satisfying to be removing stuff from the homestead, because it signaled that I was preparing to move on to new adventures, but the load of mostly steel I was dragging kept my pace slow through the rolling hill-and-swamp terrain of the North Country trail.

Steve was impatient under his 20-pound backpack, not comprehending the principles of pacing oneself, or of how much weight I was hauling. It was dark when we hit the 2-mile mark and broke for a five-minute rest. The air temperature was a balmy 35 degrees, which had turned the hardpack to the consistency of a snow cone, not exactly melting, but not really frozen either.

Steve volunteered to break trail the rest of the way, and I agreed. It really didn't make a lot of difference to me, but it would allow him to run off some excess energy. We hit the trail again with him leading, and he was soon out of sight except for the glow of his flashlight through the trees ahead of me.

I found Steve waiting for me up the trail about 200 yards. He didn't say it, but I know he was thinking that the old man was wearing down, and I suspect he might have been trying to recall how CPR is performed. He left me behind again within a quarter mile as I deliberately planted each foot to get a solid purchase with my snowshoe cleats, then heaved with enough force to carry myself and my load up the faces of the many ridges we had to cross. I was sweating hard enough to have removed my eyeglasses, but my pace was sustainable all night if need be. I just couldn't scamper up hills like someone whose load was less than a quarter of what I was toting.

When we were a quarter mile from the bridge, Steve asked me where we were in relationship to the Carp River. When I told him, he volunteered to tow my saucer the rest of the way. I agreed almost before he finished saying it, feeling just a little malicious as I turned the towrope over to him.

We set out again, and now I was on Steve's tail the whole way. My back pack was still twice the weight of his, but he'd just tripled the mass he was moving down the trail, and especially up steep ridges. I know it was mean, but I had to suppress a snicker as I watched him lean forward on the hills to plant his cleats firmly in loose hardpack, then thrust upward with real exertion. All the weight of his body and his burdens was carried uphill under the power of a single leg, one pace at a time. His wasn't quite so energetic as he had been earlier when we arrived together at his car, but his cheeks were rosy and he had a higher opinion of my physical condition.

I spent another week in town trying to write in John's spare bedroom. I had to make some cash, and it was turning out to be a bad year to be a snowshoe guide. There were plenty of low-wage jobs to be had, but I balked at the loss of freedom inherent in working for someone else, especially since I meant to be living north of the Mackinac Bridge just as soon as the situation permitted. I sold a few magazine articles, but I was hardly doing my best work. I made a few odd dollars here and there for necessities, but there were days at a time when I couldn't scrape together change enough for a chocolate bar.

When I couldn't tolerate Petoskey any more, I went back to the cabin. The North Country Trail from Carp River to the interior hadn't been traveled since Steve and I left. The portion coming from French Farm Lake had been violated by a pair of snowmobilers, however, three nights prior to my finding them. They'd squeezed through the poles we set at French Farm Creek, crossed the stream (an illegal act in itself), and held a north bearing until they ran out of passable terrain.

The machines had broken a trail through rugged country, continuing north past the intersection that led west to Carp River, and onto the main trail that led part way to the cabin. I could tell they'd come through at night because the snow had been crusted hard, breaking all around the tracks and skis. I suspect these adventurers were following my snow-covered snowshoe trail, but they didn't get within a half-mile of the cabin before turning back the way they came. Funny how easy it was to conceal something so large in a relatively small wilderness—just put whatever needs hiding behind terrain that can't be crossed except on foot.

After a relatively monotonous week at the cabin, I was ready to see people again. I walked the trail out to my van and went to town, returning four days later with a young fellow named Jason Farner, son of Mark Farner, who'd once been lead singer for Grand Funk Railroad. I hadn't liked Jason much when I'd first met him three years before; I'd wrongly tattooed him as the spoiled kid of a rock star until I got to know him, and until the realities of life had knocked some of the wind from his sails. Now, at the ripe old age of twenty-one, he'd taken enough hard knocks to have developed a good head on his shoulders, and I considered him a friend.

Jason and I arrived at the Carp River two-track in the early afternoon only to find it blocked by Jerod's truck, which forced us to park on the plowed shoulder. Two sets of tracks told me that he'd come out here backpacking with his girlfriend. I mumbled something about this place turning into Grand Central Station, and set out to find Jerod's camp. I didn't have to look far, but neither he nor his girlfriend were there. Their tracks said they'd headed down the North Country Trail several hours ago, and I figured they must have gone to the cabin.

Since they had to come back to their camp, Jason and I decided we'd meet them on the trail, then he'd drop his pack wherever we met and walk back with Jerod to jockey vehicles off the road. We went back to retrieve our gear, but met Jerod and his girlfriend coming back even before we'd crossed the bridge.

After fitting both vehicles into the two-track and catching up on current events—Jerod was leaving the next morning—Jason and I shouldered our packs and started the 3.5-mile hike to the cabin. Jerod and his girlfriend had already broken the trail, and there was barely enough snow to cover the ground except on bridges and walkways where the snow, compacted under the feet and hooves of many animals over many days, had formed slow-melting ridges. As usual, the Carp River bridge was holding up at least 3 tons of snow, but it always seemed to come out okay in spring, a testament to the strength North Country Trail Association volunteers had put into its construction.

The going was still a bit slower than it would have been in snowless months, with just enough snow underfoot to make walking a chore, but not enough to warrant strapping on our snowshoes. The saucer, to which a loaded JanSport Airwave daypack had been tied, followed like an obedient hound behind me, guided by the furrow left by footprints. I had to pick up the saucer and carry it across several narrow boardwalks that North Country Trail volunteers had constructed to keep hikers' feet out of the mud in summer, and whenever possible I made a trail around those ridges of rotting snow, whose sides tended to slide away dangerously underfoot. We sidled across those we had to cross, me with the saucer held up in front to counter-balance my backpack.

Jason and I arrived at the cabin fresh and with more than an hour of full daylight left. We sat outside in front of the cabin, me sipping coffee, and both of us nipping at a pint of Jack Daniels. When the sun set, we went inside the cabin, where a crackling fireplace and several lanterns made the place seem almost cozy.

I'd told Jason in one of our earlier conversations that I'd rejected military-type MRE foods as cabin fare, so he'd brought a couple along in his pack to show me how good they were and how wrong I was. He opened the hermetically sealed pouches of both meals and proceeded to eat crackers and peanut butter, crackers and cheese, and two compressed bars of dehydrated fruit. I watched him as I cooked up the au gratin potatoes and tuna dish I'd planned as supper that night.

"Do you know how much real fruit is in this little bar?" he asked, waving the foil package of the second one he ate at me.

"If there's that much fruit in there, it's probably going to expand in your stomach," I answered. "Maybe you'd better drink something with it."

Like every other survival expert to whom I've said, "I told you so," he ignored me. A half hour later he had a pained look on his rather pale face. A few minutes after that he was sitting in front of the fireplace on a campstool, hunched forward and holding his belly.

"I don't feel so good," he said.

I wasn't surprised. The dried food he'd eaten without drinking had coagulated into a mass inside his gut, lodged there for lack of moisture that would lubricate and soften it enough to be moved along and used as food. I understood what he'd done to himself because I'd done similar harm to myself with granola bars about ten years before. As I'd done for myself then, and for Howard last November, I forced a big cup of coffee into Jason's hands. A half-hour after drinking it he was headed for the outhouse. He felt much better after that.

Both of us got a good night's sleep. We awoke at 9:00 the next morning, made coffee, and ate pancakes with raisins in them for breakfast—odd for me, because I generally don't eat breakfast. We were leaving that day, but there was no hurry, so I washed the dishes and we spent the morning loading our packs.

Just before we left, Jason looked at my old Armscor .22 rifle hanging from the shelf support pegs over the front window. He asked if he could handle it and I said yes, but cautioned him that it was most likely loaded. He popped the clip out and opened the action without instruction from me——it wasn't loaded after all. Then he looked at me and asked sincerely, "Does this thing even shoot?"

Why did people keep asking me that about my .22? Sure, it had some rust on the exterior of its bolt, and its weatherproof coating was chipped to wood or metal in a number of places, and the parachute cord in its Ranger Sling had faded to almost gray, but it was the most eclectically functional gun in my survival arsenal. Not only did it operate flawlessly, its bedded action, floated 24-inch barrel, recessed muzzle crown, and tuned trigger had accounted for more meat than any gun I presently owned.

He didn't believe me, I could tell, so I handed him one of the empty aluminum garlic chicken cans that Jerod had inconsiderately left for me to haul out, and told Jason to take a couple of shots. He set the can up on a stump 20 yards from the doorway, walked back, and fired one aimed shot offhand. The bullet punched through the can's bottom dead center.

Jason slipped the gun's safety on and retrieved the can. "That's pretty good," he said. I told him to try it from a slightly more challenging distance before he judged.

This time he moved the can to a stump 45 yards away. He still elected to shoot offhand, but he hit the can all three times he fired. He handed the rifle back to me, saying, "Man, that thing's really accurate."

My answer was to throw the rifle to my shoulder, drop to one knee so that my supporting elbow rested on the other knee, and start shooting rapid fire. There were eleven rounds left in the gun's magazine, and it needed a fresh load anyway, so I proceeded to reduce our metal target to shredded scrap metal. The can bounced and jumped into the air, but every shot punched it through. A thin wisp of smoke drifted from the Armscor's recessed muzzle as I pulled the empty clip. I reloaded the magazine with Yellow Jacket cartridges and dropped it into a gun sock with the rifle while Jason retrieved the bullet riddled can. I tied the rifle to my pack for transport back to my van, and there was no more talk of my guns being nonfunctional.

CHAPTER

SPRING

I spent the better part of February in town, still trying to make a bit of money here and there without tying myself down to a real job. Snowfall continued to be dismal, despite frigid temperatures that routinely dropped into the subzero range at night, and there was little chance of making any money as a snowshoe guide this winter. I almost felt betrayed by the weather, but I wasn't the only one taking a beating at the hands of an uncooperative winter: One local outfitter was running radio commercials about the joys of snowshoeing a dozen times a day, which should have benefited me too, if there had been any snow. So far 2002 hadn't exactly been a stellar year for me all the way around.

It didn't escape me that if I had truly been living the life of an 1800s homesteader I would have been able to make money all winter long from the sale of pelts. Even in the northern Michigan of my boyhood there had been fur companies scattered throughout the region, and I'd often made more cash from the sale of raccoon, muskrat, ermine, and even skunk hides than men who worked regular full-time jobs. Today the fur traders were almost gone, and those still in business were offering less for prime pelts than I'd been paid in the 1970s. No one who knew how much hard physical labor was required to run a trapline was willing to do it for less money than a teenager was paid for flipping burgers. Many species whose numbers had once been held to healthy levels by trapping now suffered from overpopulation and resultant diseases like mange and rabies, but even the most altruistic trapper couldn't afford, in effect, to pay a furrier to take his pelts.

Ironically, a steady market existed for porcupine pelts, or more specifically for the quills they contained. Local Odawa and Ojibwa craftsmen used them to adorn "quill boxes" they constructed from the twigs and bark of white birches. These genuine Native American containers were a hot item in local stores, where a 3-inch-diameter quill box typically fetched in excess of $100 from tourists and year-round residents alike.

Maybe I'm a little thick, but I never could see the attraction of owning an authentic Indian quill box, some of which are held together with carpenter's glue, and I still can't understand why these uncomplicated projects demand such a high price. Perhaps hardest to understand was why the numerous Indians who pestered me to bring them porcupine hides offered a mere $25 apiece for pelts that would net them a thousand dollars' worth of quill boxes. I told them to go out into the woods and get their own damn porcupines.

Unfortunately, too many did go get their own porcupines. Porkies living on the reservation land we called "the potholes," about 10 miles west of my cabin, had been nearly extirpated by Indian hunters who didn't know or didn't care that the American porcupine gives birth to just one kit a year. Two years before, I'd warned my friend Al Colby, who was chief conservation officer of the Odawa Natural Resources Commission, that tribal hunters were driving porcupines to extinction in that area. After seeing for himself that I spoke the truth, he'd passed on the warning to tribal members, but the hunting still continued. Not unlike leopard skins or rhino horns, there was simply too much monetary value in porcupine quills to convince hunters to cease killing the animals who wore them. So long as a lucrative market existed, there would always be someone willing to fill it.

Although I was flat broke most of the time, it seemed I was always busy doing something for someone whenever I was in town. During much of my time there I was occupied with repairing and customizing rifles and pistols owned by others. I couldn't legally charge money for gunsmithing services without a federal license, but I bartered my skills at making firearms accurate and operational to get most of what I needed to live in relative comfort. Trigger jobs, weatherproofing, floated barrels, even shooting lessons for civil servants—I could have made a good living from the gunsmithing jobs I couldn't get paid to perform.

Lucrative or not, there was satisfaction in taking someone who knew nothing about guns and turning them into a marksman with proper gun-handling skills. Cheanne had treated herself to a really nice Browning bolt-action in .243 caliber for Christmas, and with just four months of rifle-shooting experience, she was routinely printing 3-inch groups at an honest 200 yards. Her success attracted others to our shooting outings, like a lady medic who was preparing to get a Concealed Carry Permit, teenagers who wanted to learn to handle a firearm, and even a federal agent who needed to improve his shooting skills beyond conventional law enforcement training. I personally fired only a few rounds during the dozen trips I made to the range with other people, but I got real pleasure from watching their smiles when they held up well-holed targets for me to admire.

While I was in town I lived out of my Chevy van, which was always parked in Big John's driveway. He and Robin both worried about me sleeping out there on subzero nights, but I politely turned down their offers of a couch. So far as comfort was concerned, the van's folded-down back seat, complete with sheets and pillows, made a much better bed than any sofa, and I actually enjoyed sleeping in the cold. The van held in heat far more efficiently than a tent, and when temps dropped too low for blankets, I had a zero-degree sleeping bag that kept me warm on the most frigid nights. If it got really cold I slept wearing pac-boot liners and my fleece jacket with the hood up over my head. As long as my nose and toes stayed warm, I slept like the proverbial baby, even when temps dropped to 15 below. I did get some amusement from the way people presumed that I must be tough or crazy, or both, to willingly sleep in temperatures cold enough to burst water pipes. It never occurred to most of them that maybe I was just warm enough to be comfortable.

I went back to the cabin several times in February, but didn't stay for more than a night or two at a time. Slowly lengthening, warming days made me crave companionship, and no one came to visit me when getting to the homestead meant an hour of hiking through snow. The forest around the cabin teemed with deer that fed on pine and cedar foliage not a hundred feet from the cabin. Porcupines, raccoons, and opossums left trails right through camp so long as there wasn't smoke coming from the chimney, and sometimes even when there was. Snowshoe hares and cottontail rabbits were everywhere, nibbling buds and gnawing bark from shrubs, but my traps and guns went unused. It just seemed wrong to kill animals I'd come to think of as neighbors.

I think the biggest problem was that there was no challenge left. From snowmelt to snowfall last year I'd been focused on creating a permanent home in the wilderness, and now that it was finished there was no sense of urgency. Practically any greenhorn could live on my homestead with a high degree of comfort at this point. I was satisfied that I'd demonstrated that a twenty-first-century man could still create civilization from untouched wilderness, and now it felt as though there was nothing left to prove. The only ordeal left to cope with was loneliness, and I figured I'd already had enough of that to speak with authority on the subject.

Even the woods around the homestead had lost its fascination for me. It was just as wild and perhaps even more feared by locals than it had been when I arrived, but to me it had become little more than a really big backyard. I knew more than 60 square miles of the surrounding forest well enough to almost never refer to the compass around my neck, and there wasn't a single ridge or swamp that I hadn't seen close up in every season. Any terrain I hadn't traveled during the homesteading project I'd covered at least twice in the previous three years of research with the Northern Michigan Wolf Detection and Habitat Survey Team. I loved this place more than I ever had, but I just wasn't getting much mental stimulation from being here these days.

Things weren't exactly going my way in town, either. My year in the wilderness was coming to an end, and I had to figure out how to get reestablished in society. I needed another grubstake to launch me someplace north of the Mackinac Bridge, enough to let me settle into civilization and write this book. That was going to require generating a few thousand dollars while I was here in the Petoskey area.

Unfortunately, my time in the woods had caused me to go a little feral (Cheanne said I'd been feral to begin with). I'd sacrificed the luxuries of civilized life to experience a freedom that can only be known from living a life in which schedules are dictated not by another person, but by wind, rain, and snow. The cost of that freedom had been high and sometimes brutally challenging, but I'd survived hardships that had killed more than a few men who'd attempted to do what I'd already done, and those often-painful victories had left me with an almost fierce sense of independence. Now the very thought of going back to a life that was centered around the wants of other people, many of whom are themselves motivated by selfishness and an illusive perception of wealth, was as repulsive to me as a rotting deer carcass.

I'd also gone a little antisocial in the time I'd been away. I'm still not sure exactly when it happened, but sometime during the last year I'd completely lost the ability to accept any amount of verbal abuse from anyone. I don't think I ever acted like a tough guy or looked for trouble, and I made a conscious effort to be considerate of stranger and friend alike, but if a man came in my direction looking for trouble, by God I was willing to grant his wish.

Fortunately for me, those with the largest mouths tend to have the least amount of heart, and I came to blows with only three guys who were really persistent. They thought they were tough because they watched football, but

I knew that real toughness comes only from suffering hardship and pain, and it isn't a trait that most people who have it developed by choice. Still, I think I understand why the trappers and voyageurs of old Michigan had such a reputation for putting knots on the heads of people who asked for them.

Pete and I saw a lot of one another when I was in town and he had the time. He was doing a fine job of making his way in society, far better than I was doing, and I suspect the month he'd stayed at the homestead had been a big step up the ladder of manhood for him. We spent many a cold winter night walking Noki and Buddydog around the streets of Petoskey, discussing the trials of life in general, and our own plans for the future in particular.

Pete and I backpacked together to the cabin in the last week of February, him to stay for four days, me to stay until I felt like leaving. There was still too much snow in the woods for us to attempt the 3-mile drive in to the dam, so we parked our vehicles at the Carp River bridge and hiked in. Most of the North Country Trail was under a foot of rotting hardpack, but there were 50-yard stretches of bare ground that promised spring was coming shortly. It seemed odd that those barren patches of freshly thawed dirt should stir such feelings of pleasure, but as much as I enjoyed the winter months, bare earth was always a welcome sign of warming weather.

After Pete left, I stayed at the cabin for another two weeks. It was reinvigorating to feel warm sunlight on my face after a winter that had been too hard and too long. Because the area hadn't received anywhere near what would have been considered a normal snowfall, spring came early in 2002, but I didn't mind at all. I took real pleasure from seeing the first green plants struggle upward through the remains of their predecessors from the previous year. The process started slowly, as it always did, then winter gradually gave way to spring, until the remaining snowbanks were contrasted by the vibrant green of young cattail shoots and swamp grasses, giving the forest an almost surreal look. By the time I hoisted my pack and headed back toward Carp River and town, the North Country Trail was nearly bare, with only a few patches of softening hardpack on its shaded sections.

Back in Petoskey there were also signs of increasing life, especially among the citizenry. People who had been more or less housebound these past several months were now using almost any pretense to get outside. There were few tourists during this hiatus between the snowmobile and boating seasons, and most of the people who were walking the streets to window shop and chat with friends they met were year-round residents. Ski resorts were still making snow to keep their slopes covered, trying to prolong their most lucrative season for as long as possible, but there was no denying that winter was fading fast.

I spent the next week in town, most of it with Cheanne. We strolled the shoreline of Little Traverse Bay on Lake Michigan and discussed our plans for the future. I still wasn't sure how to make the transition back from wilderness to civilization, but she gave me hope that it could be done. She seemed to always know what I was thinking and feeling, even when I didn't speak, and the hardness that had developed inside me this past year seemed to melt away in her presence. She made me feel humble, which is an entirely uncharacteristic emotion for me.

I went back to the cabin a few days after March became April. It bugged me that my backpack didn't have anything more in it than when I'd left for town, but the cabin was still stocked with sufficient homesteading staples to last another six months. I didn't like being too poor to enjoy the finer things in life, like Hershey's chocolate bars with almonds, but I knew there were a good many people in that other world of civilization who had it a helluva lot rougher than I did. At least I'd never have to stand in a soup line at the Salvation Army, or go begging for a warm place to sleep at some homeless shelter. So far as pure survival was concerned, I needed help from no one, but there's a lot of room for pain and suffering between the extremes of life and death.

I was still afraid to try the two-track leading to French Farm Creek, so I parked the Indian van at Carp River until I could check out the area on foot. The parking area near the bridge was nearly snow free, so I backed the Chevy down to my normal summer parking spot next to the river, where it was hidden from passing motorists by trees. The snowmobilers had put their noxious machines away until next winter, but I wanted to prevent any possibility that someone else might call the police to report my vehicle as abandoned, suspicious, or for whatever other reason a person with no life might have for being intrusive on someone else's.

I'd intended to go straight to the cabin, but the river was high, fast, and so damned beautiful that I just couldn't tear myself away from its banks. I loved the sounds made by its racing current, swollen with millions of gallons of melted snow that rushed toward Cecil Bay with enough horsepower to run a small town. Watching all that free energy simply going to waste while utility companies fouled the entire planet with toxic gases from archaic coal- and oil-burning generators—and then charged consumers for the privilege—was at the very least blasphemous to me. I don't know if the Hell of the Bible truly exists, but I'm pretty sure oil and utility company executives are praying that it doesn't.

I spent that first night sleeping in the van, where I was lulled into a sound, restful sleep by the song of rushing water. My dreams that night were happy, filled with visions of sunny flower-filled meadows and warm embraces from long-dead loved ones. I awoke the next morning to a gray overcast sky that promised rain, but my heart felt strong and filled with blessings. I'm not normally a religious man, but I felt the need to bow my head and thank the Creator of all the fine things that surrounded me for letting me be here. Then I shouldered my backpack and set off toward the cabin.

There was still a spine of hardpack snow in the center of the bridge crossing Carp River, but it was melting fast as the temperature rose to nearly 40 degrees. I paused there on the bridge for several long minutes, absorbing the serenity and spirit of these truly awesome surroundings, and I once again thanked the Great Spirit for allowing me to touch His finest creations. When I opened my eyes again the world seemed to have brightened several degrees, and I no longer felt that I was the least bit poor.

The North Country Trail leading toward the cabin was clear, with only a few patches of white scattered throughout the woods. Tracks of coyote, bobcat, and whitetails pressed into the wet sand showed that spring had brought an increase in animal activity, but there was no sign of wolves having passed through there. I knew there had to be at least one or two in the area, but gray wolves are darned hard to find from winter, when the pack splits up, until late spring when they rejoin as a family unit.

I was about 300 yards from the cabin when a flash of movement on the trail ahead caught my attention. I went to ground, dropping to one knee to reduce my profile. My 10x Leupold binoculars were hanging around my neck and tucked into a breast pocket, and when I brought them to my eyes I could see a lone whitetail feeding in a clearing where one of the ridges crossed my trail, about 200 yards ahead. It hadn't seen me, and went about feeding on young grasses and forbs as I watched its activities through the lenses.

I wasn't surprised to find that I'd already reflexively unslung my .308 rifle and laid it next to me at the ready. It was loaded with a Winchester SXT cartridge that had both the accuracy and the killing power to decisively reduce a feeding deer to venison, and the range was hardly enough to challenge the Thompson/Center. But I never exchanged binocular for rifle; I just sat there on my haunches in the middle of the trail, too far away for the whitetail to see me, and watched its graceful, almost elegant, movements. It wandered across the open meadow, tail flicking, dropping its head for a nibble of fresh greens from time to time, and I did nothing but marvel at, and perhaps even envy, the way it belonged here.

I sure could have used fresh meat, and this deer appeared to be in exceptionally good condition after having spent an entire winter in the woods, but I just couldn't bring myself to fix it in the crosshairs. I berated myself mentally for being such a modern law-abiding wimp, knowing full well that a true nineteenth-century homesteader wouldn't have hesitated to bring down a healthy supply of venison for the smokehouse.

Some of my friends would have kicked me for behaving so foolishly. Like me, they'd grown up in large, poor families where wild game and fish had made up much of their diet. None of us knew how many deer we'd put in the freezer, but I knew that most of them would never pass up the opportunity to have fresh tenderloin steaks for breakfast. I felt kind of stupid just sitting there and watching a month's supply of meat walk across my line of sight to disappear into the woods. I decided not to tell any of them about this.

The cabin was where I'd left it. I really did feel like I'd come home when I unlocked the door and went inside. It was never going to win any awards from Good Housekeeping, but it was certainly better than some of the tarpaper shacks I'd lived in as a kid.

After laying a fire in the fireplace and whipping up a filling early supper of scratch pancakes with raisins in the batter and granulated sugar as a topping, there was still enough daylight left to walk to the dam and check the condition of the two-track. I hadn't been able to park there for the past three months, and if enough snow had melted, I intended to move the van back around in the morning.

A chill had replaced the warmth of the day when I set out toward the dam, but the air felt good in my lungs as I walked. It seemed every animal in the forest was out enjoying the new spring as much as the people in town had been doing. Tiny but very noisy peeper frogs called to potential mates in a chorus of chirps so loud that I considered wearing ear plugs just to muffle them. When I'd first come out here last spring they'd gone silent at my approach, but now the peeping continued regardless of my presence—I guessed they'd come to accept my scent as part of the woods. There was a menagerie of other critters too; before I reached the dam I'd seen two deer, a porcupine, and one startled raccoon that dove headlong into a flooding at the side of the trail, then climbed out of the water onto a stump and stared at me comically, as if it couldn't believe what it was seeing.

From the dam I walked a half-mile up the two-track toward the main road. There was a little snow in the shaded woods, and a few low places on the sandy road were covered by hardpack that had compressed to become several inches of ice, but the road seemed passable. I'd have to drive carefully so as not to slide off the edges in places, but the sand was wet and packed after being weighted under snow all winter, and I figured my Indian van could get through okay.

But first I had to clean the well. With the coming of warmer weather the frogs and salamanders that had been lying dead at the bottom of the well all winter began to stink. I could smell the odor of decay in the water, and there was no way I was going to drink it, even after boiling. I clipped a plastic 5-gallon pail to the draw rope, dropped it in the well, and commenced to drain it of water, one bucketful at a time. After about ten minutes of steadily drawing and then dumping water from the pit, it was almost completely dry. I'd have to wait until tomorrow before the well refilled with clean, potable water, but I'd anticipated this chore, and the 2 gallons of drinking water tied onto my backpack would hold me until then.

I slept nearly as well in the cabin that first night as I had on the Carp River. In spite of my dire financial situation, I couldn't shake an overwhelming sense of well-being. Even running out of coffee didn't seem to be intolerable when my heart and body felt so strong. Caffeine withdrawal left me with a pounding headache that lasted a full five days before my body adjusted to doing without, but it was impossible to feel bad in a place that was so beautiful and serene.

Convinced that spring was definitely here, and that I was in no danger of being stranded even if an unseasonable snowstorm hit, I hiked to the van and drove it around Lake Michigan's shoreline to the two-track at French Farm Lake. The trail leading to the dam was rough, but I hammered the big Chevy across loose sand and rammed it through the few remaining snowbanks until we broke out of the woods into the open area leading to the dam at French Farm Creek. Once there, I wheeled the van around and backed it parallel with the posts that protected the creek from off-roaders. It felt good to park there again, further enforcing the feeling that I'd come back home.

I went back to Petoskey a couple of days later, but didn't stay long. The allure of newness that spring had brought to the forest caused me to feel bored with the goings-on in town. So when a second-year college student named Nick Bodette, whom I'd known since he was in high school, asked if I could show him wolf sign for a term paper he was writing for an English class at North Central Michigan College, I jumped at the opportunity to go back.

Nick's timing was excellent. Since the snow had melted enough for me to park at the dam there had been a lone adult wolf with better than 4-inch tracks patrolling the entire 3-mile length of sandy two-track between Trailsend Road and French Farm Creek. With runoff keeping the sand constantly damp, its track impressions there were nearly perfect, clearly showing claws, heel pad shape, and every other characteristic needed to identify the species.

I'd already shown these tracks to Cheanne, who'd been keeping three gray wolves she'd raised from pups these past six years, and now served as our wolf team's resident canine expert. She knew what a wolf track looked like even better than I did, and her knowledge of canid behavior matched or exceeded that of any wolf expert I'd met. She took one look at the track patterns I showed her and declared with an excited light in her eyes that they'd indisputably been made by a timber wolf.

Nick was also impressed when I showed him a trail of fresh prints pressed into the sand. He had no experience as a tracker, and in fact wasn't all that hot about spending time in the woods, but when I showed him illustrations of gray wolf, coyote, and dog tracks in *The Complete Tracker* he had no trouble reaching the same conclusion Cheanne and I had. I don't think he'd really expected to come away with anything concrete to put in his term paper, but now he felt as though he could pull off the highest grade in his class. As it turned out, he did just that, earning a 4.0 on his paper while at the same time convincing nearly everyone in his class that gray wolves did indeed live in Michigan's Lower Peninsula.

CHAPTER 12

APRIL 2002

The sky over the beaver flooding was blue and bright in the waning afternoon sunlight, but ambient temperatures were still in the low 40s. Cold for the latter half of April, even on the Straits of Mackinac. I'd been alone in the woods for better than a week, watching as the forest was lulled to life by a few deceptively warm summerlike days, then violently shocked back to dormancy—sometimes death—by a sudden unseasonable cold snap that left 3 inches of fresh snow on the forest floor around the cabin. Despite modern meteorological imaging, weather patterns were proving increasingly unpredictable, and the whole of nature had been disturbingly off balance for more than a year.

Adding to the feeling of cold was a stout northwesterly wind that became stronger and chillier as I peered cautiously from the windbreak where forest became open shoreline on the northwest end of French Farm Lake. I was meat hunting, and my reasons for stealth had as much to do with not freaking out people who might be visiting there as it did with not spooking off a potential meal. Despite the fact that I had a legitimate right to feed myself under both U.S. and international laws, regardless of game regulations, I figured discretion was indeed the better part of valor.

I ducked behind a stand of young spruces as soon as I peeked out from cover. There, just over 100 yards distant and swimming in the shallow lagoon surrounding a room-size beaver lodge, was a lone Canada goose. It was a mature male, and it should have been nesting somewhere among thick cattails with a mate at this time of year. That it was meandering more or less aimlessly on a small bay shallow enough for most predators to run across told me its mate, and probably the eggs, had only recently fallen prey to a bobcat, coyote, or maybe a big raccoon or otter.

Unfortunately, the widowed goose had also seen me. I was sure that it hadn't seen enough of me for long enough to determine that I was human, but it began a slow, cautious retreat toward the safety of deeper water as I quickly decided that I would definitely appreciate a flame-roasted goose dinner after nearly two weeks of dried rations. As I hurriedly plotted an ambush I felt a slight sense of déjà vu, because I'd taken a Canada goose from this same lagoon, at about the same time of year, a few years earlier.

I had my Thompson/Center Encore rifle in .308 Winchester caliber, and I could clearly see the goose in the Simmons Whitetail Classic scope as it glided around the far side of the beaver lodge. Range wasn't a problem; the Encore certainly had enough accuracy, and the explosive 150-grain ballistic-tip Winchester bullets I was shooting wouldn't destroy edible meat if I could place my shot in a 3-inch area through the bird's ribs, between wing and leg joints. That gave me a small moving target at what turned out to be 110 yards, but my mouth was watering for goose breast, and nothing sharpens the hunting skills like hunger.

When the lodge was between the goose and me, and I was sure I wouldn't be spotted, I moved low and quickly through thick evergreens to an open hummock of earth covered by tall grasses. With my rifle's forend rested across the peak of the mound, I had a stable, unobstructed view of the water where the goose would be reappearing from behind the lodge.

When it did, I had a good view of its body in profile. The big bird was still alert for danger from my direction, but I was too well concealed and too motionless for it to locate my hide. With the Simmons cranked up to 8x, the sight picture was bright and clear as its crosshairs settled almost of their own accord on the small target area amidships of the bird's body.

I thumbed the rifle's hammer back, and gently touched its trigger with the tip of my index finger. The goose was still in shallow water, where I could easily retrieve it without swimming, but it was moving offshore at about 2 miles per hour. The breeze was blowing about quarter value across my sights, but I knew from experience that its effect on my bullet's point of impact would be small enough to be ignored. Velocity, time, elevation, windage, all ran through my brain as the crosshairs tracked their target and my trigger finger delicately took a comfortable seat against the Encore's wide target trigger.

In the end, I decided that any influence nature might exert over my bullet was insignificant under these conditions, and I just aimed dead on. As always, the Encore roared as soon as I thought about pulling the trigger, and a millisecond later the goose's far flank exploded in a puff of feathers. Its wings twitched involuntarily, but the bird's head was under water, its neck limp, and I knew that its spirit had left as soon as the bullet arrived. I stashed my rifle in the bush nearby, a fresh round chambered and the empty casing in my pocket, and crossed the shoreline to where my dinner floated on gentle waves 50 yards out. The sandbar lagoon was surprisingly warm from the sun, barely knee deep, and in no time I was headed back to my rifle with the bird in hand, and from there to the cabin.

Even though this wasn't the first goose dinner I'd obtained in such a manner, I couldn't help but marvel at the sheer beauty of the big bird while I hiked, holding it by its large black webbed feet. It was a healthy adult, with thick feathers, and a stout weight of roughly 12 pounds, despite having made a recent northward migration. I felt a small sadness at having ended the life of so wondrous a wild creature, but the lower, hungry regions of my mind were already concocting recipes that used its carcass as their main ingredient. I said a brief prayer of thanks to the bird's spirit for permitting me to use its body as food, and to the Creator for judging me worthy to take its life.

Back at the cabin, I used my Gator folding knife to split the goose's hide along its spine from tail to skull, and began working the skin away from underlying flesh, removing feathers and most fat during this process. Some folks prefer to pluck their birds, leaving the skin intact, but plucking is a tedious and messy chore, and my digestive system finds greasy fowl meat objectionable. Skinning resolves both problems with a minimum of effort and mess.

Still, there were down feathers everywhere when the skinning was done. I slit the naked bird's abdomen from the anus to the bottom of its breastbone, and reached into the cavity, pulling entrails and organs out mostly intact by tearing loose the peritoneal sac that contained and secured them to the rib cage. I knew better than to split the breastbone of any bird, the way I did when butchering mammals, because the cut edges are razor sharp. I cut off both feet at the knees, removed the head, leaving most of the neck, and washed the carcass inside and out using a pot of clean water drawn from the well.

There are numerous ways to prepare a wild goose, but most take many hours, and I was already slavering over the thought of eating fresh goose flesh. Capitulating to my id, I removed the breasts first, slicing close to the breastbone as I worked them free in two pound-size chunks of lean, rich purple-red meat. I laid the breasts out on a cutting board inside the cabin and butterflied them by slicing each nearly in half across the muscle grain, then laying them open like a sandwich bun. From there, the split breasts were seasoned and placed onto a grill over hot coals in the fireplace, where they sizzled and gave off a smell so delicious that I had a hard time concentrating on anything else. I ate both breasts as soon as they were cooked.

I placed the remainder of the cleaned carcass into a large covered pot of fresh water and boiled it all night, until the meat had become tender enough to fall from its bones. I picked the meat from the legs, back, and wings, then added them to a pot of boiled rice and bracken fiddleheads. I was eating this concoction the next day when Cheanne and Jerod showed up to see how I was doing. It was good to be in their company again, but I wasn't ready to leave yet.

After walking Cheanne and Jerod back to the dam and seeing them off, I stayed at the cabin for another week. Not surprisingly, it started to rain as soon as they left, but having a cabin to stay in made the experience far more tolerable than it had been a year ago, when my house had been a tent. In fact, a hard rain pattering against the tarpapered roof while a warm fire crackled in the fireplace made the joint kind of homey.

It rained hard for the next few days, and temperatures were unseasonably cool, despite humidity and cloud cover. The snow was completely gone, but nighttime temps were still cold enough to freeze standing water with a skim of ice, while daytime highs barely reached 60. A plus was that the few mosquitoes I saw were too weak from hypothermia to be a threat, and the dreaded blackflies, whose numbers had been hellish last spring, were almost rare.

This was my twelfth day in the woods, and I'd been enjoying the experience immensely, despite a few normal hardships. At least one large gray wolf with foreprints measuring 4.5 inches had taken to patrolling the trails around my cabin, killing time in the prey-rich forest while awaiting the annual spring pack reunion when he and his adult siblings and relatives would meet the newest generation of pups. I figured it was probably the same individual I'd seen run across the trail behind me a year ago.

I'd about given up on reporting gray wolf sightings by this time. Biologists from Michigan's Department of Natural Resources weren't likely to admit the presence of wolves in the Lower Peninsula so long as it meant that control of this area would then fall under the Endangered Species Act, and therefore federal jurisdiction. Personally, I suspected there was an official desire to create another for-profit campground on the shoreline of French Farm Lake to take pressure off the overcrowded Wilderness State Park campground, 6 miles to the west. That wouldn't happen if the area came under federal protection.

Our own wolf team, the Northern Michigan Wolf Detection and Habitat Survey Team, had been idle at the official level for several months. A lot of field research was still being done, and data was still being gathered, but government biologists obstinately refused to so much as look at the proof we'd found, and not one of them would accompany us on the scores of research outings we'd conducted since 1998. I met regularly to compare notes with Odawa tribal biologist Archie Kiogima, but we'd seen that Fish and Wildlife would take no action to protect wolves in the Lower Peninsula until DNR field biologists first admitted their presence, regardless of how much proof we presented them with. It was a catch-22 situation, and none of the wolf team could tolerate attending more endless meetings where no decisions to act were made. We knew *Canis lupus* was thriving in the Lower Peninsula because we'd spent many nights in the woods and hiked or snowshoed hundreds of miles to locate hard evidence that proved it. If government biologists truly didn't know that wolves were here, it was because they hadn't done a fraction of the field research our team had done these past five years.

Pete and Noki came out to stay a couple of days at the cabin at the end of the second week. I was grateful for the company in general, and happy to see these friends in particular. Pete knew how financially strapped I was, and the candy bars he'd packed were almost as welcome as he was. We ate until neither of us could hold any more, then sat talking late into the night, feeling very much at home in this most remote of houses.

Just before midnight our conversation was interrupted by a loud, prolonged screeching that issued from just outside the cabin. The shrill screams were broken intermittently by the sounds of a scuffle atop the leafy forest floor. Noki's ears pricked up from where he was lying near the door, and Pete looked at me quizzically. Both dog and master had spent too much time in the woods to show any real concern, but neither could they identify these weird noises.

I grinned, because I knew what it was we were hearing. I looked at Pete and said, "Raccoons." He nodded his head in comprehension. Noki put his own head back down and resumed napping, unconcerned because he could see that we weren't.

In fact, there was no cause for surprise; the raccoons were regular visitors who came around each night to see if I'd left them anything to eat. Now that the cabin was secure from marauders, I'd taken to placing leftover food outside the door on a metal plate. It was gratifying to rise in the morning and find the plate empty, kind of like I'd made an offering to the spirits of the forest and it had been accepted.

Probably most authorities on wildlife would say that I was doing a bad thing by feeding the local wildlife, but my visitors were nearly always smaller species—typically raccoons and an occasional opossum—whose territorial ranges were limited to the woods. They never came in contact with other humans, so they never learned to associate anyone but me with food. My own territory was well established by this time, and it was never challenged, but every large carnivore provides its smaller cousins with a meal from time to time. I figured the food scraps I left for my animal brethren were no different than the whitetail carcasses that wolves left behind to be picked clean by foxes and other meat eaters too small to get their own deer. A fox doesn't lose its fear of wolves just because it feeds on the scraps of their prey, and neither did these raccoons lose their fear of me simply because I fed them leftover pancakes.

The screeching Pete and I heard was the sound of a territorial dispute between raccoons as they argued over who had rights to this feeding ground where scraps left by the resident boss animal (me) were usually tastier than anything they might find in the surrounding forest. At this time of year the females were pregnant, the males were filled with testosterone, and prime feeding areas were hotly contested and defended.

Pete wasn't mentally ready to leave when his schedule demanded that he return to town, and Noki was certainly willing to spend more time at the homestead, but the sharp talons of civilized life, schedules, and social responsibilities had already sunk deep into the young man's existence. I could feel Pete's reluctance as he shouldered his backpack and we walked together back to where his Bronco was parked at the dam.

We heard them long before we got to the dam. It was Saturday night, and even over the roaring of water we could clearly hear the whoops, shouts, and engines of a large group of people who had apparently come to the dam to raise a bit of hell away from the rules of civilization. Loudest among the noises was that of a jacked-up 4 x 4 truck that was stuck in a small muddy marsh at the side of the two-track. We stopped at the edge of the creek opposite the partiers, and Pete kept Noki back while I moved to a position where I could observe the scene through my 10x Leupold binoculars. The distance between us was less than 150 yards, but I made no attempt to conceal myself—they wouldn't have seen me if I'd been on fire.

They were locals, about twenty of them, ranging from preteen kids to men and women of retirement age. It was the same group I'd seen here the previous two Saturday evenings. I sort of liked the idea of what was obviously a large family getting together to have fun out here on the weekend. They were breaking a law or two with their drinking, but they had so far been careful with their bonfires, making sure to put them out completely with sand before they left, usually around midnight, and they'd policed the area commendably well. I'd never before seen the young guy who owned the rusted-out Ford that was stuck in the mud, but he was almost certainly a relative from the way the others tolerated his foolishness. I noted that no one in the group was making a move to help him get unstuck, even though there were three other 4 x 4 trucks among the five vehicles parked there.

I was a little irate over the macho stupidity of the kid whose stuck penis truck was ripping the hell out of wetland, but I was feeling laid back enough to tolerate such retarded behavior. So long as this clown's childish need to be destructive was restricted to the civilized side of the creek I guessed I could live with it.

When we crossed the dam to where Pete's truck was parked, the party was in full swing, and no one even noticed us. They certainly noticed, however, when Noki, who looked very much like a timber wolf to the untrained eye, ran into their midst in search of the hot dogs he smelled. I thought it kind of humorous the way everyone went into a near panic at his sudden appearance, but Pete was concerned that one of the more macho guys might try to harm his dog. Judging from the way they all sort of shrank away from the big friendly wolf dog, I didn't think that would be a problem, but I could understand my friend's concern.

Pete went to retrieve Noki while I unlocked my van and watched for any trouble the partiers might give him. It might not be politically correct in today's world, but I purposely leaned my rifle against the van to show them that we weren't a good choice for bullying. I of course had no desire for trouble, especially since we were outnumbered ten to one, but I know for a fact that people in the woods tend to feel uninhibited and a little lawless, especially if they've been drinking. Like everyone else around Mackinaw City, these folks already considered me half a bubble off center for living out here in these mosquito-infested, godforsaken woods, and I was taking advantage of that natural fear of lunatics to keep my friend safe from their alcohol-induced rowdiness.

There wasn't any trouble. Several of the men kept an eye on me while Pete was fetching Noki, probably just as concerned about my attitude as I was over theirs, but there were no harsh words. Pete apologized for his dog disrupting their fun, and everyone actually seemed amicable. One fellow did inquire about Noki's bloodlines, but Pete just told him that he was a malamute-mix, which was technically correct.

After Pete left, I locked up the van and hiked back to the cabin. It was dark by then, with an ambient temperature low enough to freeze water along the shoreline of the beaver pond. I could feel eyes following my silhouette across the dam and into the woods, and I smiled to imagine what they must be thinking about the weird guy who walked these trails alone in darkness and slept in a cold forest where bears, wolves, and panthers were known to reside. I'd gladly accept the onus of insanity if it kept bad people from vandalizing my Indian van again.

May 6 dawned clear and bright, with a golden spring sun that warmed air temps into the mid-60s. For the past two days I'd been packing gear from the cabin to my van in preparation for returning to civilization. I met a young blond fellow at the dam on one of those round-trips, and despite an earnest attempt on his part to convert me to his particular flavor of Christianity, I judged him to be a good enough fellow. Because of that, and because I needed to change the subject to a more mutually palatable topic, I revealed to him the secret to catching lunker largemouth bass from the flooding at the dam.

The trick lay in knowing that big bass shun bright sunlight, resting in the darkest, deepest waters until sunset. With waning daylight, top-of-the-food-chain fish begin to move toward shallower waters, where their main prey, minnows and crayfish, make their livings. These prey animals in turn telegraph the approach of large predatory fish by schooling very close to shore, in water too shallow for the big ones to negotiate.

During those twilight times of day before dawn and at dusk, a fisherman can often see the big lunkers patrolling close to shore, waiting for an unlucky minnow or crayfish to stray from the safety of shallow water. With the fishes' hunting senses piqued toward anything that moves, a medium-size Mepps-type spinnerbait cast into the pond's center, then retrieved with an occasional twitch of the rod end, usually nets a strike about every third cast. The young fellow listened with genuine interest. He left shortly thereafter, promising to return in a few hours with friends and fishing poles to try out my advice.

I fooled around with fitting the gear I'd packed out into the Indian van until about 5 P.M. There has never been sufficient room inside the big van's interior to comfortably contain all of the tools and equipment I'd used for homesteading, but I have an almost compulsive need to rearrange in search of more space. When I finally did give up, I had no more room than when I'd begun—same as every other time I'd rearranged it.

I threw on my daypack and headed for the cabin. It sure felt good to have longer days; the setting sun was still standing above the treeline on the lake's southern shore when I headed into the shadowed woods. Yet, in spite of this serenity, my brain tingled a bit from a vague, uneasy feeling that grew stronger as I left the van farther behind. There was no one else at the dam, nor did I see anyone on the trail, but the feeling of impending trouble persisted as I puttered around the cabin. I made a simple supper on a small fire in front of the cabin, not wanting to be inside on so bright a spring day, then decided that perhaps I should heed my gut and get back to where my vehicle was parked.

It was 7:30 P.M. when I shouldered my pack and headed back toward the dam. The forest was in twilight, even though the sun hadn't yet set over the lake. I "walked Indian" on the trail out, rolling each foot from the outside of the heel to its big toe as I stepped forward, making virtually no sound and leaving only faint footprints. I was hoping to catch nocturnal animals unaware as they rose from their daytime bedding places to feed, drink, and mate.

I arrived at the dam at about 8:00. As always, I peeked out from the shadows of the trail before stepping onto the open shoreline to insure that I saw whatever or whomever was there before revealing myself. There, fishing from the shoreline near the dam, were four men. I could hear shouts of excitement as spinnerbaits flashed in the waning sunlight, and one of them held up a nice forearm-length largemouth bass for the others to see.

I stashed my rifle in the usual hiding spot behind a brushy knoll at trailside, then stepped from the woods and walked toward the dam. The anglers were so caught up in their excitement that my approach went unnoticed until I was barely 6 feet from the nearest man. I startled him when I announced my presence, as I knew I would, but at least he didn't flail me with his fishing rod, the way it happened to one too-quiet fellow I knew.

Although bass season wouldn't open for several weeks, the four men, my young born-again friend among them, were having the time of their lives catching and releasing the large bass they hauled in. They, of course, credited my advice for the success they were enjoying. I accepted the praise they lavished on me with only a touch of the humility my friends say I should exhibit more often.

I was feeling pretty good from all that unwarranted credit when I stuck my key into the van's side door. It didn't click when I turned the key, the way it should have if the door was locked. I was immediately on guard, because locking the doors is more habit than procedure with me.

I looked inside the van. Sure enough, I'd been robbed, and seriously. My Eagle Creek backpack, loaded with more than $1,000 worth of gear, was gone. With it had gone a Peak 1 backpack loaded with the three pairs of winter boots I owned, and a JanSport Airwave pack, complete with a breakdown AR-7 .22 rifle, that served as my ultralight cross-country outfit. The thieves had taken my rifle-mounted long-range 35-mm camera, and even my canvas U.S. Army briefcase loaded with manuscripts, photos, and numerous other more or less irreplaceable items. Anything big and easy to grab had been taken, indicating the thieves were in a hurry, and I had a strong hunch the offenders had been a pickup-load of poorly reared high school kids from Mackinaw City.

Access to the van had been gained by knocking out the driver's side vent window, then reaching inside to pull up the lock. I'd purposely removed the knobs inside to help discourage that very thing, but at least one of the thieves had been tall enough and had arms long enough to reach through the broken vent and pull up the threaded stud that remained.

The thieves' tire tracks had been all but erased by the anglers' two SUVs, but impressions in the grass showed that they'd pulled right up to the van in a small truck, probably an S-10 Chevy. Two of them wearing tennis shoes, men's size ten I figured, had exited from the passenger side to do the breaking-in and stealing, while the driver stayed behind the wheel. They were obviously frightened and in a hurry.

Whoever they were, these morally deficient lowlifes had stolen more than $3,500 in outdoor equipment whose real value they couldn't comprehend. It was a lousy time to consider that maybe I should have spent a few more bucks for theft coverage on my van. But then, stealing a man's outdoor gear was a violation of sacred wilderness law, akin to stealing money from church coffers, and I hadn't really expected it to happen. Aside from the very serious financial loss I'd suffered, I'd miss the functionally sleek outfits that were specifically tailored to keep me alive under the most adverse conditions. But worse than that, I'd gained yet one more reason not to believe in the goodness of my fellow man, one more justification for automatically suspecting that strangers would do me harm if I let them.

To be honest, I at first suspected the anglers who were fishing a mere 50 feet from my vehicle, but it took only a few seconds to determine that none of them were guilty. They couldn't have secreted the gear in their SUVs, which I could see into, and my own judgment told me they hadn't committed this crime. Somehow, in the short time between 5 and 8 P.M., I'd been parted from nearly all of my most valued worldly possessions by people of low character and flawed upbringing, and the thieves had been lucky enough to not be seen. I shuddered to think how long my prison sentence might have been if I'd caught the bastards in the act.

My good mood was as gone as my gear. I retrieved my rifle amidst curious stares from the anglers, unloaded it, and sheathed it in its gun sock. None of the fishermen had seen anyone else since they'd driven in, which narrowed the time of the robbery to between 5:15 and 6:30 P.M. There was only one thing I could do now; I fired up the Indian van and headed for Mackinaw City to make out a police report.

The police station in Mackinaw City was deserted, as I knew it would be, but it was a small town, so I parked in front of the municipal building and waited for the only cop on duty to drive by. When he appeared, I stepped into the street and flagged him down.

The sergeant in the cruiser didn't get out of his car. He rolled down the passenger window, listened to my story, and told me that because the crime had occurred outside the city limits, it wasn't his job. Instead, he radioed the state police post in Petoskey, and told me I'd have to drive 35 miles from the crime scene to make a report.

It was 11:30 P.M. when I got to Petoskey, and I was completely exhausted. Aside from that, there was no point in trying to preserve the integrity of the crime scene now. I drove to Big John's place and attempted to call the Petoskey state police post to reschedule my police report, only to find that after 9 P.M. all calls were routed through the Gaylord post, 50 miles away. The lady dispatcher there told me not to worry about it, I could make a report any time. Boy, was she wrong.

I called the Petoskey post at 9:30 the next morning, and was told to come on over. When I arrived, a mustachioed blond sergeant with a donut belly and a serious attitude of superiority told me I'd have to come back in an hour. I told him I had a lot to do that day, and asked if he couldn't take my report. He looked at me with a sneer and said with thick sarcasm, "No, I can't take your report."

I handed him a written summary I'd prepared of what had happened, along with a list of the most identifiable items that had been stolen. He actually stepped back from the counter, refusing to take the documents. I slid them onto the counter and left them there. I didn't have a very good feeling about this.

The next morning I called the Petoskey post once again. The same sergeant answered, and when I asked him if I could make out a theft report the same day, he flew into a tirade and accused me of standing up whoever it was who wrote police reports by not returning as ordered the day before. Stupid me for not understanding that a specially trained officer had to make a special trip to take a routine report.

I gave up; it was glaringly obvious that there was nothing I could do to make this sad excuse of a police officer earn his pay. I could almost understand that he didn't give a damn about my being robbed, but I figured that having a stolen semiautomatic rifle out there in the hands of people who were indisputably of a criminal bent would be worthy of his concern. I also couldn't believe there was only one state cop in northern Michigan who'd been trained to write a report, as he'd inferred. I was reminded of a quote from Robert Heinlein: "Specialization is for insects."

I never did make out a police report, and whoever the thieves are, they're still at large and still armed with a stolen gun. Unfortunately, they can never be arrested for having stolen that gun, or any of the other identifiable items I'd lost, because there's no police record to show that the theft ever occurred.

CHAPTER

SAYING GOOD-BYE

After failing to get any help from the police concerning the robbery that had deprived me of most of my worldly possessions, I returned to the cabin. I'd considered parking my van at the Carp River, where it would be less likely to be found and robbed again, but a stubborn streak wouldn't permit me to let the bad guys think they'd run me off. Besides, I really had nothing left to steal. I parked my van at the dam in exactly the same place it had been.

I'd managed to trade a rifle for another backpack while I was in Petoskey. It was an old Kelty Red Cloud that had been well used from Alaska to Michigan, but it was comfortable and serviceable, despite a few scars. I missed my Eagle Creek pack with its detachable daypack, and I sorely missed the many useful to very important items it had contained, but at least I was back in business. I hoped the thieves who had robbed me were proud to have virtually wiped out one of the poorest men in northern Michigan.

Even so, the homestead remained a place of safety and solitude for me, and I still very much enjoyed the time I spent there. The days were warm and the weather was fair most of the time, and when the weather was foul, I had a fine cabin to protect me. The trees seemed reluctant to sprout leaves again after the earlier cold spell had killed off their first attempts, but they'd recover well enough. Ground plants seemed not to have been harmed at all by the late snowfall—in fact, the shock appeared to send most species into high gear. That was good, because if the herbivores had plenty to eat, that meant the carnivores did too. I regarded at least the first 60 square miles of forest around the cabin in much the same way as a groundskeeper might think of his garden, and it warmed my soul to see the place so vibrant and healthy.

Spring also heralded an increased diversity in my own diet, just as it had for settlers and Indians of old. In terms of availability, one of my favorite

171

wild vegetables has always been the fiddleheads, or young shoots, of the bracken fern. This woodland fern is ubiquitous throughout the forests of North America, and it continues to sprout from April to July in the north, making it an invaluable survival food if for no other reason than its sheer abundance. It was once a staple of American Indians, and some tribal hunters ate nothing else for several days prior to going after deer because a diet of only fiddleheads purified the body and helped to eliminate scent.

But even though I'd been cooking with them for decades, I was never all that fond of bracken fiddleheads. Eaten raw, the cores have a slimy texture that I find objectionable, although the taste isn't bad. Boiling them for five minutes eliminates the sliminess, but renders the shoots limp and almost tasteless. I'd often mixed them with other dishes because they contain vitamin A, at least, but my use of them had so far been merely supplemental.

Now I was looking for a method of preparing bracken sprouts that would make them a palatable stand-alone dish. Since fiddleheads have always reminded me of green beans, I decided to try frying them in lard. I'd eaten green beans prepared that way and liked them, so I figured the same recipe might work with fern shoots. I gathered a half pound or so of them from around the cabin, washed them with well water, and tossed them into a hot skillet with a tablespoonful of Crisco. I seasoned the sizzling greens with salt and pepper and fried them until they were firm and browned.

The result was surprisingly good. After a first tentative nibble, I scraped the contents of the skillet onto a plate and consumed them with more relish than I'd anticipated. I can't say exactly how much nutrition the fried fiddleheads contributed to my diet, but they tasted pretty darned good. Funny how there's always something more to learn about doing any given thing, no matter how long you've already spent doing it.

With the warm season in full swing, there were plenty of animals around the homestead. Deer, rabbits, and other herbivores were drawn to the grasses and forbs that were sprouting in profusion along the forest's open ridges, and I frequently walked the trails in early evening just to see what I might find browsing for supper.

One of my favorites was a huge black porcupine that seemed to have no care other than eating. Most porcupines are a grizzled gray, but this one was notable for having the blackest coat I'd ever seen, and it appeared to have virtually no fear of me. I could almost count on seeing the big critter during evening walks, when it would typically be sitting on its haunches, nibbling at the tops of fern and other sprouts.

The porcupine never ran from my approach, even though I sometimes passed by within 10 feet of where it was feeding. It would simply stop eating and watch me walk by, then resume its nibbling. It knew my scent, and I suppose it just didn't see me as a predator. Whatever the reason for this apparent lack of fear, it made me feel good, like I was indeed a citizen of this forest community. The downside, so far as emulating a genuine pioneer was concerned, was that I obviously hadn't hunted these animals.

Every night after dark I was serenaded by family packs of coyotes that gathered at regular rendezvous spots, usually on one of the higher ridges that extended inland in concentric half circles from the bays along Lake Michigan's shoreline. I'd gotten to know the different packs well enough to identify them, one at Carp River, one in the thick forest a half mile east of the cabin, and a third along the southern shore of French Farm Lake.

Howling coyotes have been a normal feature of my camping experiences since I was a kid, and I love hearing their high-pitched howling and yapping. The pack east of the homestead had me puzzled, though, because I could swear that its nightly sessions were initiated and led by a wolf. Every night they'd start with a low monotonal howl that was unlike any coyote I'd ever heard, and then the low howl would be joined by a chorus of shriller howls and barks that were definitely made by coyotes.

Two years before, during one of our regular wolf team meetings at the Odawa tribe's Natural Resources Commission, Cheanne had posed the question of whether migrant wolves might crossbreed with resident coyotes if there were a lack of suitable mates. At first I merely dismissed that suggestion as implausible, since wolves under normal conditions perceive coyotes as competition and prey.

What I was hearing and the tracks I was seeing now caused me to rethink that opinion. We knew from the photos we'd obtained using infrared-triggered cameras that the French Farm Lake area was home to some of the biggest coyotes in North America, with individuals weighing in at better than 60 pounds, and our assessment had only been confirmed by the very large coyotes that had been taken from there by local hunters. Later I was to learn from a DNR biologist that nearly all of the wild wolves in Minnesota whose DNA had been sampled showed traces of coyote in their cellular makeup, so apparently the two species are more apt to interbreed than had been previously believed. Still, it was damn peculiar to think that a gray wolf was the head of a coyote family.

I'd been at the cabin just a few days when my radio died. The worn out 12-volt battery from Pete's Bronco hadn't been charged since I'd hauled it by saucer to my van in February. Even then it had been so weak that it wouldn't power my Grundig Yachtboy shortwave receiver for more than a few hours after being charged, and now it wouldn't run it at all. The receiver needed only 9 volts from the supposedly 14.5-volt battery, but the Yachtboy has a large appetite for amperes, despite having state-of-the-art digital circuitry. Even with six fresh AAs, which it was actually designed to use, I only got about one hour per battery.

When the Yachtboy stopped working, I switched to my Grundig Traveler II backpack receiver, the one that had been briefly occupied by a colony of pismire ants the previous summer. The TRII had terrific battery life—about forty hours on three AAs—but I'd been too broke to buy fresh batteries during my last trip to town, and now those in the radio steadily faded until it, too, ceased to operate. Since the TRII actually needed just two batteries to run its receiver, with the third operating its clock, I replaced them with the nearly dead cells from my Mini Mag flashlight and got three more days' use out of it. The Maglite got my last pair of fresh AAs, because I needed the flashlight a whole lot more than I needed to hear news of the outside world.

When the almost depleted batteries in the receiver finally died, I needed to get creative to keep my only contact with the outside world in operation. The problem now was getting whatever voltage was left in the tired old car battery down to a level that worked the little Grundig without frying its internal circuits.

Among my small supply of electrical gear was a 6-volt battery tray from Radio Shack that held four D-size cells. The cells in it were dead, but by connecting the car battery in series-parallel with the battery tray, I was able to use them as a shunt load, siphoning off enough power from the battery and running it through them to safely run my radio for another three weeks. I felt a bit like the professor on the old *Gilligan's Island* series when I considered that not only had I accomplished this simple modification with electrical equipment not invented when the first homesteads were built, but I'd manipulated those components using scientific knowledge that hadn't existed in the nineteenth century. I was more convinced than ever that replicating the experiences of early pioneers was a sheer impossibility; modern humans knew too much about too many things.

My time at the cabin passed almost blissfully, until I began to lose track of days. Temperatures remained unseasonably cool for the most part, with midday highs seldom reaching beyond the 60s, but I was comfortable enough to finally shed the long underwear that had been part of my daily apparel for more than six months. It still got downright frosty at night, but the cabin was warm and cozy, and cold rains pattering softly against its well-sealed roof didn't bother me at all.

I honestly contemplated staying for another year—it'd be easy now that the cabin was finished and all those other hard, time-consuming jobs had been done. I could concentrate on growing a garden, especially potatoes, in the sandy soil back of the cabin, and the deer were so accustomed to my spoor that they'd be mine for the taking. Then I slapped myself back to reality, recalling those cold, mournfully brief days of December and the terrible depression they'd created in me. I also remembered that the days of earning a living from the homesteader's life were long gone in northern Michigan, and in that respect alone I faced a lot tougher situation than had the fur traders of old. Sure, I could survive, but life would purely suck insofar as having the finer things were concerned.

Before I knew it, the Memorial Day weekend had arrived. With it came the first real T-shirt weather, and the start of the blackfly hatch. Thanks to a cold spring, the bloodsucking gnats weren't nearly as plentiful as they'd been the previous spring, and this time I had a fine cabin in which to take refuge from their torments. I spent most of the holiday weekend sitting inside at the fold-down table I'd constructed, jotting down notes for this book with the door and windows wide open to allow a cooling breeze to flow through the little house. Throughout the daylight hours a cloud of hungry blackflies hovered around the open doorway, but they were as reluctant to come inside as the vampires of ancient lore. The few that did wander in bounced about, apparently blind, and were too preoccupied with escaping to feed on me.

I finally left for Petoskey on Tuesday, after the crowd of Memorial Day tourists had gone back to their more southerly homes and it was again safe to drive on the highway. In keeping with my luck, it was raining, not hard and not too cold, but a steady drizzle that was deceptive in the way it robbed a body of warmth.

I spent most of the day outside in this rain, getting thoroughly soaked as I hunted for something to take with me for Big John's freezer. Neither he nor Robin were gainfully employed right then, and I knew they were having an even tougher time of making ends meet than I was. I was more impoverished than they were in regard to having money, but I didn't have a monthly rent bill to pay, and my cabin was well stocked with at least the most fundamental of food staples. Beyond that, I had a smorgasbord of fresh meat, fish, and wild vegetables at my disposal that weren't available to my friends. It made me feel kind of stupid to realize that I couldn't bring myself to kill for my own rather desperate needs, but willingly took up my rifle to put meat on the table of a friend in more need than myself.

I've always liked to hunt in the rain, which probably explains why I was so oblivious to the fact that I was being chilled to the bone. Rain softens fallen leaves and brittle twigs, permitting even a mediocre stalker to walk in near silence through untracked woods. Animals enjoy that same advantage, but wet earth and damp air lessen their ability to detect an approaching human, while our own superior vision is actually enhanced by the reduced contrast of a gray day.

I saw several deer that didn't see me, but getting a shot in the thick swampy whitetail yards of northern Michigan isn't like hunting the wide open spaces of Montana, where even the deepest woods seem sparse by comparison. Almost never does a hunter have the luxury of seeing all of the deer he's about to shoot—a phenomenon that accounts for probably most of the so-called accidental shootings that occur in the north woods—and if a targeted whitetail takes two or three steps, or one good leap, it's likely to be out of sight entirely.

It was nearly dusk when I broke from the woods onto Linsley Road, a remote dirt dead-end almost 4 miles southeast of the cabin. Air temperature was still relatively warm, and the rain was still little more than a steady drizzle, but I'd begun to feel a vague achiness in all of my joints. I attributed it to lack of sleep the night before.

There was plenty of game along Linsley Road, but so were there dense thickets of willow, dogwood, and alder that could have concealed a fire truck. I was scrutinizing these thickets for anything out of place when a large animal suddenly broke out onto the road less than 100 yards in front of me. I had the rifle to my shoulder and was looking through the crosshairs before I realized that this was a wolf. The big canid hadn't seen me as it stopped in the middle of the road to sniff at deer tracks in the dirt.

I watched the wolf in my scope for as long as it remained in sight. It was uniformly black, or at least a very dark gray, which coincided with many of the reported sightings our wolf team had received from this area. I estimated its weight at about 90 pounds, making it roughly three years old, and it looked healthy, with no evidence of mange or malnutrition. The animal lingered in the open for only twenty seconds or so before disappearing into a thicket on the opposite side of the road, but that was long enough for me to know a good deal about it.

I walked quietly along the road until I cut the tracks where it had crossed. It was getting dark now, but I could see in the beam of my Maglite that its front prints were better than 4 inches long. I said a prayer of thanks to the Creator for letting me see this elusive creature. It was my fourth sighting of wild wolves in this area, and I treasured the memory of each of those encounters more than any worldly wealth I could have possessed.

When the thrill that always accompanies seeing a wild wolf had subsided I remembered my mission that evening was to bring some meat to Big John. I set out walking toward an old apple orchard, about a mile away, that had once been part of a genuine homestead, but had been abandoned since World War II. There weren't any apples so early in the year, but there was an abundance of sweet grasses growing on the open terrain where the orchard sat, and I knew from previous experience that it was a preferred feeding ground in all but the deepest months of winter.

The drizzling rain continued nonstop as I hiked, just as it had all day, and I began to feel a slight chill as the coolness of night settled in. I buttoned up my wet BDU shirt and ignored it. When I drew to within a quarter mile of the abandoned orchard I went into hunting mode, walking more slowly and carefully, and listening intently for any sound of movement in the darkness. The Maglite was in my right palm, beside the forearm of my rifle, and my thumb was on its pushbutton switch. It wasn't an easy method of taking deer, but I'd shined whitetails while on foot numerous times over the years, and I had good reason to believe that I'd be successful tonight. If nothing else, shining on foot always gave a hunter the element of surprise, because wild animals never expect to see a human walking in the woods at night.

My footfalls made no sound as I stepped gently along a washed-out overgrown two-track that had once provided vehicle access to the orchard. Most of my attention was focused on the right, where the apple trees grew, but I halted midstride when a deer leaped almost nonchalantly across a narrow runoff ditch bordering the trail's left side and landed in the middle of the track not 30 feet ahead of me. The night was moonless and too overcast to see clearly, but my eyes had adjusted well enough to see objects in varying shades of gray and black, and I could tell that the deer crossing my path was an adult doe.

I could also tell that the doe hadn't seen or scented me as it moved at an unhurried walk into the grassy feeding area. I waited until it was about

50 feet from the two-track and had started to feed, then uncapped my scope lenses and brought the rifle stock to my shoulder. I could see the whitetail stepping calmly through knee-high grasses as I peered through the scope. I couldn't see my crosshairs, but the trick was to first get the animal in the lenses. When I had the clearest and brightest sight picture I could get, I thumbed back the Encore's hammer with a soft metallic click and pressed the flashlight's button.

The gray shape silhouetted in my lenses instantly became one well-illuminated and extremely surprised whitetail. The deer was standing broad-side to me, and since its body was already fixed in the scope, I merely fine tuned my point of aim and pressed the gun's trigger. In the time it takes to blink an eye, the deer was dead.

Out of habit I opened the rifle and reloaded, dropping the expended casing into a breast pocket, and walked over to where the deer lay. Its legs kicked a bit, but the eyes were already glazed with death. The 150-grain ballistic tip bullet had entered just behind its left front shoulder, and exited in the same location on the animal's opposite side. Tissue damage between those holes was severe and immediately mortal.

Still, I gripped the deer's snout tightly with one hand to expose the underside of its jaw, then drove my Ka-Bar knife hard upward through both palates and into its skull, twisting the blade after it was inserted to literally scramble the whitetail's brain. I'd been using this seemingly harsh technique for years to guarantee that the deer and other animals I'd shot were truly dead, after learning the hard way that the old redneck method of cutting an animal's throat was ineffective at best.

The Indian van was parked 1.5 miles from here by foot, and 7 miles by road. I needed to leave the deer while I walked to get it, then drive it around. Doing so would take an hour, minimum, and while I don't mind sharing with my wild brethren, I didn't want the many carnivores living in these parts to abscond with all the best pieces while I was gone. I wasn't too concerned about coyotes and bobcats, but a wolf, cougar, or black bear might carry off the entire deer. To help discourage all of them, I urinated in the grass all around the carcass. My scent wouldn't deter a hungry predator for long, but I hoped it would keep them away until I got back.

I found the Chevy still in one piece at the dam—I was always half expecting to find it burned up or otherwise destroyed these days. The old girl fired right up, as always. I considered how much I really hated driving the behemoth van as I bounced along behind its headlights, but I figured that was probably why it continued to run so well.

I arrived at the end of Linsley Road just past 10:30 P.M. There was little chance of seeing even a drunken off-roader out here at night, especially right after Memorial Day weekend, so I went to work on the deer straightaway. From inside the van I took a large cardboard box lined with a plastic garbage bag to contain the quartered sections after I'd butchered the animal. The big Maglite went into a cargo pocket of my BDU trousers as I switched over to using the Mini Mag on my belt—the next steps required having both hands free, and I needed a flashlight I could hold between my teeth.

The doe was a healthy hundred pounds. Its back molars had grown in, so I knew it had to be at least two years old. It wasn't overly fat, but neither did it appear to have seen many hungry days. I judged it to be the kind of deer I'd like to eat. I drew my knife and went to work.

Butchering a deer on the ground violator style is a skill that most sport hunters never need to learn. I started by making a long cut along the spine, slicing the hide from neck to anus, so that it could be peeled away from either side to expose the back muscles, or tenderloins. After removing these long strips of meat and placing them in the box, I extended the cuts in the hide down to the knees of either hind leg, than peeled the hide away from the hams. When the hindquarters were exposed, I ran my knife around the knee joints to sever the tendons and weaken them. Then I placed my own knee on top of the deer's, and snapped them in two with a hard upward jerk against the ankle just above its hooves.

With both hams skinned and the ankles removed, I used my Ka-Bar to hack through the spine just forward of the hips and removed both hindquarters in a single piece. I separated them into two pieces by hacking through the anal bone and spine where they joined—I really missed the SP-8 machete that was stolen, because its heavy blade made that chore a lot easier than it was using only my survival knife.

With both hams in the box, I repeated the skinning process on the shoulders, separating the ankles from them in the same way. The shoulders were easier to remove because deer, like nearly every mammal, have a floating shoulder blade that isn't connected except by soft tissue. I simply began my cut at what might best be described as the armpit, and made a long cut upward toward the spine until the entire limb came free. Finally, I skinned the neck from the base of the skill to where the shoulders had been, and hacked it free of the spine—there aren't any large cuts of meat on a deer's neck, but it makes a fine pot roast.

The entire process took about twenty minutes, and I didn't have to open the gut cavity the way conventional hunters did. I wiped off the little blood

I'd gotten on my hands in the wet grass and closed the wet cardboard box. I was sweating and feeling overly warm as I carried the box of venison back to where my van was parked, even though my clothes were thoroughly soaked by rain. I was feeling chilled when I started the van, so I put on an insulated shirt over my wet T-shirt and turned on the Chevy's anemic heater.

It was nearly 1 A.M. when I stuck my key into the lock at Big John's apartment, and both he and Robin were fast asleep. I tried to be quiet while lugging the box of meat to their kitchen. I put the quartered deer in the bottom of the refrigerator to keep it cool until I could process it into edible meat the next morning. When I had it all packed into the fridge, I went out to my van and fell fast asleep, still feeling a little chilled and not quite up to speed.

I awoke at 9:00 the next morning with a searing pain in both my lungs. The pain was low and in my back, and I couldn't seem to draw a full breath. It was a warm day, with temperatures reaching near 80 degrees, but I was shivering. My temperature was only 102 degrees, which wasn't bad considering the way I felt, but when I coughed it felt as if someone had poured boiling water into the bottom of my lungs. It was pretty clear that I had a good case of bronchial pneumonia.

Still, I tried to process the venison I'd stored, but after just fifteen minutes or so I crawled back into my van and slept for a couple more hours. Big John had gone to work cutting cedar trees for a local furniture maker. I kept coming in throughout the day to continue the work, but never more than a few minutes before heading for the van to sleep again.

I don't recall much of the next three days, except that I know I slept through most of them, and that it hurt like hell whenever I coughed. Robin had a supply of cudweed (*Gnaphalium obtusifolium*), an herbal antibiotic that I'd brought her earlier, and I drank several cups of tea made from it to help bolster my body's defenses. Finally my immune system got the better of whatever had taken hold of me, and I awoke in the morning of my fourth day in town drenched with my own sour-smelling sweat, but feeling much better. I still felt weak, but the congestion that had been stuck at the bottoms of my lungs like concrete began to break up and be hacked out in godawful gobs of green-yellow mucous. I spent the next three days coughing up the horrible stuff, but my normally strong immune system combined with a regimen of walking 2 to 3 miles each morning soon had me feeling as good as new.

I still didn't have enough money to interest a mugger, but I'd sold a magazine article that I'd written at John's place the last time I was in town, and I figured to use the small check to show myself a good time. I was still set on crossing the Mackinac Bridge and living in the Upper Peninsula as soon as I could, and whichever direction the winds of fate blew, it was obvious that I'd have to leave the homestead very soon. I had no intention of leaving quietly; too much of my blood, sweat, and tears had spilled there, and there was far too much of my very soul invested in the place to just leave it behind without some sort of celebration.

I set my party date for the second Saturday in June. This gave anyone I wanted to join me several days' notice to prepare. Big John had grown too fat and too disinterested in the woods to hike out to the cabin, but I invited several other friends and acquaintances. I was a little surprised that absolutely no one wanted to go. Most of them said they did, but I knew from the looks in their eyes that they didn't. Pete certainly would have gone, but he was working as a stonemason on Beaver Island, and Jerod had to work the whole weekend as a tribal cop.

That honestly didn't hurt my feelings, because the party was actually for myself and the homestead I'd built any way, and I'd have a good time all by myself if it came to that. To help insure that, I picked up a fifth of rum, a fifth of bourbon, mixer, and snacks. When Saturday came I hung around at Big John's until 3 P.M., and when no one showed up to go with me, I left for the cabin alone. I was feeling pretty good about the situation as a whole, but I really couldn't comprehend why anyone wouldn't want to spend a Saturday night getting drunk and having a good time at the fine homestead I'd built. Maybe they just didn't think it was as fine as I did, even though most had never seen the place.

To protect my vehicle from assholes, I elected to park at the Carp River bridge and hike the long way in. My Red Cloud backpack was loaded with booze, pop, and munchies, but I could easily make the 3.5-mile hike with it. There were a few mosquitoes in the air as I shouldered the pack, but the afternoon was sunny and blissfully warm, perfect for backpacking. I truly enjoyed the walk to my cabin, even though I'd traveled this same trail hundreds of times, and I was a little surprised at how much I didn't mind not having company. Maybe it was better this way, saying farewell to the homestead that had been my home for the past year without distraction or input from people who couldn't comprehend what I was doing.

In fact, I had a wonderful time all by myself. I placed booze and mixers into mesh bags and dropped them into the well to keep cold, started a small fire in a portable grill that had gone unused since I'd brought it out there the previous summer, and just sat on a bench in front of the cabin, listening to the radio while I proceeded to get plastered. I drank bourbon while eating sausages on buns with mustard and ketchup until late into the night. I re-tired sometime after midnight, feeling just a little shy of great.

I rose in the morning without a hangover to bright sunshine and the beautiful "dee-dee-dee" song of chickadees hunting for bugs outside the cabin. After drinking a cup of fresh-brewed black coffee, I started flavoring subsequent cups with bourbon, and my solo party was on again. Every-thing was prettier, brighter, and nicer than I'd perceived it to be in a long, long time, and I was surprised at the serenity that filled my being. I've never believed in the concept of destiny because I think it's an excuse for not taking control of one's own pathway through life, but I do believe that things sometimes happen for a reason, and it seemed the Creator had in-tended for me to be alone on this trip. I couldn't have felt the deep sense of peace I was feeling if there had been other people around to distract me from the forest.

I've also never believed in mixing guns and alcohol, but sometime dur-ing the afternoon I got a hankering to squeeze off a few rounds. I sat on the bench in front of the cabin, my .22 pistol beside me, and between sips of bourbon I'd plink away at those damned chicken cans that Jerod kept leav-ing out there—at least I'd found a suitable use for them. The cans were set up at ranges from 25 to 50 yards on stumps of trees that I'd felled, and they were satisfyingly well holed by the time I grew tired of setting them back up.

I finished the bottle of bourbon, but never uncapped the fifth of rum that lay at the bottom of the well. I slept like a log Sunday night, and once again awoke without a hangover on Monday morning. I was almost a little sad to be leaving my homestead after having such a remarkably good time there, but unless I planned on spending another year there I had to find a way to generate another grubstake that would let me move across the Mack-inac Bridge. I threw the empty chip bags, plastic wrappers, and bullet-riddled cans into my backpack and headed for the van.

The feeling of serenity persisted as I hiked the North Country Trail to-ward Carp River. The mosquitoes were tolerable enough, and I didn't find it necessary to wear a head net. Even my pack seemed light, so when I reached the Carp River bridge, I struck off upstream on a vague trail that I'd created a few years before. The trail was unused by all but a handful of people I'd shown it to, and it led to one of the most peaceful spots I've ever found. There was a regular campsite there next to the river, and a small rock pier that I'd built to make drawing water easier jutted about 6 feet into the stream. The water was high this year, flowing over the top of the pier, but I was glad to see it was still there.

I dropped my backpack and sat on the bank for the next hour or so taking in the beauty of the place. Life in these woods over the past year had hardened me, mentally as well as physically, but here, now, I felt as though I was being caressed by God. Maybe it was because I knew that I'd be leaving this place for good very soon, even though I still didn't know how that was going to happen, but even my bones felt as if they were softening. It was dark before I picked up my pack again and headed for Petoskey.

CHAPTER 14

NEW ADVENTURES

Back in Petoskey all of the serenity I'd felt in the woods vanished, crushed by the reality that I still needed to find a way to move on to new challenges and adventures that didn't include the Lower Peninsula. As much as I loved the homestead I'd built, and the forest it sat in, I hated seeing what had become of the once majestic area surrounding it. Condominiums that had blighted the shoreline of Lake Michigan since the late 60s were multiplying, and places where I'd once hunted and trapped had been bulldozed to build yet more subdivisions and housing projects. People with more money than I could comprehend were coming here in droves, buying tracts of forest for their natural beauty, only to flatten them with heavy equipment so they could erect gigantic houses with lawns and asphalt driveways. New roads made area maps obsolete on an almost weekly basis, and local highways that had been considered lonely and desolate in my youth were now congested with traffic nearly twenty-four hours a day.

I couldn't stand seeing the wild places of my boyhood disappear forever, nor could I hide the tears that sprang suddenly from my eyes when I drove down any number of suburbanized roads and realized how many species of wildlife no longer had a place to live. Whitetail deer were actually living within the city limits, hiding in dogwood bushes along Bear River to sleep during the day, and I'd seen their hoofprints along the sidewalks of Petoskey's busy downtown streets. Tourists thought that was charming, but the disturbing truth was that these deer had habituated to living in town because there was no place left within a whitetail's range for them to live as nature had intended.

More disturbing were the black bears that had been coming into town with increasing frequency. In the previous summer an adolescent bear had been seen scavenging around the DNR's fish hatchery in Charlevoix, along the Lake Michigan shoreline. A crowd of people scared the two year old—a teenager in bear years—up a tree, where it was kept by a growing mass of curious onlookers until police arrived.

Unfortunately for the bear, police aren't trained to handle such situations, so they acted in the only way they knew. The bear was shot out of the tree and killed. It was a sad conclusion that could have been avoided if all of the curiosity seekers whose presence was forcing the terrified animal to remain treed had just gone about their business and provided it with an avenue of escape back to the woods.

A similar incident occurred in Petoskey on the evening of July 4, 2002. Cheanne and I had just returned from Mackinaw City, where onlookers are treated annually to simultaneous fireworks displays from Mackinaw City, Mackinaw Island, and St. Ignace at the northern end of the Mackinac Bridge. It was a little after 10 P.M. when we stopped at Big John's, where the police scanner he kept going 24/7 was buzzing with reports of a young black bear that had been treed near Bay View, a resort community along Lake Michigan's shoreline at the northern edge of town. Aside from causing consternation among local residents, the bear had caused a traffic jam along U.S. 31 as motorists stopped to gawk at the activities of local police who were trying to keep people away in hopes that the frightened animal would climb down and leave on its own.

Fearing that this bear might be killed, I immediately dialed 911 and offered my assistance. The officers in charge took my offer seriously, but thought that my plan for climbing the tree and forcing the bear to ground with a long stick was too risky, especially since the mob surrounding the scene refused to withdraw. The dispatcher didn't say so, but I suspect they envisioned a scenario in which the bear hit the ground in a rage and took it out on bystanders. In fact, there was no chance the bear would charge madly into the crowd, but I had to admit that with so many people pressing in for a closer look there was no telling what one of them might do.

Still fearing for the bear's life, I called Archie Kiogima. Bay View wasn't on reservation land, but it was within a mile of Kegomic to the north, which was, and I hoped the two of us might at least bring enough attention to the situation that anyone with an itchy trigger finger would think twice about shooting. It was late at night on a holiday, but Archie said he'd call his biologist contacts at the DNR and get them involved.

Just in case Archie couldn't get hold of anyone, I called news reporter Kate LeBlanc of TV channels 9 and 10 and told her what was happening, figuring that she could bring media attention to what was obviously a newsworthy event. She was definitely interested, and said she'd do what she could to get press coverage on the scene.

I can't say that any of what I did made the difference, but the black bear wasn't killed. DNR biologists arrived on the scene and, after deciding the two-year-old bear was too big to handle using "capture sticks" (long metal tubes with a steel-cable noose at one end), they contacted Emmet County animal control officer Jack Balchik, a man I know and like, in spite of his job. Balchik was the only official there who owned a tranquilizer rifle.

To their credit, DNR officials were careful not to overdose the bear, but a conservation officer erroneously told Balchik that the two-year-old bear weighed about 60 pounds, which was in fact about half what a black bear weighs when its mother sends it off on its own. Balchik had a local veterinarian prepare a dose of (probably Zylazine [Rompum]) for that size animal, so it was hardly surprising that he fired four darts into the bear's rump without knocking it out. Moreover, adrenalin is an effective counteragent to tranquilizers, and this bear was scared to death. The darts did eventually bring the bruin down from its perch, but it hit the ground running.

For some reason I'm not privy to, the biologists gave chase—maybe they wanted the darts back. Predictably, the bear climbed another tree, then jumped back to the ground when DNR officials found it again. This game continued into the wee hours of morning, until the young bear had been darted a total of five times—four times in its butt and once in the shoulder. The poor critter finally succumbed to the sedative in the middle of Petoskey's business district, where conservation officers finally "gained control of him and put him in a pet carrier" (a large portable kennel). From there they reportedly transported the bear to a large swamp 20 miles north, and administered a "reversal" drug (Yohimbine or Tolazaline), whereupon it ran into the woods. That's one bear I doubt will ever want anything to do with people again.

Kate LeBlanc phoned me at Big John's the next morning and asked if I'd consent to do an interview for her 6 P.M. news broadcast that evening. She told me that a black bear—probably the same one that had been relocated—had been caught earlier rummaging through the dumpster at a deli a mile from where last night's action had occurred. Incredibly, the deli manager had run out of the store waving a knife and chased the bear into a nearby cedar swamp. I don't believe Kate thought that response was any more heroic—or any less idiotic—than I did, and she wanted me to offer advice about the proper way to handle such an encounter.

It was sunny and already 85 degrees when I met the news crew at the swamp where the bear had been last seen. I don't think I was quite what they expected when I showed up in the Indian van wearing cutoff shorts, a tank top, and sandals, but she clipped the microphone to my shirt and we started shooting. I'm never as articulate as I should be during a TV interview, and when she asked me point blank what I thought of how the deli manager with the knife had handled the situation of a bear in his dumpster, I'm afraid I wasn't very diplomatic either. Still, the interview aired that evening, although I didn't see it—as usual. Others who did see it told me that it went pretty well, but I suspect that had more to do with creative editing than with my skill at speaking to the camera.

The summer sped on like it had wings, and still my plans to go north lay dead in the water. Foremost in my mind was the fact that I was under contract to write this book, and that I was already well beyond my deadline. More than a legal document, a contract is a promise, and I'd broken mine. I needed to get myself reestablished in a place where I could set up an office and work, but that took money, and I just didn't have any.

Worse, people were starting to refer to me with terms like "bum" when they thought I couldn't hear. No one ever accused me of being lazy or shiftless, yet it was pretty apparent that I refused to work for anyone for longer than a day or two. It was pure stubbornness, I guess; I'd spent the past decade working myself into a position where I owed nothing, paying cash for everything I bought or doing without. It hadn't been easy getting to this point, and now I'd be damned by God Himself before I gave up the freedom I'd worked so hard to earn. This past year of hardship and privation had only served to strengthen that resolve.

It was with a hard swallow of pride that I finally called my publisher to ask for yet more money on the advance for a book he hadn't yet seen a word of. He refused, but to my great surprise offered me yet another book, along with the biggest advance I'd ever received. I almost couldn't believe what I'd heard, but when the contracts arrived by mail I knew that my dream of moving north was about to become reality.

It was a hot August day in 2002 when I gassed up the Indian van one last time at the Speedway station north of Petoskey. I checked the oil, transmission and brake fluids, and tire pressure, then pulled out onto U.S. 31 and pointed the big Chevy north. My tires were mismatched and nearly worn out, and there was a disturbing scraping sound coming from the right front wheel bearing, but I was almost desperate to escape the Lower Peninsula. I reckoned the old mule would make the 125 miles I needed it to take me, even overloaded with computer, desk, and other meager possessions I'd taken out of storage.

Traffic through Petoskey was bumper to bumper, which had become usual for this time of year, and it served to remind me why I was being driven north. I had the van windows wide open to circulate as much air as possible through the ovenlike interior, and the stench of sulfuric automotive exhaust was thick and acrid enough to make me gag. I was very much aware that my van was contributing to the noxious smog that enveloped the once quaint village, and even though I'd put less than 4,000 miles on it in the three years I'd owned it, of late I suffered a guilty conscience whenever I drove the thing.

Traffic thinned north of Petoskey, and my foot grew heavier against the accelerator pedal the farther north I traveled. There was a feeling almost of joy when my tires rolled onto the Mackinac Bridge under the bluest skies I'd ever seen. I paid my buck-fifty at the tollbooth on the bridge's northern end and sped off toward M-28 west.

I was headed for the little town of Paradise on Lake Superior's Whitefish Bay, where the legendary SS *Edmund Fitzgerald* had been making for safe harbor when the gales of Gitchigoomie broke her in two in November of '75. It was a tiny town with big winters, bug-infested summers, and forests still large enough for a man to disappear forever if he desired. I didn't know if Paradise would live up to its name for me personally, but it looked to be a place where a social outcast like myself could live and write in peace. Whatever awaited me there, it was sure to be a new adventure, and I was never coming back.

ABOUT THE AUTHOR

L en McDougall is a full-time outdoor writer, professional photographer, and illustrator with more than thirty years of experience in the northern woods. He teaches survival skills and tests products for the outdoors. He also works as a field guide and tracker, and is a member of the Michigan Gray Wolf Team that monitors the wolf resurgence in the state's Lower Peninsula. McDougall is also the author of *The Complete Tracker, The Field & Stream Wilderness Survival Handbook,* and *Practical Outdoor Survival.* After spending most of his life in and around Petoskey, Michigan, he now lives in Paradise.

Practical Outdoor Survival
A Modern Approach
ISBN 1–55821–228–0
US $16.95 / Can. $25.95
A potential lifesaver for anyone who ventures into wild country.

The Encyclopedia of Tracks and Scats
ISBN 1–59228–070–6
US $19.95 / Can. $32.95
A comprehensive guidebook for identifying, understanding, and collecting
the tracks and scats of the animals of the United States and Canada.